DATE DUE

GAYLORD

The Rise of the Expert Company

The Rise of the Expert Company

*HOW VISIONARY COMPANIES ARE
USING ARTIFICIAL INTELLIGENCE TO ACHIEVE
HIGHER PRODUCTIVITY AND PROFITS*

Edward Feigenbaum

Pamela McCorduck

H. Penny Nii

EXPERT SYSTEMS CATALOG by Paul Harmon

𝕿𝖎𝖒𝖊𝖘 BOOKS

Library of Congress Cataloging-in-Publication Data

Feigenbaum, Edward A.
The rise of the expert company.
Includes index.
1. Management—Data processing. 2. Business—Data processing. 3. Expert systems (Computer science)
I. McCorduck, Pamela, 1940–   . II. Nii, Penny.
III. Title.
HD30.2.F45 1988   658.4'05   87-40588
ISBN 0-8129-1731-6

Manufactured in the United States of America

9 8 7 6 5 4 3 2

FIRST EDITION

Contents

Foreword

THE RISE OF THE EXPERT COMPANY by Tom Peters

THE WORLD OF ORGANIZING HUMAN ACTIVITIES is undergoing its first genuine revolution since the correctly labeled industrial "revolution" of the late eighteenth century. The information-processing technologies that are powering the new revolution may eventually have even more impact on human organization—public and private—than did the mass production revolution, powered first by steam. It is even plausible to state that this information-technology-inspired transformation in the way we organize and execute affairs is the most fundamental since the Chinese developed hierarchical models of administration to pull together their vast empire several thousand years ago.

The still-youthful applications of artificial intelligence (along with the accelerating spread and deployment of high-speed, high-storage-capacity microcomputers) really provide our first inkling of what that revolution will eventually be all about. Most new technologies are initially applied to peripheral or even frivolous tasks (for instance, the first tape recorder, which was developed in Japan, was used in bars, where drunks enjoyed listening to their own slurred voices). So, too, with information technology. For its first twenty-five years or so, following the beginning of widespread use after World War II, the only serious impact was on the most mundane of tasks, such as payroll processing.

Miniaturization and the microcomputer user's growing

ability to break the barriers of the plodding, conservative Management Information Systems (MIS) baronies have begun to change this, attested to by 9 million personal computer (PC) sales in 1987 in the U.S., and the explosion of software houses, which have introduced 15,000 new programs in the last three years. But most current PC uses will surely be viewed in twenty years, perhaps even in ten, as small potatoes, too. AI is increasingly where the action is. And, thanks to this pioneering book, even the skeptical layman will readily see that.

Artificial intelligence is a harsh term, as threatening to "us professionals" (most readers of this book) as the powered loom was to artisans two hundred years ago and "automation" was to the blue-collar worker some forty years ago. After all, tools to date, starting with the wheel, have simply replaced brute physical labor (even the most blue collar of white-collar work, such as the laborious task of doing payroll). But now the quintessential human trait, intelligence, is at risk to machines. That was the vague fear we all harbored, and the AI gurus did not help allay it. They sang of a revolution that would replace skilled professionals. Yet the first applications of AI seemed trivial, which added to the confusion.

While this one book will not by itself cause the world to reverse its direction of spin, it is, in my view, the first motivating, demystifying exposition of the real, practical—and yet exciting, even inspiring and definitely revolutionary—world of AI.

You will find no theory here, though there are enough definitions and explanations to stoke your interest, if you are a total novice to the field. What you will find, painstakingly provided by pioneer and renowned AI scholar Ed Feigenbaum and his colleagues, Pamela McCorduck and H. Penny Nii, are cases. Beautiful, rich cases. Practical cases that you can sink your teeth into. Compelling cases about people (impassioned AI champions) and turf fights (usually practical AI experimenters taking on the often-reactionary central MIS function). In all, there are some twenty cases. The manufacturing sector is well represented (Navistar, FMC, IBM, Du Pont, DEC, Westinghouse et al.), and so is the service sector (American Express, Arthur Andersen). The public sector (British National Health Service, British Pension Advisory Service) is here, too; and Japan's pathbreaking firms are also examined in detail—Kajima in construction, Canon, Fujitsu, steelmaker Nippon-Kokan, Toyota and Nippon Life.

The book, you might say, consists of twenty good yarns. The first comes from Northrop. A pair of relatively powerless (junior) engineers tackle the laborious, essential, and high-skill task of translating engineering drawings into a detailed plan for manufacturing complex aircraft parts. One of the upstarts builds his first expert system on an Apple computer at home, with surreptitiously acquired resources and lots of cover provided by his partner. User number one is his wife, naive to engineering, who is awakened at 3:00 A.M. to be the guinea pig. From such a humble beginning, startling results are achieved. A difficult task that used to take several days is reduced to ten to fifteen minutes, and reliability soars. Moreover, the expertise of aging engineers in short supply is captured forever.

If Northrop's way of backing into AI (albeit involving a critical task) is at one end of the spectrum, the monster IBM is at the other. AI, says its grandees, *is* the future. But the lovely description of the beginning of the AI revolution at Big Blue is again practical. There are now fully four dozen significant AI systems up and running at IBM, with at least 120 significant systems under active development. We are allowed to peek at one that aids production of the state-of-the-art one-megabit chip at IBM's Burlington, Vermont, facility and another that helps with final inspection of big disc drive mass storage systems at IBM–San Jose. Yet a third IBM system is a pioneering attempt to apply AI to complex, expensive internal processes, which are so far resistant to productivity improvement efforts.

Other "bet the company" AI sagas emerge at such places as DEC and, most surprising of all, Navistar (the old International Harvester). Both of these firms' pioneering—and revolutionary—systems are aimed only secondarily at increasing efficiency. The chief objective is adding value for the customer by substantially customizing every product.

Big systems with giant payoffs are also explored in a case study from American Express, where credit approval process expertise is captured, causing big efficiencies, and even greater (revolutionary is, once more, not too strong a word) improvement in effectiveness, an improvement the customer can feel. The sometimes almost lurid details of the tortuous implementation process at Amex are in themselves a dandy guide for would-be AI champions.

But most exciting to me was the Du Pont story. Du Pont certainly wins hands down at the numbers game. It has two hundred expert systems already up (a staggering number, considering the authors' estimate that 1,500 systems were up and running worldwide by the end of 1987) and a whopping six hundred in the works!

It's at Du Pont that we learn about "Mike-in-the-Box," the actual name of one expert system that is the essence of this exciting and eminently practical book. The real Mike is simply the best engineer Du Pont has at purging a distillation column of impurities, one of the most demanding of human tasks in the real world of commercial chemical engineering, especially when it comes to producing 99.9 percent pure material for solid state electronics applications. A great deal of the real Mike's unique expertise is boiled down to hundreds of "rules" and captured in an expert system run on a PC. (Almost all of Du Pont's applications are PC-based.) The overall Du Pont AI champion, Ed Mahler, oversees his "pirate-ship operation" with just a tiny full-time staff. He largely eschews giant investments and instead urges engineers, by the bushelsful, to spend just one month and five to ten thousand dollars in developing each new PC-based system. The average impact of each is about a hundred thousand dollars! The pleasantly nonthreatening term for a Du Pont system is Partners for Experts.

Mike-in-the-Box, "God in the works" (the captured expertise of an aging, irreplaceable blast furnace expert at Nippon-Kokan), "Geoff's Book" (thousands of expert rules from the head of the senior, top estimator at building contractor Lend Lease of Australia), and J. A. Gilreath (Schlumberger's ace oilfield data interpreter, whose expertise is now enshrined in that company's Dipmeter Advisor system) are among the stars we meet. Much of the priceless skill of these experts has been captured by "knowledge engineer"-translators. These very special, very human characters breathe life—and even more realism—into these pages.

Though at each of the companies studied, even those with "bet the company" programs, AI is in its infancy, one is nonetheless staggered by the success that has already been achieved. At IBM Burlington (the chip operation), a 10 to 20 percent increase in throughput has been realized; this adds up to tens of millions of dollars' annual savings from just the one system. At the British National Health Service, a demanding and critical evaluation task that took six experts two hours is now done (better) in nine minutes. At American Express, the "decline rate" (decisions not to grant credit) has been reduced by fully one-third, and the value of the single, new AI system is already estimated at $27 million a year. A Westinghouse system (a new service which that firm sells to utilities), aimed at enhancing the utilization of giant electric power generation turbines, contributes a whopping $2 to $3 million per year per customer machine. Then there's a sales support system at Digital, called XSEL, which has reduced a three-hour system configuration/alternative generation task to fifteen minutes; moreover, less than 1 percent of the systems so specified turn out not to be manufacturable, down from 30 percent before the system was installed—all of which is worth $70 million a year, says DEC, not including immeasurable added customer satisfaction that accrues from providing the customer with more options. And an AI system that aids product design at Canon has made scarce, highly skilled lens designers fully twelve times more productive!

The list of advantages is as impressive as the numeric results. Advantages include order-of-magnitude increases in speed of complex task accomplishment; reduced capital expenditure (another Digital Equipment system, in manufacturing, is presumed to have saved the construction expense of six final assembly and test factories); the capture of top experts' perishable experience; the freeing up of top experts to take on more exceptional problems; remarkable speed-ups in training would-be experts; consistency in decision-making;

the promotion of teamwork (frontline people now have all the information needed to make decisions and work together better as a result, at such places as IBM–Burlington); the challenging of vital but long-buried assumptions (at American Express, system construction led to many productive policy discussions); the generation of more, and more creative, options for customers in a short period of time (such as in the personal financial planning service operation at Sanwa Bank); and the ability to generate many, many more design trials (e.g., Canon).

One benefit is of special note, and it emerged at DEC. The major expert systems there, though still youthful, get at the heart of the true AI revolution to come. As experts' rules there were unearthed, codified and elaborated, the essence of "the way the company works" was discovered. The true nature of "organization" was in many ways revealed for the first time—and substantial modifications in basic schemes for organizing are already under way. Startling truths (often counterintuitive) about the way people work together, evaluate information, and get things done are also emerging at Navistar and IBM. This is precisely what the eventual AI story will be all about. The Du Pont tale is one form of exciting result: fast, cheap, practical, and valuable—AI as a partner to numerous experts in a big, decentralized operation. But DEC's journey is a glimpse at AI's future—the redistribution of decision-making rules, the reconfiguration of (and redefinition of) the process of organizing, and a shift of influence and power inside the firm.

It turns out that our true understanding of hierarchy and organization is limited, despite our thousands of years of experience with them. In the business study of organizational behavior, researchers are just starting to move beyond such ideas as certain, mandated "laws" about "span of control," for instance. The combination of radically changing market conditions (true globalization, new competitors), the true technology revolution and now the fast-charging AI revolution, which is of a whole different order, will leave little conventional wisdom about business practice intact, ten or so years from now.

I came to this book and to the task of writing this foreword interested, even fascinated by this topic, about which I am largely naive. I leave the process of digesting the manuscript and writing the foreword mesmerized. The emerging world, brilliantly and pragmatically described in *The Rise of the Expert Company*, is not the world we now know. The consequences are exciting and a bit frightening—and clearly monumental.

I conclude that any senior manager in any business of almost any size who isn't at least learning about AI, and sticking a tentative toe or two into AI's waters, is simply out of step, dangerously so.

The Rise of the Expert Company

Chapter 1

Working Smarter

> Standards of living rise not because people work harder
> but because they work smarter. If you want to see people
> working hard go to almost any underdeveloped country
> and you will see people working like no one in America
> works. Economic progress is the replacement of physical
> exertion with brain power.
>
> —LESTER C. THUROW (1983), DEAN, SLOAN SCHOOL OF
> MANAGEMENT, MIT

AMONG THE NATIONS, rising standards of living are at stake. The wealth of nations once was brought forth from fertile soil, abundant mines, hardworking cheap labor, and money capital. Today national wealth arises from knowledge, expertise, innovation, and intellectual capital.

Walter Wriston, the former CEO of Citicorp, spoke to this in 1985: "If capital is what produces a stream of income, then it follows that knowledge is a form of the new capital. . . . A strong argument can be made that information capital can be more critical to the future of the American economy than money capital."

The Knowledge Worker Drives the Wealth Machine

The factory is a symbol of the corporate wealth machine. It brings to mind images of fabricating and assembling, not planning and decision making. When we think of the factory, we think of things that are solid and "hard," that are touched, assembled, handled—unlike knowledge, which is intangible, "soft," "nontouch," evanescent. The first ideas about robotizing factories, a decade ago, involved the solid, the "hard." Build machines to grab and move things, to shape and weld them. The costs of robotizing were great, the productivity gains disappointing, and the question was why? The reason uncovered by the follow-up studies was that, broadly speaking, the "touch" work in manufacturing represented one third of the costs, the "nontouch" two thirds! If robots were costless, and you could eliminate all the "touch work" of manufacturing with these robots, you would save only a third of your costs. Unaffected were other "nontouch," knowledge-based costs of doing business associated with procurement, design, engineering, quality assurance, management coordination and control, and other manufacturing functions involving decision making and information flow, as well as the nonmanufacturing costs of sales, service, and financial management.

To make major productivity gains, we discovered that the automation net would have to be cast farther out than the factory floor—to cover the information handlers, those doing the planning, the problem solving, and the decision making. In short, it was necessary to bring the power of automation to the knowledge worker.

Knowledge workers are found in all the offices, all the skill jobs, and all the professions of a modern economy. The competitiveness of nations and of corporations derives from the expertise and productivity of this worker. *Competitiveness*, the big C word, and *productivity*, the big P word: these dominate the political discussions in Washington, Tokyo, and Brussels. Nations strive for small percentage-point gains in productivity. They understand that major shifts in wealth, in national standards of living, flow or ebb from small changes in national productivity in a relatively few years. As a nation, we understand (to paraphrase the well-known television commercial) that we can grow national wealth only the old-fashioned way, by earning it with productivity gains.

In the agricultural revolution, the engines of productivity

were the farm machines; in the industrial revolution, the heavy factory machines. In the knowledge workers' revolution, the engine of productivity—the engine of "working smarter"—is another big C word, the *computer*.

The computer is omnipresent in the economies and societies of the advanced nations, as likely to be found on the CEO's desk as in the design bureau or the purchasing department, as likely in our doctor's office and our bank as in our child's bedroom. Our planes are run by computers, and most of our cars have a dozen. Computers are everywhere.

The Computer as the Power Tool of the Knowledge Worker

The computer is the most general machine ever invented. It is a "universal symbol processor," capable of manipulating information for us in whatever way that we choose. Surprisingly, throughout most of the computer era, we have chosen to use the remarkable generality of these universal machines for the most mundane of our information-processing needs: for calculating numbers, for filing and retrieving data, and most recently for easing the burdens of typing. Yet even the mundane can be of immense value, enhancing the productivity of the knowledge worker and propelling the information-processing industry into the first rank of the world's industries.

As this industry and its customers, the businesses and governments of the world, reach out to satisfy the demands of knowledge work, data processing is being supplemented by knowledge processing—a technology born in the 1950s that has become practical and widespread in the 1980s. In conventional computer data processing, the computer uses processes of arithmetic, filing, and retrieving on numbers and characters. In knowledge processing, the computer uses facts, rules of judgment, rules of expert decision making, and logic to discover lines of reasoning leading to the solutions of problems. *The hallmark of knowledge processing is reasoning by computer*. Reasoning, not calculating. The power of the universal symbol manipulator is turned toward the symbol manipulations that occupy most of us most of the time: assessing relevant knowledge, solving problems, and making decisions.

The computer is the engine, and the engine is used to drive software "power tools" called *expert systems*.

Expert systems are computer programs that couple a collection of knowledge with a procedure that can reason using that knowledge. The knowledge can be factual, as one would find in textbooks, manuals, and journals. Or it can be heuristic: experiential, judgmental, "soft." Heuristic knowledge is what distinguishes expert from novice, though both may know the same facts about a field. The reasoning procedure of an expert system is usually based on simple forms of logic that allow conclusions to be drawn in an orderly way. The syllogism is an example of such logic ("Socrates is a man; all men are mortal; therefore Socrates is mortal").

Across the spectrum of human knowledge work, in businesses and the professions, expert systems are being used to enhance the productivity and skill of the knowledge worker. Recalling the great machines for assisting human muscles—our continuing legacy from the Industrial Revolution—we can think of the expert systems of today and tomorrow as power tools for the knowledge worker, tools to assist minds, not muscles.

Prologue to the Pioneers

This book is a collection of tales of pioneers. Of the hundreds of expert systems in use today, we have chosen to focus on a few dozen. The pioneering companies have opened new territories and have found in these uncharted places great economic gain for themselves and their customers. It has been said that a technology can be called "revolutionary" if it changes people's physical or mental capabilities by a factor of ten (10X). For example, the automobile revolutionized personal transportation by introducing a factor of ten in speed between a brisk walk and a drive. This factor of ten radically changed the way we live. We saw revolutionary change, factors of ten or more in the productivity of human knowledge workers.

A Brief History

Where did this technology come from? It emerged in the late 1970s from university computer science laboratories doing research in the science of artificial intelligence (AI). In the mid-1950s speculation about the possibility that the newly arrived electronic computers could perform acts of cognition that we call reasoning, learning, perception, and language understanding was followed by the hard work of experiments with computer programs. These were aimed at developing the basic concepts and methods for a science of computer cognition and a better understanding of human thinking. Many ideas were tried, but the one that emerged as today's most important principle is one that in retrospect seems obvious (the best of science always seems obvious in retrospect). The Knowledge Principle says that the power of artificial intelligence programs to perform at high levels of competence on problems of intellectual difficulty depends on the amount of knowledge, and the quality of the knowledge, these programs contain about their problem domain. The reasoning method, while necessary, plays a secondary role. Knowledge is what gives rise to understanding and to effective problem solving. "Smarts" equals knowledge.

The vehicle for moving this insight into practical application emerged as the expert system, software for problem solving that uses the knowledge of human experts skilled in solving narrowly defined but difficult problems. Often, but not always, the knowledge is transferred from human expert to computer by technologists called knowledge engineers. Knowledge engineers take the knowledge, the experience, the hard-earned intuitions of experts and put them in computer software.

A dozen or so successful experiments by university engineers and AI scientists in the 1970s, and the pioneering industrial efforts of Schlumberger Ltd. and Digital Equipment Corporation, gave birth to the revolution whose stories of challenge and success in the 1980s we tell in this book.

What We Sought and What We Found

Ours was a journey of discovery. Having been present at the birth, having helped to send the youngster to its corporate finishing school, we sought out the young adult—in Dallas and Wilmington and Boston, in Tokyo and Sydney and London—to understand its power and its problems, its nurture and its growing pains.

We looked for the economic muscle—the higher productivity and higher profits. And we looked for the human stories behind the corporate nurturing of the new technology, stories of champions who took big risks, of managers whose vision arched high above corporate goals, allowing them to see paths hidden to ground-huggers. We looked for innovative developers taken by the sheer fun of doing something frontier-new and frontier-exciting.

We set out on this journey as optimists and believers and we were amazed and sometimes awed by what we found. The systems were powerful and productive, and they ranged across corporate life in an unexpectedly general way. As we moved from place to place, we found common themes. Some were no surprise. Others were of the greatest importance.

Across all applications we found expert systems used as intellectual assistants—intellectual power tools—for decision makers and professional problem solvers. Nowhere was the expert system conceived as "stand alone." Assistant or colleague, or sometimes servant is the assigned role, never boss or replacement.

We expected to find, and we did find, large cost savings from expert system applications to internal operations of firms. In the application of a new technology, a company usually looks inside. We were amazed by the size of some of the savings realized. Indeed, for systems of small scope and limited dollar returns, we were struck by the extraordinarily high return-on-investment (ROI) percentages. Savings of tens of millions of dollars per year were seen, and savings of more than half a million dollars per year were common. ROI figures for small and even medium-size expert systems were in the thousands of percent.

An advertisement in a national newsmagazine shows a computer and asks, "What if it could multiply thought as easily as it multiplies numbers?" The issue is speedup. Is the intellectual power tool fast? We know the computer is super-fast at calculating, but is it fast at reasoning? Can a person using an expert system as an intellectual assistant do his or her work faster? Savvy as we are about expert systems, we were not prepared for what we saw. Almost everywhere, expert systems were speeding up professional work by at least a factor of ten. Speedup factors of twenty, thirty, or forty were common. And today's expert systems, powerful as they are, are still Model-Ts! If we look across the economy, the gains in white-collar productivity are very low, almost zero. Considering that economists and business planners tell us that we should strive for productivity gains of 5 percent or 7 percent per year, even the "small" speedups we saw were huge.

We also saw improved quality and consistency of work. This results from the ability of the expert system to manage large bodies of knowledge more thoroughly and consistently than people can. No big surprise. Sometimes quality and consistency of the outcome were the main reasons the company undertook the expert system development. In a competitive world, quality is one of the important dimensions of the challenge. In one case, an IBM expert system, consistency was the target. It helped to deter legal action by competitors who might feel wronged by IBM's (occasionally inconsistent) pricing of one of its customer services.

By its very nature, an expert system is a collection of specialized know-how and facts. In a company, it can be the "corporate memory" of some product or process. The corporate knowledge is the company's biggest asset, yet it is the most volatile. Everyone is an expert at something, and everyone changes jobs, retires, or dies. We saw cases in which somebody's expertise was strategic, critical for the company's success in one of its lines of business. The experience of Lend Lease Corporation in Australia that we describe in Chapter 8 is an example. The desire to capture the company's best expertise and pass it around, not only to current employees (for use and for training) but to a future generation of employees, was much stronger than we had expected.

The other reason for capturing company knowledge is to sell it. Knowledge is a valuable product. Professors, publishers, and consultants know that. In the era of the knowledge worker, companies are discovering new lines of business, new sources of revenue from knowledge-intensive products. When a new technology is introduced, companies rarely look outside to new markets because the visibility of those new "top line" opportunities is limited. Companies focus inward as they assimilate the technology. We had expected to find few new products and services, but we were surprised. We found an entirely new line of business at Texas Instruments, a valuable new service from Westinghouse for its electric utility customers, and several products in the financial industry. Some consumer products and services are in the wings.

Many different motives energize the expert systems revolution. Operations managers need an attentive, thorough, twenty-four-hours-per-day "cool head in a crisis." An expert system is currently receiving test trials at the console of a nuclear power plant in Taiwan. The Nippon-Kokan system that we describe later monitors steel-making blast furnaces for two different types of catastrophic failure. An American system by the FMC Corporation monitors a phosphorus-making furnace for optimum performance and to avoid big trouble.

We found expert systems in most business sectors and in most of the business functions of companies. Applications of very high leverage are found in manufacturing, where expert systems, like those at DEC, IBM, and Navistar, are assisting in tasks of scheduling, planning, and configuration design. High leverage also seems to be characteristic of financial industry applications, such as the transaction-oriented charge authorization advisor of American Express. Service functions are mainline for expert systems applications because they are by their nature knowledge-intensive. Diagnostic systems predominate, but close behind are the knowledge advisory systems, delivering knowledge. These simple but useful systems are essentially "active books," providing users the right piece of knowledge to fit the situation. Think of them as corporate rule books, performance guides, standards books, maintenance and operations manuals—except that they tell you what you need to know in a particular situation. You do not need to search. Expert systems make knowledge immediate, available, accessible, always useful.

Engineers are always early adopters of technology, so, as expected, applications in the engineering function have proliferated. Engineers use expert systems in design and in the interpretation of instrument data. Schlumberger Ltd., the expert system pioneer, sells the data service of an expert system, and uses another system to design exotic electric transformers for its oil-industry service equipment.

Getting close to customers with expert systems means putting the systems in the hands of salespeople. The experience at DEC with their XSEL advisor shows the great promise of expert systems in sales. Navistar proposes to extend its emerging truck-manufacturing expert system to the sales situation. If and when Navistar does it, a milestone will have been reached—to give the ordinary customer the product he wants to buy rather than one of a limited range that you want to sell. The trick is how to couple customer choice with assembly-line technology. That power of computers, to add to consumer choice rather than to consumer frustration, has been a long time in coming.

Company Champions and Their Tactics

The tactics companies have used to get going in expert systems are as diverse as the expert systems' applications. Some company managers have decided that the long-term prospects within their companies for expert systems technology demand that the first system make a big splash. These are the "boulders," like the FMC furnace-monitoring system or the American Express authorization advisor. It takes a great deal of money, company clout, and risk taking to toss a boulder, so other managers choose to do many small systems, making their waves by tossing many "pebbles in the pond." We saw both strategies work well.

An important tactic, and one that is generic to the introduction of any new idea in a company, is the end user buy-in, the art of getting the ultimate user to feel ownership of the new idea, the new system. Throwing it over the wall, from techies to end users, doesn't work. Over and over we saw the successful managers seducing their end users into the emotional commitment of ownership, made tangible by the commitment of budget to help fund the system development.

How do the successful managers we saw "work the organization" to weave the web that will ensure corporate resources and the commitment of others? They do it by networking, the corporate "old boy network." They call on friendship and trust, reopen lapsed friendships, do some arm-twisting, cash in chits accrued for past favors.

The managers, and in some cases the engineers, who hosted us were remarkable people, tirelessly championing their ideas throughout their companies. There seemed to be no end to the energy they brought to the task of championing. Talk, talk, talk, dozens of talks, even hundreds. Fight the battle. Or find a work-around. Never give up. Hide what they're doing, if necessary, until the right moment. Where do they learn this? (Is one born a champion?) They carry around inside themselves a great vision that directs their energy, in searching, finding, and deciding. They are a tiny bunch. What would we do without them?

Some of the champions are young, low in the company hierarchy. They work bottom-up, and their job is tough because they have to persuade both their peers and their superiors. They have the advantage, however, of being in the right place, the operating level. Some of the champions are at the top, vice presidents and even CEOs whose job is to form, hold, and push the strategic company vision. They, too, have a tough job, because they work top-down and are far from the operating level. But perhaps the most difficult position of all for a champion to be in is middle management. He has to work both ways, up and down. He has limited resources, lacks the clout of the people at the top, is not himself at the operating level, and can find his career stalled or ruined if the project he is championing fails.

Government Champions and Their Strategies

Governments too have acted as champions to enhance their national interests in the knowledge-processing technology. The Japanese industrial planners whose superb strategic vision brought about the Japanese lead in steel making, shipbuilding, and semiconductors, caused the most visible international fuss when in 1981 they set forth their ten-year plan for the Fifth Generation computer project. The plan was exciting, far-reaching, revolutionary. It was a blueprint for building a new "knowledge industry." It caused competitive alarms to sound in America and Europe. The United States had little trouble responding. It had a twenty-year history of major Defense Department funding for the science of artificial intelligence, and a tradition that looked favorably on big Defense Department funding for projects of general national interest. And the United States was leading from a position of great technical strength and deep resources of trained scientists in the area. The Europeans responded from a position of technical weakness, the usual fragmentation, smaller budgets, but, happily, excellent leadership. The EEC built a large, multifaceted, supranational project that included knowledge-processing technology, and supported it with Community funds from Brussels. It is called ESPRIT (for European Strategic Program for Research in Information Technology) and also continues. The individualistic British, stronger than their European counterparts in artificial intelligence technology, began a separate national program, called Alvey (and inside that, Intelligent Knowledge Based Systems), that ended in 1987.

It is not national pride that is motivating these actions of governments but national economic interest in staking out a position in the emerging new technology. Dr. Kazuhiro Fuchi, the charismatic head of the Fifth Generation laboratory (ICOT), has said, "Our project was predicated on the prospect that applications of artificial intelligence would become the mainstream of future information processing."

In a 1987 conference titled "Global Information Society," held in West Berlin, Swedish professor Ake Andersson spoke of future "C-region" (competence, communications, culture) cities. He called these cities "knowledge factories," whose work was principally "knowledge handling" by the new methods of advanced technology, not "goods handling" by traditional means and technologies.

Knowledge Processing and the Competitive Edge

The struggle among nations, as among companies, is for competitive edge and, as we look forward, the edge of "working smarter, not working harder." What gives the edge? Resources, and the productivity and creativity of a nation's people. Singapore is a tiny nation, with few natural resources. How do Singaporean opinion makers envision their future? The dean of the faculty of science of the National University of Singapore, Professor Bernard Tan, wrote this in 1985:

> Can Singapore play a vital and pivotal role in the coming information-rich age by exploiting and developing to the fullest its capabilities in information technology and the relevant branches of artificial intelligence? . . . To fulfill its role as a nodal point in the future world information network, I envisage Singapore performing the role of a "knowledge broker" for the world, capable of bringing information and knowledge of every conceivable kind from source to user. As a knowledge broker, most of the knowledge and information

transacted through us would not be actually generated by us, as we could not hope to be able to originate even a minute fraction of the useful knowledge in the world. However, we would need to be adept at all the techniques for manipulating and processing knowledge, so that we could deliver it from source to user more efficiently and cheaply than anyone else. . . . It is imperative that if Singapore is to have such a role, we must make a new start now in equipping ourselves with the requisite expertise in information technology and the relevant fields of artificial intelligence.

The expert systems whose stories are told in the pages that follow are power tools for thinking. The edge they provide is productivity and creativity. It has been a long time since we have seen the arrival on the business scene of a tool of such power and strategic importance. The time to grasp this tool is now.

Chapter 2

The Microcosm Called Northrop

AMERICAN MANUFACTURING, once the nation's pride, has had some hard knocks lately. Not only is it accused of high cost and low quality compared to the manufacturing of other nations, but the foundation upon which U.S. manufacturing has rested—a skilled, well-educated work force—has eroded. Is there any way to recapture the respect *Made in the U.S.A.* once inspired? We offer here a story that says there is: manufacturing better by manufacturing smarter.

Northrop Aircraft in California manufactures jet fighters. These sophisticated aircraft require some 11,000 different types of parts, each of which requires a plan for its manufacture on Northrop's factory floor, or at an off-site vendor's. In addition, these parts must be assembled, and each assembly also requires a step-by-step plan. For a jet fighter, the total requirement can exceed 20,000 plans.

Northrop's problem was that a plan for a typical sheet metal or extrusion part would take six to eight hours of a planner's time, and often required revisions when it was tried out, which added days to the planning process with further impact on manufacturing. Even with experts in charge, the process of drawing up plans for manufacturing parts was error-prone and lengthy. But worse than the time problem was the fact that the experts were getting ready to retire, and nobody was available to take their place.

But now a manufacturing process planner using the expert

system ESP experiences a startling gain in his own productivity. An hour of work in planning the steps needed to manufacture a part is reduced to a few minutes. The speedup seen at Northrop is somewhere between twelve and eighteen times faster (12X–18X). In practical terms the saving is even greater. When people do the process-planning job without ESP's help, up to three different individuals are involved in composing any one particular plan. There is handoff time between the individuals, during which the partially completed plan is sitting on a desk awaiting the next planner's attention. The entire time to completion may be several days. Using ESP, because all the work is done by one person in one session, the time of completion for the average plan is reduced to ten to fifteen minutes.

We begin with Northrop because this company's experience foreshadows many of the major themes of our book: the ten times or greater speedup we've discovered that an expert system introduces into professional work, with multiple payoffs of time and money saved; a way of successfully carrying out tasks of inhuman complexity; the permanent capture of expertise that won't retire or change jobs; a consistent and accurate approach that improves quality; and transforming a hard job into an easier one, freeing the human expert to think more—and better—about tasks he might not have considered before. Last but not least, our Northrop story also illustrates the genuine difficulty of inserting a new technology into existing processes, a problem that demands ingenuity and tenacity.

Manufacturing Smarter

In the dreary, hangar-like structures of its Hawthorne, California, plant, a setting of chain-link minimalism, the aircraft division of the Northrop Corporation manufactures some of the world's most sophisticated jet fighters.

Once an aircraft's design is approved, then its manufacture must be planned. These complicated aircraft, F-5s or F-18s, require some 11,000 to 20,000 different parts and assemblies.

The manufacture of each part and assembly must be planned, step by step, from materials and subassemblies through to the finished item. Drawing up such plans is exacting and complicated, requiring an expertise that combines knowledge of processes and materials. The quality of the manufacturing plans is critical to Northrop's manufacturing efficiency and hence its costs.

To heighten the complexity, Northrop manufactures these fighters for the government, which along with Northrop sometimes mandates a small but essential midstream design change. That too can interrupt Northrop's production process for days while the new part's manufacture is planned and executed.

How does planning for parts manufacture take place? An experienced planner, familiar with shop processes, looks at a part or assembly design and translates that design into written process instructions for the rest of the shop to use. But planning the manufacture of a jet fighter with 20,000 parts and assemblies is a difficult and complex task with great opportunity for error. When errors inevitably occur— a discovery often made on the factory floor—manufacturing is further delayed while the plans are returned to the planners for revision. These revisions may result in rescheduling assembly tasks or, in the case of manufacturing individual parts, delays of hours, days, or (where tooling is affected) weeks.

In early 1983 two young Hawthorne engineers ("literally at the bottom echelons of manufacturing engineering—except for being a trainee," they'd joke later) named Ken Lindsay and Bob Joy were instructed to find some way of automating the manufacturing planning process for making all those jet fighter parts and assemblies.

The planning process was considered a terrible problem, not only because it was expensive and error-prone but also because retirements and death were beginning to wipe out the very experts who had the knowledge to accomplish this task, the eyes and brains that looked at a part and translated it into a step-by-step shop process. Most of the manufacturing planners had been hired in the decade following World War II.

One obvious answer would be to hire replacements. But where? The kinds of people Northrop wanted to hire weren't coming out of the schools. At a meeting Northrop convened with deans and chancellors from many different universities, Northrop complained that it simply wasn't getting the troops it would need to build airplanes in 1995. The academics shrugged: they weren't getting them either.

As for the few qualified college graduates Northrop has been able to hire, about a hundred have undergone a two-year training program, rotating through every manufacturing function. At the end of this expensive training process, the trainees are permitted to pick where they'll work, but only a few have elected to return to a full-time position as planners.

If the universities couldn't help, perhaps good candidates could be found in less exalted schools. Since this was an industrywide problem, the entire aerospace industry formed a committee to talk to junior college and high school educators. They made an offer: If the junior college and secondary schools would just teach some shop math and how to read a drawing, the companies would do the rest. But for one reason or another, the lower schools have barely been able to do even that.

Northrop had to cope. If it couldn't find the people, it had no choice but to explore automation. Thus Lindsay and Joy's task.

Ken Lindsay, a chunky, mustachioed man who might have played linebacker, and Bob Joy, a slight man behind enormous aviator glasses who might have played the oboe, began by considering several different technologies for automating process planning. All these were conventional software solutions, except for one. That exception was artificial intelligence and its expert systems.

It was on a field trip to Palo Alto—sponsored by Computer Aided Manufacturing International, known as CAM-I, an industrial consortium for the cooperative development of computer-aided planning systems—that Lindsay and Joy first heard about AI. The field trip included a visit to Teknowledge, a Silicon Valley startup that was one of the first firms to sell expert system software tools and services.

At the tutorial, Lindsay and Joy were shown examples of expert systems that could solve problems of considerable difficulty, problems that previously were the province of highly skilled specialists, in some cases people with Ph.D.s and M.D.s. They learned that the expertise of these specialists—the knowledge that gave them their expert edge— could be extracted and put into a form for computer use. They were told about the methods by which a computer could be programmed to reason with this knowledge to arrive at solutions to problems of diagnosis, interpretation of data, design, and planning. These methods, they were shown, came from logic and involved the processing of symbols, in contrast to the traditional computer methods that are based on arithmetic and involve processing of numbers. They saw how IF–THEN knowledge forms, called rules, could be used by logical inference steps like the syllogism to create quite complex lines of reasoning. They were shown how these lines of reasoning could be explained to the user of the expert system, and also how the expert system could interact with its user to get the user's statement of the problem to be solved. Finally, the Teknowledge tutorial exposed them to software building tools that make the job of building expert systems easier by providing packaged knowledge forms, reasoning methods, and user interfaces.

Lindsay and Joy couldn't help thinking about their problems back in Hawthorne—the complexity of planning, the wasted time, the lack of skilled people. "No one else saw the relationship between MYCIN [an early medical expert system] and manufacturing automation. But Ken and I knew right away that this was it," Bob Joy says now. At the end of the conference they were so excited they delayed their flight back to Los Angeles so they could talk privately with Teknowledge executives.

Exciting it was, but the entry fee seemed staggering. Ken Lindsay recalls the Teknowledge people saying they couldn't do anything without a hundred-thousand-dollar commitment from the CAM-I program. "Many of the other CAM-I members were unsure about committing to the technology. And everyone was kind of, well, we don't know . . . I remember one comment—two months ago we couldn't even spell AI, and now we were considering shelving other software projects that were already under way."

Yet Lindsay and Joy were convinced they'd found what they needed. Their past experience had shown them how hard—maybe impossible—it was to capture the knowledge of manufacturing processes in conventional computer languages. Rules used in expert systems, on the contrary, provided a means of embedding logic in an English-like format (in fact, in cozily familiar aerospace jargon) that could be easily manipulated when changes came along. As they drove to the airport they vowed to each other, We're going to do *this* thing with *this* technology, "We came back to Hawthorne with evangelistic fervor."

As a corporation, Northrop encourages new ideas, and Lindsay and Joy immediately went to their superiors brimming with new enthusiasm. Teknowledge executives were invited to Hawthorne for talks.

Meanwhile, as part of the handouts at the Palo Alto conference, the two had been given a sample expert system reprinted from *Byte* magazine. This was something of a toy program; its rules concerned the properties of zoo animals, and it was very much like playing Twenty Questions, except it could evoke more than yes-or-no answers. The program would ask about characteristics of an animal you had in mind and then, based on your answers, would guess what that animal was. *Is it a mammal?* the program might ask. *Yes*, you'd say. *Is it carnivorous? Yes. Is it striped or spotted? Spotted*, you'd reply. *Is it a leopard?*

The program was written in the Basic language, and since Lindsay had just bought himself a new Apple, he tried implementing the program on that, lugging the machine in from home to show people the possibilities.

Their immediate manager at the time was less than impressed. Ken Lindsay remembers: "He had a very particular idea of how we should approach these problems, and we were starting to deviate further and further from it." The two gave him a demonstration, showing how the sample expert system could reason about zoo animals. "Bob and I ecstatically said, Look, it said zebra, and that's what I was thinking about! We were superexcited, while the manager could not quite understand what guessing cheetahs and zebras had to do with process planning."

Obviously they had to adapt the program to a context people around Northrop understood, transforming the rules about animal taxonomy into rules for manufacturing airplane parts. Almost surreptitiously, Lindsay began to formulate rules and write them into his Apple, while Joy acted as a smoke screen, dutifully doing what their supervisor expected them to do. In retrospect, it's something of a miracle the little toy program could be adapted; if Lindsay and Joy had been forced to take the high road, asking for a Lisp machine and expensive AI specialty hardware, and praying that if they got it, they could make it work, the stakes would have been much higher and the delay far longer.

Even the zoo-animals-turned-to-fighter-parts program certainly didn't work right away. Lindsay had problems debugging it. He'd take it home and rewrite and debug, until he had spent two or three weeks, day and night, preoccupied with it.

One morning at 3:00 A.M. he woke up with the insight that his problem probably was occurring at the level of the knowledge the program was using, and that he could trace its erroneous reasoning at this level by using the expert system's explanation service, which would give him at each step of the way an explanation of the program's line of reasoning. He sat down at the Apple, spending another hour debugging, until at long last it worked. He was so excited he woke his wife, Jan.

"I said, Honey, honey, get up; and she's like, What? What? I sat her up on the bed and said, Here, you can plan a part! I pulled out an engineering drawing and said, I'll help you read the drawing and answer the questions." Lindsay's wife, sleepy but agreeable, did it; was in effect the first user.

A planner is given an engineering drawing of a part from which he must specify in detail how to manufacture that part. With the expert system, however, Lindsay hoped a planner could merely enter into the system selected descriptions of the engineering drawing, and then the system would itself generate the manufacturing plan. Ken and his wife showed it could be done.

A few hours later that morning Lindsay rushed in to work, telling everybody his program worked. The demo showed that somebody unfamiliar with process planning, unfamiliar with sheet metal parts (indeed, torn from sweet sleep) could do something that normally requires the expertise Northrop had such a terrible shortage of. The demonstration program and accompanying evangelical lecture, fondly known as the Ken and Bob Show, began to be given everywhere. Lindsay and Joy wheeled Lindsay's Apple on a dolly from conference room to conference room, wherever they were invited.

As a consequence of the Ken and Bob Show, management above their immediate boss had begun to get enthusiastic, and the skeptic had to give way (eventually a new manager was assigned to the group). "In every case we've encountered resistance to our work, it's always been an individual," Lindsay says. "It's never been the policy of the company because in general, and especially in the upper levels, we've had excellent support."

With the ball now rolling, they decided to add momentum by hiring one of the small firms specializing in the expert systems area. A Teknowledge vice president, Frederick Hayes-Roth, was invited over to give an assessment of some of their technical ideas and goals, and to deliver a major talk on expert systems to an interdivisional Northrop audience consisting of every manager of manufacturing and engineering (and every other manager Ken and Bob could think of).

"We thought this was going to be a one-shot deal, this would fire everyone up, and away we'd go. So the day came, he arrived, and we had a large conference room scheduled. We invited way too many people and the place was packed, the air conditioner wasn't working. So it was dark, and crowded with every manager that could have any impact on my career at Northrop for the next fifteen years."

Hayes-Roth gave what everybody agrees was a thorough presentation on the state of the art of expert systems in 1983. The Northrop group had pleaded with him to make the talk pertinent to manufacturing, because that was what drove the company, but Hayes-Roth, following an old AI rule that says talk about what you know, used examples from medical expert systems, and talked about the importance of expert systems as a corporate resource. There simply were no manufacturing examples in 1983 to talk about.

"It was the same presentation that had fired us up," Lindsay says, "but we knew it had to zero in on how it could apply to building airplanes. That's what's important at Northrop. It was hot and stifling in there, uncomfortable, hard to concentrate. There was a shop nearby and an operating wind tunnel. The presentation was intermittently drowned out by the *whoosh* of the wind tunnel and the clamor out in the machine shop. What was going on behind those walls was the building of airplanes—parts shortages, all the things these manufacturing managers worry about—and they're hearing *blood diseases*. It just didn't go. It didn't work. I remember going home a wreck. Our expectations were so high about generating enthusiasm and it came out just the opposite. Those few who stuck around for the question-and-answer period got the most out of it, but . . ."

Fortunately, the Ken and Bob Show was already scheduled to be shown to a group of twenty-one managers of manufacturing engineering in the aircraft division, so taking a lesson from what had just happened, they worked late into the night getting their presentation together, making it as pointedly appropriate to local problems as they possibly could. And the results were completely different. The only questions were Where do we go next? and When do we start?

For six months the Ken and Bob Show was on the road around Northrop, moving up higher and higher through the management hierarchy. Lindsay and Joy felt themselves the prophets of the future, and the future was expert systems.

And then they heard that somebody named Steve Lukasik, who could be found at something called the Northrop Research and Technology Center in Palos Verdes, was also talking about expert systems and artificial intelligence. Lindsay and Joy were more than a little peeved: who was this parvenu, and how come he hadn't heard that Lindsay and Joy owned AI at Northrop? It was high time to deliver a lesson in turf and getting there first. They called Lukasik's secretary and told her they'd like to give the man a demo

—the Ken and Bob Show, actually—and when would that be convenient, like *right now?* Appointments were set up, appointments were broken, and always with vague apologies about senators and trips to Washington. The Hawthorne group was mystified, perturbed. Until this guy came on the scene, they hadn't even known Northrop *had* a research center.

Finally the Ken and Bob Show was booked firmly into Palos Verdes. Just before they were about to load the Apple and its dolly into the car, somebody went to the corporate directory just to check out Lukasik's title. There it was: corporate vice president for research.

Indeed, Steve Lukasik had a long and important relationship with artificial intelligence research. As director of the Defense Department's Advanced Research Projects Agency, he'd stood in front of DARPA contractors in the early 1970s and told them that although most programs were funded in a burst and then funding died away, "artificial intelligence is my long-term bet." When he'd moved on to industry, to the nonprofit Rand Corporation and then to Northrop, he'd been one of the first industrialists to see IntelliCorp's expert system software (called KEE, for Knowledge Engineering Environment), which ran on a Lisp machine, an ensemble that in 1983 cost some $150,000. It took Lukasik about three minutes to buy KEE, and how soon could it be delivered?

Lindsay and Joy knew none of this. But as bottom-of-the-hierarchy engineers, they certainly knew what a corporate vice president was. The nervousness factor shot up sharply. When they drove into the Palos Verdes site, they weren't reassured. The research center was about as different as you could get from the grungy real estate of Hawthorne: a corporate Shangri-la on a bluff overlooking the Pacific Ocean, manicured lawns, even a duck pond. The building loomed up over what looked to the Hawthorne group like the steps of the U.S. Supreme Court.

They pulled and tugged the Apple on its dolly up the grand stairs and into the plush reception area, only to discover that a second staircase, even grander, stood between them and Lukasik. Luckily, somebody told them that down the hall was a dumbwaiter that went up to the next floor, so they stashed the Apple onto that, hoped it would take the weight, pressed the button, and dashed up the stairs and along the hallway to receive their baby. Somewhat disheveled, they gave their demo, a boffo performance.

Lukasik was in fact delighted. He became a powerful, crucial ally to the brave little Hawthorne AI group. Palos Verdes was the end of the Ken and Bob Show and the beginning of big-time expert systems at Northrop.

The Northrop expert system, called ESP, would eventually contain knowledge about how to manufacture sheet metal or extrusion parts with the company's current manufacturing facilities. How does ESP work?

For ESP to help make a plan to manufacture a part, it must first obtain information about the part as specified in an engineering drawing. It asks the user, usually a planner, about the part: What is the material type? If it's aluminum, what is the alloy type? Is there any variation in the part thickness? It only asks questions consistent with what it's already been told. If the plan is for an extrusion part it won't ask questions that relate to a sheet metal part, for example. After getting two to three dozen such aspects of the part's description, the system applies the rules in the knowledge base.

Some of the specific rules in its knowledge base have to do with selecting the correct manufacturing machinery:

IF   the edges of a sheet metal part are irregular,
         and the minimum internal radius is greater than .156 inch,
         and the length is between 90 and 140 inches,
         and the width is between 2 and 45 inches,

THEN rout this part using the Marwin router.
     Or:
IF   a sheet metal part is to be drilled

THEN the operational sequence is drill, scribe the tool tabs [remove tabs used to hold the part in place], and deburr [smooth the rim of the drilled holes].

The expert system can also advise on types of tooling:

IF   a sheet metal part needs to have holes drilled
and the part has contour [is not flat]

THEN   use apply-drill template.
   Or:
IF   a sheet metal part needs to have holes drilled
and the part is flat

THEN   use drill template.

Internally, the system generates a rough outline of a plan: saw, rout, drill holes, test, and apply coating. Using this rough outline as a guide, the system applies detailed rules (some were shown above) about each part of the rough plan. The result, or the output of ESP, is a "planning control plan," which lists the sequence of manufacturing tool stations that the raw material must pass through on its way to becoming a specific part, and instructions to the tool operator at each of the tools: " . . . drill per tool instruction; vapor degrease per PI-8008 and K-129; tumble deburr hole edges per PS20016; perform in-process check to prevent damage. Note: edge and surface conditions shall be acceptable provided the surface roughness is 250 RHR or better. . . ."

The problem of planning the manufacture of a plane part is an exacting one, requiring much knowledge from many different sources. A manufacturing plan begins with a part to be manufactured, and then each step in the process must be specified in detail, from raw material to finished product. Before the expert system was introduced, a planner would examine the part drawing and begin to develop the manufacturing plan. Perhaps the part would remind him of one he'd worked on before: he could get out the earlier plan, adjust and revise it, hoping the new version would work. Each planner had his own favorite plans, his own preferred machines for manufacturing, and would sometimes impose them inappropriately or inconsistently. "Inconsistencies in manufacture can be as costly as incorrect manufacture," says Bob Joy.

These are the essentials:

- ESP speeds up an individual's work in producing process steps for the plan by a factor of between twelve and eighteen. When the individual is a trainee or a novice, the speedup is considerably greater. This is the reduction in pure think time. The typical job that heretofore needed three hours of think time is reduced to ten to fifteen minutes of think time by the computer.
- Not all the work of generating the plan involves think time. Approximately four hours are spent in gathering and analyzing information and doing some other necessary procedures and forms. ESP does not assist with this work.
- The three hours of think time are typically done not by one person but by up to three people. As one passes his work to another, there is a loss of flow time because the paperwork sits on a desk awaiting attention. The total time to completion of a process-planning task is typically several days. Because ESP pulls that work together at one time in one place, the typical time to completion is reduced to four and a quarter hours—the ancillary time (four hours) plus the ESP session (ten to fifteen minutes).

As effective as the expert system proved to be, obstacles like gremlins continued to pop up. There was much skepticism on the part of those people trained only in conventional computer systems, and they were in a position to obstruct. Behind this sanitized and bland statement, couched in these terms to protect Lindsay and Joy from vengeful corporate warriors, lies a story rich in bureaucratic turf protection, human inertia, the frustration of alert champions, anger, patience, perseverance, and year-long delays. We have used the Northrop situation to announce our major themes, and this sadly turns out to be one of them. In company after company we were told of the struggles between the expert system champions in functional areas such as manufacturing and engineering and the powerful corporate service bureaucracy known as Management Information Systems, the dreaded MIS. The theme is so striking and important that we have given it a special place of its own in Chapter 6. Lindsay and Joy stuck at it.

ESP's planning time will soon be reduced significantly through a change to faster software. ESP develops a whole new plan, unique to a particular part. The step of checking the plans for correctness has also been drastically reduced because the rules have been supplied by an expert in the first place. If an expert writes incorrect process rules, he can easily change the rules; the system speaks the language of planners, not computerese. Joe Venskus, whose rules are incorporated into the expert system, says that although he has zero programming experience, using KEE it took him less than two weeks to learn how to write and coordinate rules for the knowledge base.

Those roving company ambassadors called management trainees are now exposed to the expert system environment. In the one to two months they spend in the Hawthorne process automation department, they can easily familiarize themselves with the system. Drawing on their experience with the planning expert system, they've already begun to provide significant innovations in manufacturing elsewhere within the company. An unexpected extra: it takes only a few weeks' training for a novice trainee to begin behaving like a master planner of ten or more years' experience, thus freeing the precious skills of the master planners for more important, unusual tasks.

Finally, with the expert system, the corporation is gradually gathering a living library of planning expertise. Knowledge resident in the system represents Northrop's accumulated, collective manufacturing wisdom: "It represents how well we can make aircraft," says Bob Joy.

Because of their experience, the Northrop automation group can now tell very quickly which processes will lend themselves to the expert system treatment and which won't—"and we're asked a lot," Joy says. He praises the software KEE for making the job of automating decision processes much easier. Unlike a conventional computer system, this and other successful expert system development software contain methods that produce software that is human-like in utilizing knowledge, deducing the answer to a problem, and explaining in English how it solved the problem.

Asked to pass on his advice, Joy cautions against biting off too big and difficult a problem in the beginning. "A lot of domains are tempting to tackle because of their criticality. But unfortunately they really involve the conglomeration of many different areas of expertise, and there's no easy short-cut there. We bite off a small chunk, master it, and go on to the next chunk, and then make the first chunk communicate with the second. Been a very effective strategy in here."

Like many manufacturers, Northrop has been concerned about its manufacturing effectiveness, and AI is proving to be an important solution to some of the biggest problems. The company early on recognized that some major costs in manufacturing are no longer on the shop or factory floor, the so-called touch costs. Much of the manufacturing cost is nontouch: the white-collar work, the decision making, problem solving, and data processing that support manufacturing.

"In aerospace, we're trying to carve down the cost of our product, which is very high," says Bob Joy. "We want to automate the processes that are most costly. We've chosen expert systems as a principal tool, and we're kind of proud of our progress to date. We see many more ways to apply it in the future."

Chapter 3

What's an Expert System?

AN EXPLANATION of expert systems requires a few specialized concepts. To fully appreciate the promise of the expert systems in this book, it is worth familiarizing oneself with the concepts and terminology at this point. A glossary is also provided in the back of the book.

Artificial intelligence is a part of computer science. AI's scientific goal is to understand intelligence by building computer programs that exhibit intelligent behavior. It is concerned with the concepts and methods of symbolic inference, or reasoning, by a computer, and with how the knowledge used to make those inferences will be represented inside the machine.

Of course, the term *intelligence* covers many cognitive skills, including the ability to solve problems, learn, and understand language, and AI addresses all of those. But most progress to date in AI has been made in the area of problem solving—concepts and methods for building programs that *reason* about problems rather than calculate a solution. For example, creating a sales plan is a reasoning process, not a calculation process. Expert systems have their roots in this particular area of AI.

AI programs that achieve expert-level competence in solving problems by bringing to bear a body of knowledge are called *knowledge-based systems* or *expert systems*. Often, the term *expert systems* is reserved for programs whose knowledge base contains the knowledge used by human experts, in contrast to knowledge gathered from textbooks or nonexperts. More often than not, the two terms—*expert system* and *knowledge-based system*—are used synonymously.

The area of human intellectual endeavor to be captured in an expert system is called the *task domain*. *Task* refers to some goal-oriented, problem-solving activity, and *domain* refers to the area within which the task is being performed. These days, the most common task for expert systems is diagnosis: Toyota's automobile engine diagnostic system, Westinghouse's systems to diagnose problems in different components of steam turbine generators, and Nippon-Kokan's real-time diagnostic system for a steel blast furnace are examples we'll encounter in this book.

But other kinds of tasks are important to other companies. The task for the Northrop expert system is to plan manufacturing processes of fighter plane parts. Later we'll see Navistar's expert system to specify a truck assembly, one of Schlumberger's expert systems that interprets data gathered from oil wells, and an expert system at IBM that helps deal with bureaucratic paperwork. The range of tasks and domains for expert systems is as wide as the world of professional and semiprofessional work.

Building an expert system is known as *knowledge engineering*. Practitioners are, of course, *knowledge engineers*. The knowledge engineer must make sure that the computer has all the knowledge needed to solve a problem. The knowledge engineer must choose one or more forms in which to represent the required knowledge as symbol patterns in the memory of the computer—that is, he (or she) must choose a *knowledge representation*. He must also ensure that the computer can use the knowledge efficiently—he must select from a handful of *reasoning methods*. We'll describe knowledge engineering later. First, the components of expert systems.

The Building Blocks

Every expert system consists of two principal parts: the knowledge base and the reasoning, or inference, engine.

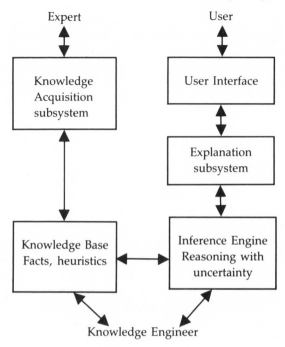

Basic Structure of an Expert System

The *knowledge base* of expert systems contains both factual and heuristic knowledge. *Factual knowledge* is that knowledge of the task domain commonly agreed upon by those knowledgeable in the particular field. For example, in automobiles, "The carburetor system controls the mixture of air and gasoline" is a fact.

Heuristic knowledge is the less rigorous, more experiential, more judgmental knowledge of performance—the knowledge that constitutes the "rules of good judgment" and the "art of good guessing" in a field. "If the car fails to start after several tries, the problem might be a carburetor flooded with gasoline" is heuristic knowledge—an educated guess, since the problem might be a dead battery or some other problem. *Heuristics* also encompasses the knowledge of how to solve problems efficiently, how to improve performance, and so on. Such knowledge, concerned with problem-solving strategy and not with the nuts and bolts of the task domain, is sometimes referred to as *meta-knowledge* (to contrast it with *domain-specific knowledge*). In diagnostics, a strategic piece of meta-knowledge might be: "If there are several possible defective components, check the most accessible components first."

Knowledge representation formalizes and organizes the knowledge. One widely used representation is the *production rule*, or simply *the rule*. A rule consists of an IF part and a THEN part (also called a *condition* and an *action*). The IF part lists a set of conditions in some logical combination. The piece of knowledge represented by the production rule is relevant to the line of reasoning being developed if the IF part of the rule is satisfied; consequently, the THEN part can be concluded, or its problem-solving action taken. For example, IF several attempts were made to start a car and there is a gasoline odor, THEN the carburetor is probably flooded. The meta-knowledge above about diagnostic strategy is also represented in a rule. Expert systems whose knowledge is represented in rule form are called *rule-based systems*.

Another widely used representation, called the *unit* (also known as *frame*, *schema*, or *list structure*) is based upon a more passive view of knowledge. A unit-based system is an assemblage of associated symbolic knowledge about the things to be represented. Typically, a unit consists of a list of properties of the thing and associated values for those properties. "A modern carburetor system consists of the main carburetor, the idle system, the accelerator pump, and an automatic choke. In cold start the choke is closed and the idle system is on."

Since every task domain consists of many entities that stand in various relations, the properties can also be used to specify relations: "a throttle valve is operated by the accelerator pedal"; the throttle valve and the accelerator are related to each other by a particular causal relationship. One unit can also represent knowledge that is a "special case" of another unit, or some units can be "parts of" another unit. "A fuel injection system is a kind of accelerator pump." Or, "a throttle valve is part of the main carburetor." The carburetor system can be described as a network of units, each unit representing a part, with links that relate each part to other parts. The carburetor system itself is a part of the fuel system, which is a part of the engine system, and so on.

The *problem-solving model* (or *paradigm*) organizes and controls the steps taken to solve the problem. One common and powerful paradigm involves chaining of IF-THEN rules to form a line of reasoning. If the chaining starts from a set of conditions and moves toward some (possibly remote) conclusion, the method is called *forward chaining*. If the conclusion is known (for example, it is a goal to be achieved) but the path to that conclusion is not known, then reasoning backwards is called for, and the method is *backward chaining*. These problem-solving methods are built into program modules called *inference engines* or *inference procedures* that manipulate and use knowledge in the knowledge base to form a line of reasoning.

Let's assume that the knowledge base of our automobile diagnostic system contains, among many others, the following two rules: "If the carburetor is flooded, then the car won't start" and "If the battery is dead, then the car won't start." We get into our car one morning, and it won't start and we ask the expert system for help. Using a backward chaining procedure, it determines that either the battery is dead or the carburetor is flooded. The system then tries to establish whether the battery is dead. (Remember the meta-knowledge about testing the most accessible components first.) It asks us to take a voltmeter reading, but not everyone happens to have such an instrument lying around in the garage. We can't provide the answer, so the system uses a well-known heuristic—"If the headlights are left on for a long time when the engine isn't running, then the battery will die." It asks if we left the headlights on, for how long, and whether the engine was off. We suddenly remember we forgot to turn off the headlights last night. And the expert system provides us with a most likely solution: the battery is dead.

Another scenario: At breakfast we remember that we left the headlights on. With a little forward chaining it can be inferred that the car is probably not going to start. The chain of reasoning in either case is simple: the headlights were left on, therefore the battery is probably dead, therefore the car probably won't start.

In diagnosing our car problem, the diagnostic system used pieces of knowledge stored in the knowledge base. Knowledge bases aren't the same as the *data bases* we hear so much about. Confusion about them is common, so it's worth exploring the difference. If you go to the same mechanic for all your automobile problems, he has on file a record, a *data base*, of services he's performed on your car, indicating the last time he changed the oil, did a tune-up, tightened the brakes, replaced the clutch, and so on. If your mechanic doesn't keep such a data base for your car, there is at least a sticker on the front door post with some data.

The knowledge base the mechanic uses is what he learned at mechanics' school, from colleagues, and from years of experience. Presumably the more experience he has, the larger his store of knowledge. Knowledge allows him to interpret the information in the data base to advantage in servicing the car. Missing, inadequate, or incorrect knowledge causes some mechanics to perform poorly. In this respect, data are passive and knowledge is where the action is (or isn't!).

Though an expert system consists primarily of a knowledge base and an inference engine, a couple of other features are worth mentioning: reasoning with uncertainty, and explanation of the line of reasoning.

Knowledge is almost always incomplete and uncertain. Earlier, when we stated that the problem might be a flooded carburetor, what was meant by "might be"? It could have meant that the carburetor is flooded "with certainty," "most likely," "possibly, but probably not," and so on. To deal with uncertain knowledge, a rule may have associated with it a *confidence factor*, or a weight. Using uncertain knowledge in combination with uncertain data in the reasoning process is called *reasoning with uncertainty*. Incomplete knowledge can sometimes manifest itself as uncertain knowledge. Expert systems use knowledge gathered from experts in the task domains to capitalize on their breadth of knowledge.

Because an expert system uses uncertain or heuristic

knowledge (as we humans do) its credibility is often in question (as is the case with humans). "Might be" is a phrase that instantly put us on guard, especially when uttered by a mechanic. When an answer to a problem is questionable, we tend to want to know the rationale. If the rationale seems plausible, we tend to believe the answer. So it is with expert systems. Most expert systems have the ability to answer questions of the form "Why is the answer X?" Explanations can be generated by tracing the line of reasoning used by the inference engine. There might be a dialogue of the following form: "Why doesn't the car start?" "Because the battery is dead." "Why?" "Because the headlights were left on." Rationale can be used to find errors in the line of reasoning as well. Ken Lindsay, struggling with his expert system in the middle of the night, used the explanation facility of his system to find incorrect rules in the knowledge base.

Tools, Shells, and Skeletons

Today there are two ways to build expert systems. They can be built from scratch, or built on a shell. Let's briefly review what knowledge engineers do. Though different styles and methods of knowledge engineering exist, the basic approach is the same. A knowledge engineer interviews and observes a human expert or a group of experts and learns what they know and how they reason with their knowledge. He or she then translates the knowledge into some form usable in the computer, and designs an inference engine, a reasoning structure, that uses the knowledge appropriately. He also determines how to integrate the use of uncertain knowledge in the reasoning process, and what kinds of explanation would be useful to the end user.

Now the inference engine and facilities for representing knowledge and for explaining are programmed, and the domain knowledge is entered into the program piece by piece. It may be that the inference engine is not just right; the form of knowledge representation is awkward for the kind of knowledge needed for the task; and the expert might decide the pieces of knowledge are wrong. All these are discovered and modified as the expert system gradually gains competence. As an aside, *incremental development* and the extensive involvement of experts all through the program's development are key features of the expert system building process.

Compared to the wide variation in domain knowledge, only a small number of AI methods are useful in expert systems. That is, currently there are only a handful of ways in which to represent knowledge, or to make inferences, or to generate explanations. Thus, systems can be built that contain these useful methods without any domain-specific knowledge. Such systems are known as *skeletal systems*, *shells*, or simply *AI tools*. Like prefabricated houses, the major shape and components are predetermined, and the buyer chooses and adds features that make the house uniquely his or her own. Of course the resulting house looks essentially like all other prefabricated houses from the same catalog, but the advantages are obvious: Building is cheaper and faster, and avoids all the headaches associated with dealing with architects and contractors, not to mention having to specify in very great detail exactly what one wants.

Building expert systems by using shells offers the same kinds of advantages. A system can be built to perform a particular task by entering into a shell all the necessary knowledge about a task domain—the inference engine that applies the knowledge to the task is built into the shell. Northrop's expert system to aid in the planning of manufacturing processes was built using an AI tool called KEE. A system described in Chapter 5 and developed by American Express uses a shell called ART. If the program is not very complicated and if an expert has had some training in the use of a shell, the expert can enter the knowledge himself. Du Pont has dozens of expert systems, all developed by experts or their assistants using Insight (a rule-based shell for personal computers) and an internally developed shell called the Tool Kit.

Many commercial shells are available today, ranging in size from shells on PCs to shells on workstations to shells on large mainframe computers. They range in price from hundreds to tens of thousands of dollars, and range in complexity from simple, forward-chained, rule-based systems requiring two days of training to those so complex that only highly trained knowledge engineers can use them. They range from general-purpose shells to shells custom-tailored to a class of tasks, such as financial planning or real-time process control.

How does one decide which shell to use for a given application? There are only a few agreed-upon criteria for choosing the "right" tools and methods for a given problem, although more criteria are emerging. Our stories here show that rule-based systems with simple inference engines seem to serve well for a wide range of applications. But large and complex problems still require the expertise of highly trained knowledge engineers. The need for expertise is the same in any field.

Although shells simplify programming, in general they don't help with knowledge acquisition. The choice of reasoning method, or of a shell, is important, but it isn't as important as the accumulation of high-quality knowledge. As we indicated earlier, the competence of our mechanic is directly related to the breadth and depth of his knowledge. The power of an expert system lies in its store of knowledge about the task domain—the more knowledge a system is given, the more competent it becomes.

Bricks and Mortar

The fundamental working hypothesis of AI is that intelligent behavior can be precisely described as symbol manipulation and can be modeled with the symbol-processing capabilities of the computer.

In the late 1950s, a special programming language was invented by Professor John McCarthy (then at MIT, now at Stanford) that facilitates symbol manipulation. Called Lisp, for LISt Processing, it allows computer programmers to avoid dealing with all the complex details of symbol processing. Because of its simple elegance and flexibility, almost all AI programs are written in Lisp, including most of the commercial shells. In the past few years special-purpose computers, known as *Lisp machines*, whose architecture is especially tailored to Lisp, have been built. Several companies manufacture and market them, including Symbolics, Texas Instruments, Xerox, and Fujitsu.

In the early 1970s another AI programming language was invented by Professor Alain Colmerauer at the University of Marseilles. It's called Prolog, for PROgramming in LOGic. Lisp has its roots in one area of mathematics (lambda calculus), Prolog another (first-order predicate calculus).

The basic operations in Lisp are adding a symbol to a list of symbols (in many different ways), retrieving a symbol from a list (again in many different ways), and evaluating expressions—for example, "Is the third word in a list (battery is dead) 'dead' or 'live'?" Using these basic capabilities, Lisp programs can freely manipulate arbitrarily complex symbols and symbol structures.

Prolog, on the other hand, consists of English-like statements that are facts (assertions), rules (of inference), and questions. Assertions might be: "The float-chamber is a part-of the carburetor. The induction-pipe is a part-of the carburetor. The throttle-valve is a part-of the carburetor." An inference rule: "If object-x is part-of object-y then one component-of object-y is object-x." A query in the form "What are the components-of a carburetor?" returns "Float-chamber, induction-pipe, throttle-valve."

Programs written in Prolog have behavior similar to rule-based systems written in Lisp. Prolog, however, did not immediately become a language of choice for AI programmers. In the early 1980s it was given impetus with the announcement by the Japanese that they would use a logic programming language for the Fifth Generation Project. Prolog became *prolog*, standing for a variety of logic-based programming languages. One of the first products to come out of the Fifth Generation Project is a *PSI machine* (Personal Sequential Inference machine) manufactured and distributed by Mitsubishi Electric Company. PSI is a *prolog machine*, a counterpart of the Lisp machine.

In concluding about expert systems, if one accepts the hypothesis that human intelligence arises from a human ability to manipulate symbols, then we can see why a computer has the potential for intelligent behavior. Knowledge, a conglomeration of concepts, can be represented in the computer. Knowledge engineers do not yet know how to represent all knowledge. Today's expert systems lack common sense, because not much is known about how to represent some commonsense knowledge. But knowledge engineers do know how to represent substantial bodies of useful knowedge.

And reasoning, a goal-directed manipulation of knowledge, can be performed by a computer. There are many ways to reason, and some are poorly understood by today's AI science—no expert system today can reason by analogy, for example. Today's expert systems are confined to narrowly defined task domains. Expertise, even in well-circumscribed tasks, can consist of hundreds of thousands of facts and heuristics. Today's pragmatics of knowledge acquisition, knowledge base maintenance, and computer size and speed preclude systems that can reason over broad task domains. But then we don't expect our favorite mechanic to be a car designer or to know that carburetor design is based on Bernoulli's law, either. We are at a stage where we know enough to build economically viable expert systems.

Knowledge Engineering

Knowledge engineering is the art of designing and building expert systems. Knowledge engineers are the practitioners of knowledge engineering. Gerald M. Weinberg said of programming in *The Psychology of Programming*: " 'Programming'—like 'loving'—is a single word that encompasses an infinitude of activities." Knowledge engineering is the same, perhaps more so. We stated earlier that knowledge engineering is an applied part of the science of artificial intelligence, which in turn is a part of computer science. Theoretically, then, a knowledge engineer is a computer scientist who knows how to design and implement programs that incorporate artificial intelligence techniques. The nature of knowledge engineering is changing, however, and a new breed of knowledge engineers is emerging. We'll discuss the evolving nature of knowledge engineering later.

The discovery and accumulation of techniques of machine reasoning and knowledge representation is generally the work of artificial intelligence research. The discovery and accumulation of knowledge of a task domain is the province of the domain expert. Domain knowledge consists of both formal, textbook knowledge and experiential knowledge—the *expertise* of the experts.

A knowledge engineer is an intermediary who combines AI methods and techniques with knowledge about the task domain to create expert systems. Like experts in other domains, an expert knowledge engineer brings to the task of building expert systems many diverse sources of knowledge. Much of the knowledge is "hard" knowledge, like the knowledge of programming. Some is heuristic knowledge, like "Use backward chaining if the task can be formulated as a classification problem." A knowledge engineer must keep abreast of the results of AI research—a new knowledge-representation formalism or a new twist in a forward chaining technique—and be aware of their strengths and weaknesses and their applicability to different types of problems.

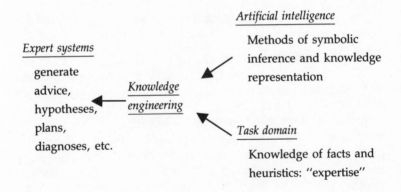

Knowledge Engineering Task

As an intermediary between a human expert and a computer that will emulate the expert's expertise, a knowledge engineer has two primary tasks—getting the expert to articulate what he knows about his field, and encoding this knowledge in the computer. How might a knowledge engineer go about these tasks? First, since the expert and the knowledge engineer must be able to communicate, and since the expert cannot be expected to translate his knowledge into computerese, the burden falls on the knowledge engineer to understand the expert's language and jargon that pervade every field. By reading textbooks and articles, the knowledge engineer can get some rudimentary appreciation of the field.

The knowledge engineer is now ready for a series of interviews with the expert. There are two types of information a knowledge engineer must glean from these interviews. One is, of course, specific pieces of facts and heuristics the expert uses; we had an example earlier in the statement "If a carburetor is flooded, a car probably won't start." Another type of information is a bit more indirect—the knowledge engineer must figure out how the expert manipulates the knowledge, that is, figure out his thinking process. This information forms the basis for the design of the reasoning engine of the expert system. Example: If a car won't start, the expert may hypothesize all the possible causes of the malfunction and gather all the necessary data at once (breadth first), or he may focus on the most common cause and only gather the data needed to support that hypothesis, and if that turns out not to be the cause, focus on the next common cause, and so on (depth first). Whether the expert tends to solve the problem in one way or the other makes a difference in the design of the expert system. Why not directly ask the expert how he goes about his reasoning?

Asked to describe how he solves a problem, an expert generally gives a very sanitized, textbook version. Invariably, that is not the way he really solves the problem. Not that textbooks are wrong, but the real world seems to hold more exceptions to the rules than described in textbooks. The only way to find out how problems are really solved is to have the expert solve example problems and have him verbalize what he is doing. Even then, he may say that piece of data indicates something while he is looking at another piece of data. Or a piece of knowledge that worked in one example doesn't work for a new example. All this is not to say that experts are dishonest, but that their expertise is so ingrained they are often unaware of the details of what they are doing. It's like trying to explain how to tie shoelaces to a child—if we can describe it at all, we leave out subtle details that make all the difference. Articulating what one does naturally is a very difficult thing to do.

Whether by working through examples or by critiquing the performance of the evolving expert system, the knowledge engineer must get the expert to verbalize knowledge he wasn't aware that he even had. For computer scientists, who never enjoyed a reputation for being great communicators, the interview process can be one of the most challenging aspects of knowledge engineering.

During the initial interviews with the expert, the knowledge engineer is not necessarily looking for the actual pieces of knowledge used in solving problems. Instead, the knowledge engineer is looking for things that affect the performance and the design of the system. How diverse is the knowledge being used? (If too diverse, the knowledge acquisition may take too long.) Are the concepts and techniques being used generally agreed upon within the field? (If not, the system will have a very difficult time being accepted by others.) How long does it take the expert to solve a problem? (If more than a few hours, the problem may be too difficult given the current state of the technology.)

While listening to the expert, the knowledge engineer begins to form a mental model of the expert system—use rules for heuristics, use units for facts of the domain, use primarily backward chaining but allow for some forward chaining, save rules used during system execution for use in explaining the line of reasoning, and so on. If a knowledge engineer is experienced, he may have come across a similar problem before and can use a similar system design. If not, he must try out in his mind many different models made up of different combinations of methods and techniques.

After the initial interviews, the knowledge engineer designs an expert system with a reasoning method that closely matches the expert's problem-solving process. It is programmed, and knowledge used to solve the example problems be encoded. Psychologically, it is very important that the first version of the system be built quickly—experts, like everyone else, like their gratification sooner than later, and nothing can make a busy expert lose interest faster than a project that seems to disappear into a black hole. The first version will have many things wrong with it: the knowledge engineer may have misunderstood the expert, he may have made an inappropriate choice of reasoning method or knowledge representation, or pieces of knowledge might be wrong. The knowledge engineer and the expert hold another round of interviews. The process of updating the system and the expert critiquing the system that is supposed to mimic his problem-solving behavior is repeated over and over again.

Sometimes the behavior of the program may inspire the expert to reevaluate the way he performs his task, and he may come up with a better way to do the job. Or as the knowledge in the system accumulates, the knowledge engineer might think of a better way to represent the knowledge. All this calls for changes to the system. The development of an expert system is an evolutionary process of extracting the expert's knowledge, transferring it into a computer program, testing, and modifying the reasoning method and the knowledge base.

This incremental software development practiced by knowledge engineers is in direct contrast to the practice of traditional software engineers. In software engineering the application task is analyzed, and the requirements, and the knowledge necessary to meet the requirements, are specified by the expert and the software engineer. The software engineer then builds a program that meets the specified requirements exactly. This approach often raises the issue of whether the expert knew what he really wanted at the beginning and whether that information was correctly communicated. In knowledge engineering the determination of the requirements, system design, and implementation occur concurrently. The desired system unfolds in stages, each stage improving on the competence or the desirability of the system at the previous stage.

Whereas practices and guidelines exist to manage software engineering projects, there still are no well-defined guidelines for managing knowledge engineering projects. How does a manager evaluate a knowledge engineer's performance when there is no existing metric to show how far he has progressed toward an acceptable expert system? This and other "cultural" differences are sources of tension that are seen over and over again in this book between the old and the new breed of system developers.

Why can't expert systems be developed in a traditional manner? Why is it that throughout the book we hear people say they couldn't solve the problem with "conventional" programs? A part of the answer lies in the kinds of problems that AI has addressed and in the methodologies that evolved in the process of tackling these problems.

AI scientists like to study ill-structured problems. Ill-structured problems are characterized by a "solution" that is not precisely defined and by the absence of a predefined way of obtaining the "solution." Let's say a businessman travels often between San Francisco and Washington. He's communicated to his assistant his preferences: nonstop, wide-body, leave San Francisco in the early afternoon, leave Washington in the late afternoon, and so on. Often there is no flight that exactly suits his preferences. How does his assistant cope? Suppose there is no nonstop. If it's in the winter, he might avoid a flight with a stopover at a northern city; he might decide to avoid flights with a stopover at O'Hare altogether on a certain carrier, because he has often been delayed there while the plane waited for a gate. Although people face ill-structured problems all the time, they are capable of coming up with acceptable solutions, if not optimal ones. They are able to do so, not because there are prescribed ways of solving the problem, but because they know a lot. They can apply knowledge in a reasoned manner and come up with a reasonable solution—people who know more do better than people who know less. As will be seen in this book, many of the expert systems are able to "mimic" the problem-solving behavior of human experts, and are able to handle ill-structured problems quite well.

Currently, there appear to be two types of knowledge engineers. The first type, who fit the mold we just described, designs and implements reasoning systems that closely mimic the cognitive behavior of the experts. The second, new class of knowledge engineers organizes and encodes knowledge in forms dictated by expert system shells. They generally do not have an academic background in artificial intelligence; they often have no programming experience. Whereas the first type of knowledge engineer is not very common, the latter type of knowledge engineer is on the rise. It includes experts who build their own expert systems. The "old type" knowledge engineers tend to migrate to research labs or to cutting-edge development projects. The new breed of knowledge engineer, more an expert-system-shell expert, can be trained quickly, and they are capable of building many useful expert systems. This is a very fortunate turn of events, since the universities are unable to produce knowledge engineers fast enough to meet the rising demand.

Summary

Expert systems involve techniques for representing human knowledge, and methods by which that knowledge can be used by the computer to reason toward the solution of problems that are difficult enough to require significant human expertise for their solution. Every expert system consists of two principal parts: the knowledge base and the reasoning methods, or inference engine.

Knowledge bases contain factual and heuristic knowledge. The factual knowledge—like knowledge in textbooks or journals—is widely shared and easily obtained. In contrast, heuristic knowledge is rarely discussed, and is largely private among experts. It is the knowledge of good practice, good judgment, and plausible reasoning in the field. It is the knowledge that underlies the "art of good guessing."

The inference methods used by expert systems are often

based on mathematical logic. Most commonly used are "forward chaining" methods that reason from conditions to conclusions, or "backward chaining" methods that reason from goal statements to conditions.

The most important ingredient in any expert system is knowledge. The power of expert systems resides in the specific high-quality knowledge they contain about task domains. AI researchers will continue to explore and add to the current repertoire of knowledge representation and reasoning methods. But *in knowledge resides the power*. Because of the importance of knowledge in expert systems and because the current knowledge acquisition method is slow and tedious, much of the future of expert systems depends on breaking the "knowledge acquisition bottleneck" and in codifying and representing a large knowledge infrastructure. Chapter 13 is devoted to the future of knowledge systems.

Chapter 4

Internal Cost Savings and Product Quality Control

WHEN A NEW TECHNOLOGY appears above the business horizon, companies usually try it out on problems involving internal operations. Internal problems are more visible and better understood than problems involving markets and customers. The possible gains, risks, and costs can be more easily assessed on internal problems, and the effect on corporate performance more accurately measured. So it was with the early adoption of expert systems.

Expert systems provide great opportunities for internal cost savings and the quality control of products. We begin with IBM, perhaps the world's most admired corporation, and show how this computer manufacturing giant has introduced expert systems into internal manufacturing processes, and—a charming surprise—into office procedures, to guide employees through the (alas, inevitable) bureaucracy.

We follow with another industrial giant, the conglomerate called FMC, which has introduced an expert system into a heavy industrial manufacturing process—the manufacture of phosphorus—to help control costs, avoid waste, and prevent premature equipment failures and catastrophes, all this by capturing a lifetime of furnace expertise.

Finally, the Toyota Corporation and Britain's National Health Service have also introduced expert systems to help them control costs and quality in auto repair and human repair, respectively.

IBM: The Great Mountain Moves

Harrison: Our Middle Name Is Business

IBM, one of the world's largest corporations—and one of the most admired—came to expert systems somewhat late compared to two of the other computer firms whose stories we'll tell later, Digital Equipment and Texas Instruments. However, in the usual IBM tradition, once the corporation decided to move, it was grand opera, not chamber music.

IBM's relatively late arrival wasn't because no one at IBM was watching. In the mid-1960s, as the first expert system was being designed at Stanford, Horace Flatt, a senior staff member of IBM's modest-sized Palo Alto Scientific Center, used to make periodic visits to the Stanford people just to see what they were doing in AI, and he found it all very interesting. During the 1970s and early 1980s, certain small-scale expert system projects were under way all around the IBM corporation, and at the company's distinguished research laboratories in Yorktown Heights the topic was under intense study, if not intense development. But among all these efforts there was no coordination and very little communication; and there was certainly nothing like a grand plan.

And then, in 1985, IBM's Management Committee, consisting of its board chairman and CEO, and its senior vice presidents, received a report it had commissioned on the whole question of artificial intelligence. In essence, the report declared that the technology was maturing enough for IBM to take official corporate notice of it; that it would sooner or later permeate all areas of the corporation's activities, internal and external. The report noted research and development already under way, but asked whether the corporation was doing enough.

Wasn't it possible, the report suggested, that the inevitable—and its attendant benefits—could be hastened with careful strategic planning? To be sure, at IBM that did not mean appointing an AI czar to impose the technology on IBM's far-flung masses; nor did it mean establishing an independent business unit to produce, make, or otherwise be in charge of AI.

Instead, the report recommended that IBM establish a small, high-level group with open-door access to top management, a group that could facilitate this inevitable change wherever it was taking place, stimulate it if need be, but all the while making sure that resources put into AI would be consonant with corporate strategic goals.

It would be a group that asked whether IBM was doing enough development, and whether the development was the right kind; it would be charged with ensuring ways of preparing the marketing people and their customers, identifying *strategic* opportunities, the opportunities with a big payoff. The group would make sure AI was properly organized and that researchers, developers, and customers were all communicating, so there was minimum redundancy. It was an unorthodox approach for IBM, which likes more conventional organizational units and usually measures success in terms of revenue and expenses. But this was different, the report argued; this would be to the next decade's business what conventional computing had been thirty years ago. So radical and far-reaching a change in business practices required a novel approach.

However persuasive the report's rhetoric, its authors were unsure just how clearly the *idea* of expert systems had jelled in the minds of top management. The Management Committee comprised very bright but very busy men; they had parallel processing and supercomputers and ten other things besides AI to think about for IBM's future. Maybe a demonstration would help.

Roger Goldwyn, an animated, almost elfin man, who was a manager of technical planning for systems at Yorktown Heights, remembers finding a systems engineer out in the field who'd put together a little expert system to help in making decisions about insurance underwriting (a topic the man happened to be interested in because he was pursuing a Ph.D. in it). "We must have rehearsed this thing two dozen times, and we kept telling him to stay away from the technical details." In fact, Goldwyn told him to breathe not a word about the Ph.D.; the management people might think he was more of a scientist than he really was.

When the demonstration was over, somebody on the committee asked a question. Suddenly the engineer got excited, broke out of his carefully rehearsed patter, and, as Goldwyn puts it, began selling his system: look what I can do, if I want to change the underwriting rules, or add a rule to the knowledge base; now let's see what the system does, and how it changes.

John Akers, the board chairman and CEO, watched all this. Finally he spoke. "You mean these are the kinds of software changes that normally I'd get back from my information systems shop in nine, eighteen months?" The engineer nodded enthusiastically. Akers understood all the implications of that perfectly and immediately.

"It was high-risk, plucking this person out of the field and putting him in front of the Management Committee; it was one of the first live demonstrations they'd ever been given, and it went across very successfully, really gave people a feeling for what expert systems were all about," Goldwyn says. Even better, the demo answered a big question: Did expert systems require high-priced talent to implement? "This was a mortal who could do it, not a Ph.D. in computer science." The Management Committee put the report's recommendations into effect at once.

To head this new high-level group they chose Herbert Schorr, vice president of systems in the research division and a longtime IBM research scientist from Yorktown Heights. Schorr has a rare combination of technical and business savvy that makes him credible to both sides of IBM's house. He holds a Ph.D. in electrical engineering and is so serious a collector of contemporary art that museums ask to borrow from him. He descended from the *haute moderne* halls of Yorktown Heights to the *bas-blah* buildings of IBM's Harrison, New York, site—a trip that must have been as aesthetically dispiriting as it was professionally exciting.

"My mandate? Oh, to bring the technology into the company, and make IBM a world leader at it," he says cheerfully.

To Schorr, developing AI was the easiest part. One benefit of a late corporate decision to pay attention was that no selling, no consciousness-raising, no persuading had to be done; IBM's best and brightest were clamoring to work on expert systems. It would, however, be much, much harder to bring the marketing people and their customers around. They responded to different pressures.

As IBM always does, the AI group went around talking to customers. Which do you prefer, they asked, Lisp or Prolog? People looked blank. It was like asking commuters whether they preferred a rotary to a piston engine. All they wanted to know was would it get them there.

And then there was the problem of identifying the really strategic applications internal to IBM, distinguishing the garden follies from real architecture, so to speak. Which internal application would make the big difference, deliver the big payoff?

In July 1985, when Schorr and his group got started, their first task was to sort out the problems, choose among the seemingly endless possibilities. Bob Bachman, who'd come to Harrison with Schorr, asked himself the big question: How much is enough? Bachman was educated in North Carolina, which from time to time colors his voice. His history of science master's thesis on information across scientific disciplines had come to the attention of IBM, which thought Bachman's would be an interesting mind to have around the corporation. Bachman calculated that two years later, in 1987, IBM would have 150 internal applications in some stage of development. By 1988 it would have 5 significant applications, and in 1989, 5 others that were critical. Is that enough? he asked himself. If that's enough, I can take the rest of the year off, because IBM's pioneers are going to do that, and no one will stop them. That's simply what will happen by natural means. The flip side of that, he'd say later, was that anything more would have to take place by unnatural means.

And indeed, as he and his colleagues surveyed the expert system activities throughout the IBM empire, they found many being developed by adventurous experts with a flair for technology. Why had a given expert picked a certain system to do? Because that was what he or she knew. "Finding out whether that bit of expertise is of true value is an extraordinarily difficult task," Bachman would say later. "At this stage, the biggest gating factor to the development of this technology is a good method for evaluating expertise. What is it? How much of it is there? What would you gain by automating it? If you knew that, business cases could produce the rest."

As it turned out, Bachman's projected schedule of the significant applications was way too modest. By 1988 there were some four dozen significant expert systems in use at various IBM sites, and there were more than 120 major systems in the works. These ranged from systems that help control manufacturing processes to those that aid computer engineers and salespeople, and detect defects in computing equipment. "I mean major systems," Schorr emphasizes. "Nobody has the faintest idea how many expert systems exist on personal computers around the company."

"The area was going to grow, no matter what anybody did," says Roger Goldwyn, who also came with Schorr from Yorktown Heights to Harrison. "But Herb was able to put intellectual content into it. This, coupled with the fact that there was a growing business awareness, made it more successful than it might otherwise have been."

The AI group has stayed small. "Our view is, if we grow, then we haven't been successful in driving this technology into the mainstream," says Goldwyn. But IBM's august Management Committee is taking a very close interest in the group. Schorr himself meets nearly monthly with a subcommittee to make what he calls midcourse corrections toward the strategic goals, and reports between two and three times a year to the full committee. "This is a very fast-moving field, and different marketing conditions require different tactics."

Among IBM's many successful expert systems is one similar to DEC's XCON/XSEL, to be described in Chapter 11, which IBM is using to help sales representatives determine the exact components needed in minicomputer configurations. Schorr has said publicly that the problem of configuring such a custom machine is so hard that without an expert system the product virtually couldn't be sold. But IBM also has expert systems in many other places, including an innovative one to create intelligent courseware for graduate students in music.

We've chosen three of their most interesting applications—one from product manufacturing, one from product assembly, and a final one from office procedures. Though the office procedures system may be the simplest, it may also symbolize the most significant applications expert systems will come to have. For when Schorr looks ahead, he sees that the so-called front office functions are going to be automated by this new office procedures technology just as thirty years back office functions were automated by conventional computing.

In one interesting way, IBM's careful planning has gone awry. Schorr won't disclose numbers, and chuckles as he says it: "Our revenue picture is much rosier than we foresaw; we're getting a significant return on expert systems much faster than we ever expected."

Burlington: Making the Complicated Easy—Almost

Gary Sullivan, the manager of advanced industrial engineering at IBM's Burlington, Vermont, chip fabrication plant, says it plainly: "The only words any bigger than artificial intelligence or expert systems in industry right now are *continuous flow manufacturing*. That stands for the minimization of waste, the reduction of the time to flow the parts from launch to delivery to customer. The Japanese use terms like *kanban* (just in time). Our approach was to take advantage of some of the leverages that we thought would be available in current expert system technologies."

The plant where Sullivan works makes IBM's most advanced chip: 1-megabit, 80-nanosecond cycle, the fastest, biggest chip in production. If the fastest and biggest such items qualify as the most complicated devices ever fabricated (and they do), it stands to reason that their fabricating process is also among the most complicated on earth. And sure enough, every day at Burlington, chips move through a fabricating process of between 200 and 300 steps. "There's a lot of room for things to get out of control, and a lot of human expertise involved in keeping it under control," Sullivan says.

The making of microelectronic chips is most easily thought of as an extraordinarily refined printing and etching process. The printing and etching is done on thin round wafers of silicon, the same material found in sand, but purified as much as possible. The wafer is coated, repeatedly, with a photosensitive material to record the millions of lines of the chip design. The wafer is exposed to radiation that will "print" the lines. Since there are millions of lines in a tiny space, the photolithography machines that do this are extremely refined and expensive. Other steps in the process wash the wafer, fill etched channels with metal, implant impurities as necessary (but very carefully), and go through dozens of other procedures, then do them many times over in a carefully controlled sequence. The finished wafer contains dozens or hundreds of the desired microchip, and is diced into the individual chips.

A wafer travels many days on this journey. Its home is a box of similar wafers, and the box is often transported from step to step by robot machinery. The factory in which microchips are made is a huge "clean room," since the slightest contamination from dust or human skin cells can ruin the wafer production. An eerie quiet prevails as operators, clothed in protective disposable "bunny suits" to inhibit contamination, move through the filtered air doing their jobs.

Consider the problem: an operator on the fabrication line is responsible for the work-in-process stream through a number of fabrication tools. Some of the tools—the photolithography machine, for example—are very expensive, perhaps costing a million dollars or more, and so there is a relatively small number of these. Other tools are quite cheap, and plentiful. Chip wafers flow quickly through the low-utilization, cheap tools, and then get in line to go through the highly utilized expensive tools, the so-called pinchpoint, or bottleneck, tools. This lineup delay causes imbalances in the production line, which can actually start the work-in-process oscillating, because as wafers wait to go through the expensive pinchpoint tool, their photosensitive coating begins to deteriorate. Now the coating will no longer accept sharp, definitional images; the wafers have to be pulled from the line and reworked, and the whole process started over again. "That's a cost, and every time you cycle through the system, you get breakage and new losses. So there's real incentive to straighten out the logistics of the production line."

The operator responsible for all this has other worries, too. Tools he's responsible for can't all run the same kind of products, and since he has a mixed stream of products, he has to think about which product is going where. Furthermore, tools are idiosyncratic about when and how they age, and what effects that produces. The operator remembers them and compensates for them; he must also observe the status of all the tools he's responsible for, not only from the instrument readouts, but, from time to time, by personally verifying those readouts by randomly checking the tool. Meanwhile, of course, he has to keep in mind process specifications, the sequence of fabricating steps. Each wafer must go through, say, a photo process ten or fifteen times, each process building a layer resulting in a three-dimensional complexity—you can't build level B before you build level A. All this is compounded by a difficulty other line workers don't share. That is, if an auto comes down an assembly line, it looks like a car in some stage of assembly, but all boxes, as the wafers are called, look alike: the box coming down the line looks exactly the same whether it represents ninety-nine pieces of work, forty-nine pieces, or even two pieces. If an important customer comes in with a special request in a hurry, then everything's up for grabs. *Modern Times* at its worst.

"It's a big job," says Sullivan, "and the operator gets very, very busy. Frequently he gets overloaded. He responds as humans always do to high levels of work-in-process ahead of them, by trying to work faster, or panicking, or getting depressed."

So the industrial engineers faced a challenge: find the optimal match between the work-in-process stream and the tool capacity, given all those constraints of tool use and timeliness. Good operators do it routinely up to a point, and then they break, go into cognitive overload, and start making erratic decisions.

"Our objective was to capture the knowledge a good operator has working at his best, the expertise of where to send a given kind of wafer, and when. If we could capture that knowledge in an expert system, emulate that set of decisions, we could give the operator a cognitive amplifier; when he approached his breaking point, he could turn to it." But conventional industrial engineering models of process control and logistics (generated by existing software) simply didn't work well. Soon after the process began, the steady state plan offered by those conventional models was no longer any good. And anyway only industrial engineers could understand the results.

"We weren't getting much decision confidence from people. We'd run the model, we'd work to get all the factors in. Everybody'd say, That's cool, but I'm not gonna bet the ranch on it."

Sullivan's group regrouped. Obviously people weren't interested in neat mathematical models; they wanted a model that included objectives and judgmental decisions involved in managing a line. In 1984 the industrial engineers requested funds to develop an expert system. "We built a rule-based modeling scheme, with an inference engine that was separate from all of the rules; thus we could reuse an inference engine over and over again." In other words, Sullivan and his group built a shell, eventually to be called XEN, for eXpert ENvironment. They added a good user interface with graphics, so that it would be easy to use.

As they set about the knowledge engineering, the industrial engineers soon discovered that an operator's decisions were driven not only by the work-in-process stream but also by the expectations of his high-level boss, the superintendent, the person responsible for the fabrication process from start to finish. Therefore they decided to model not only the operator's best decision processes, but also the superintendent's. In this case it was a man named Tom Henry, then in charge of the smallest fabricator at the Burlington site.

Henry himself was extremely cooperative, not only permitting his own decision processes to be modeled and opening his organization to the knowledge engineers, but also acting as an early corporate sponsor. He would later become superintendent of the largest fabricator at the site, and would take the knowledge engineers with him, giving them a whole new set of problems to solve.

For operator and manager alike, the whole manufacturing process is like a giant chess game—except the complicated sequencing, combinatorial complexity, and unpredictability make it harder to think through than even that most demanding of games.

To understand and control the complex manufacturing process, when IBM built the plant they put in place a computer-based factory automation system to track the progress of the boxes of wafers as the work made its way through the numerous processing steps. Operators and their managers can access the computer to track the flow of work through the plant. The system is a window on their work that allows them to manage the flow intelligently. But the tracking system as initially installed provided no decision-making aids for the operators and managers, no intellectual power tool to assist them, but only data to allow them to do their job. The project to supplement the data-collection system with an expert system was an attempt to give plant personnel a power tool to manage the complexity of their tasks, and help them do their job better.

The Logistics Management System, or LMS, as everyone at Burlington calls the expert system, is now embedded throughout the plant, helping managers and operators control the processes. It advises operators and managers on the prioritization of work in the queues, on the rerouting of work if a problem develops at one of the workstations, and it automatically sends messages to workstations upstream and downstream of the problem advising them of a specific change of schedule. LMS is a rescheduling advisor, operating moment by moment to ensure that the work in process never exceeds certain limits. It maximizes the utilization of tools while minimizing rework.

LMS also eases another difficult problem. The ordinary problem of shutting down the line for the weekend is fraught with complexities because etching must be done on certain chips within a certain time, or else the process must restart from the beginning. One IBMer says, "You want to shut the line off at a good enough time where the last shift will have work to do, but not a time where the new shift is gonna have to rework it. It's too tough for us humans to figure out."

The system also permits exploring alternative line controls. When something acts to destabilize the line, a rule might say: Run the model to see what the best way to rebalance the line is, so that we can shorten the queue on this machine; or, Force this batch through the process ahead of some other things that are already in the queue, perhaps to take advantage of the knowledge that certain machines or tools down the line are not working. Thus LMS maintains a constant awareness of the state of the line and possible alternatives to keep it moving at peak efficiency.

When Tom Henry saw it he loved it, and immediately embraced it as a management tool. Of course, as Sullivan now admits, Tom Henry's personality is all over that particular system; most of the decision models were drawn from him and his team. "We were fortunate in having a really superb manager as our sponsor. A manager who's confident can take advice. Tom Henry is confident." And operators loved the system, too, and were eager to add rules and views. Mary Ann Westover, a programmer and system analyst, explains: "We started with some fairly simple rules, but as you use LMS and explore it, the possible rules you could put in there to make your life on the manufacturing floor so much simpler become apparent. It's very evolutionary."

"All we did was provide an enabling environment," Sullivan says. "They created it, and it fits them."

The expert system is now in every building at Burlington. By the spring of 1987 the system had some four hundred users, of whom sixty to eighty use it regularly, such as managers who use it every morning, during the day, and just before they leave at night. The numbers of both part-time and regular users were expected to quadruple by the end of 1988. The system is in a constant process of improvement. For one thing, each application of this system to help somebody do his or her job is customized to that person's own way of looking at things.

However, a new problem has arisen: people don't want to work without it. "One day we were in prototype mode," says Westover, "and the next day, every line was saying I've gotta have this or I'm gonna die. I just won't survive without this." If the system goes down over the weekend, nasty notes end up on the knowledge engineers' desks. One of them compares the situation to using a calculator: if your battery goes dead and you have to go to paper, you don't like it; you want your calculator back.

Besides saving human wear and tear, does the system have any other benefits? It does. First and foremost, thanks to a set of dynamic rules Mary Ann Westover wrote, a feedback loop has steadily reduced average cycle time, the amount of time wafers sit in the system.

As Moe Gaboriault, one of the manufacturing managers at Burlington, explains, "It's not just getting the product through fast, but it's getting the right amount out fast. A lot of people think that if you load up a line and just keep pumping the products through, you're going to get what the customer wants. It doesn't happen that way. The trick is getting the right amount of the right part number out every single day."

The overview LMS affords is very important to the Burlington managers. In midspring 1987 the system only signaled operators to pay attention to and solve a flagged problem. The knowledge engineers hadn't thought operators would want to know *why* a flag was up. But the site manager objected to that: were the knowledge engineers under the impression that operators did less thinking than other people involved? Abashed, the knowledge engineers added explanations.

Bill Brueckner, manufacturing manager of hot processes, says, "I don't think any one person can see the whole picture. But the system allows you to see the whole picture at once, just like you're looking down from the top of the room, and you see everything working, what's going on." In particular, it helps people recognize problems before they become critical. Moe Gaboriault adds: "The biggest thing about LMS is the picture it gives me of my area of responsibility. Just by looking at it I can see if it's in trouble or not, where I have to put my attention, and not waste my time checking each individual tool." Later he elaborates: "It really comes in handy too when you go on vacation. I send my output from the expert system to the next manager who's covering for me." "It's your rules in absentia," Westover agrees. "You're not there, but your rules are."

Westover sums up LMS: "It makes a very, very complex environment—with many different variables and different products—simple."

If shorter production time and a real management overview are two of the big benefits, so is better utilization of tools, especially the important expensive ones. And as the production time goes down, better line utilization goes up, so yields also go up. "With reduced cycle time," says Westover, "you have more opportunities to feed product through the entire cycle of the line, and therefore to tweak the line to make it more efficient, more effective, improve the processes, boost the yield, so you have to start fewer parts to get the same number out at the other end. It's just more opportunities to see how your line is functioning, and that cycle time drives learning." The opportunity to see and study the changes in the lines also makes smarter operators.

And, of course, with the amount of work in process diminishing, there's less inventory carrying cost.

Perhaps unsurprisingly, another advantage of the system is better communication. "It doesn't replace the human-to-human communications, but it can definitely supplement them—if a tool goes down, LMS can activate the rule that notifies maintenance automatically, and if lots go on hold, notify engineers—that sort of thing. So nothing falls through the cracks," says Westover, adding that this is much more reliable than the telephone messages, notes on desks, and general whatnot it replaces.

One manager mentions another unexpected dividend: "I see it promotes teamwork. Even though a person might only own one small section, it gives them the opportunity to see how they fit in the whole picture. In other words, they aren't a little Caesar who runs this square foot of floor tile and says, Come hell or high water, that's all I'm gonna do is manage my piece of floor tile. It lets them look at the other guy, talk back and forth, and say, Well, maybe I should step off my floor tile and give this guy a break."

This all brings about what the Burlington site strives for, better service for the customer, usually another IBM site. Though customers can be users, putting these chips into machines for sale, they might also be chip designers, shopping around for a fast turnaround time in design implementation.

The first two buildings where LMS was running achieved the target: cycle time equaling only three times the (absolute minimum) raw process time. In a special study of the effect on throughput of the expert system in one critical pinchpoint area, photolithography, the results were remarkable. For that one pinchpoint, throughput increased 35 percent, and the savings from that were $8 to $10 million per year on a continuing basis.

But the bottom line, so to speak, is the overall increase of throughput of the manufacturing plant, the overall increase in productivity of manufacturing. Gary Sullivan estimated this at 10 percent, Herb Schorr at 20 percent.

How much is this productivity gain of 10 to 20 percent worth to IBM on an annual basis? For competitive reasons, IBM carefully guards the figures on the value of the microchips produced by the Burlington factories. But informed guesses by industry sources and journalists put that value in the many hundreds of millions of dollars per year. The requirement for less capital equipment also saves tens of millions of dollars per year. So the value to IBM of working smarter in this factory setting is at least many tens of millions of dollars per year, a handsome return on the investment in the expert systems technology.

To stand back for a moment from the getting and spending (and making) is to see that LMS is a new kind of entity. It's a *community* intelligence, born from the collective wisdom of various disciplines, experiences, and points of view, which dynamically disseminates the new intelligence around the same community that engendered it, solving problems that are "too tough for us humans to figure out."

Burlington's LMS regulates the complex manufacturing tasks of an entire plant. It automatically picks up data and, using the knowledge that has been given to it by scores of human experts, it reasons so thoroughly about manufacturing production, and makes corrections and changes based on that reasoning so quickly, that no individual or group of individuals can match its performance.

San Jose: Improving Quality and Reducing Cost with DEFT and ESE

How does a technician fix a faulty product when the problem might be in any one of some five hundred parts? Very carefully.

IBM's storage products manufacturing division is a business unit within the General Productions Division (GPD). It assembles components from various sources (other GPD business units, other IBM sites, and outside vendors) into storage devices such as the 3380 disk drive. From assembly the product moves into a "unit test" area, where for the first time the whole newly assembled box is tested as one unit and must run for fifteen to sixteen hours free of defects. Then the disk unit moves into "final test," where it's put through a series of simulations that mimic how it would be run at the customer's site.

The disk drive is a very complicated piece of equipment. It has perhaps 500 replaceable parts—cables, power supplies, electronic and mechanical components. Any set, or subset, of those parts can fail, bringing the entire mechanism to a stop.

On the premise that expert systems will contribute to a major IBM goal of computer-integrated manufacturing by 1990, a bubbly engineer, Don Palese, from the storage products manufacturing division began working in August 1985 with the head of final test operations, Quinton O'Neal, to put together an expert system that would help technicians diagnose failures at the final test stage. They chose that stage because problems there are reasonably limited and because that stage had built up a lot of good historical failure analysis; any rules put into an expert system could be well justified.

They engaged two top-rate technicians, Craig Diltz and Steve Viallet, who'd had a lot of experience in solving problems at the final test stage, and convinced their department heads to release them unconditionally for the six months it would take to build the system. Though neither technician was a programmer, both were well respected and were often consulted when problems would arise in the final test area. The two learned enough about knowledge engineering and rule-writing to begin to put together a knowledge base of diagnostic and remedial recommendations. Using IBM's expert system shell ESE (for Expert System Environment, which, like all shells, contains everything except specific domain knowledge) the first knowledge base about the most common problems was completed in two weeks. The entire system was completed in under a year.

For this, Diltz and Viallet drew upon their own knowledge and six months of accumulated history of defects. They also had manuals, a directory, and a product guide. "Wonderful stuff," Palese says. "Thirty pounds of engineering-level documentation. Most doctors in Santa Clara County could recommend it for insomnia, because you start reading it, it's gonna put you to sleep. It's good stuff, the right stuff, but it's very hard for somebody to go through on a daily basis to try and solve problems." Nevertheless, when the expert system would later offer advice, it would also refer a technician to the exact page in the manuals if he wished.

DEFT, the Diagnostic Expert for Final Test, was introduced to the other technicians in the final test area as a tool. They were well aware that two of their own, technicians they knew as the best, had designed it. It spoke to technicians in their own jargon. They were encouraged, but not ordered, to use it.

DEFT, they were told, would help their productivity; it was a tool like the screwdrivers and voltmeters they also used to do their jobs. "We wanted to dispel the fears of artificial intelligence," Palese says. "You know what that means? Job's gonna be gone! We didn't want anybody to think that their job was gonna be gone because clearly that's not the way IBM operates."

Acceptance among the technicians was immediate and enthusiastic. Third-shift technicians would stay over to the first shift so that they could work with the experts, explaining that a problem had come up during the night, and if it wasn't in the knowledge base it ought to be. Let's see if you've got it, they'd say, and if you haven't I wrote down everything it took to solve the problem. "They were doing it themselves," Palese says, "it wasn't an outside group coming in, taking their requirements, delivering a product that says, Well, who needs your job? They felt good about it; they were encouraged." Other technicians would take Palese aside: When am I going to go to class? I want to learn how to write rules; I have ideas, too, and want to put them in.

One night a visiting customer was escorted into the final test area during the second shift and struck up a conversation with a technician. What would you do, he asked her, if they took the expert system away? She almost said, Go home, the visitor's escort remembers. "I mean, she came as close as she could without saying it." The customer was suitably impressed.

Not every problem that can possibly come up has been entered into the knowledge base. Of approximately four hundred problems that might, knowledge needed to solve only two hundred was chosen for the knowledge base, the others being problems that might creep in once a year or less.

In practice, DEFT has about a 98 percent success rate. Specifically, it is able to do diagnostic work on 98 percent of the problems that occur, and within the 98 percent it is always correct (100 percent accuracy). The other 2 percent includes the two hundred rare problems, and engineering changes that introduce temporary bugs into the system. That 98 percent accuracy compares very well with the best technicians. IBM says that the average consultation of DEFT by a technician takes one minute or less.

Typically it takes from fourteen to sixteen months to become a certified technician, but with the expert system, that training time has been cut to between three and five months. "That's productivity," Palese says. "They've learned, and they've learned the right way, as opposed to going all the way around the mulberry bush to get there." Palese also points out that novice technicians feel more comfortable about consulting a terminal again and again until they assimilate some piece of knowledge, in a way they wouldn't feel comfortable asking their shift supervisor six times in a row.

"People used to ask us weren't we just going to have a bunch of robots out there after a while, people who don't really know what they're doing?" Mike Burnett, a systems analyst for advisory systems, says. "It's turned out not to have happened—in fact, the exact opposite. People out there have increased their expertise generally across the board by using this system."

The system has its own monitor that asks the technician, Did the expert system succeed in giving you advice or not? If it didn't, if a problem's solution doesn't yet exist in the knowledge base, it can be added by the domain experts in a matter of a few hours. "That means the other technicians don't have to go through trial and error from their own knowledge. It keeps the boxes moving through the production facility on time. The other technicians learn because when they see a new defect they're not familiar with, they generally go through and exercise the explanation subsystem, asking 'why' and the 'hows'; they learn remarkably fast from that," Palese points out.

In addition to the high performance and the reductions in training time the system brings about, fewer good parts are erroneously rejected. "Prior to the expert system, 38 percent of the parts that were rejected were actually later shown to be NTF, no trouble found. Shortly after the expert system was in place, that number dropped to 19 percent, and the good news today is that the number is now below 3 percent, and we've been able to do away with the verification step to validate whether a part is good or bad. We just assume now that if the expert system kicks it out, it's failed. From 38 percent to less than 3 percent is very significant."

Mike Burnett elaborates: "The no-trouble-found parts never got put into another box and out to a customer; it was just too risky. And that was really a waste. So we're talking about a change in waste from 38 percent to less than 3 percent; quite significant."

Palese adds: "The last point I want to stress is that consultations are five to twenty times faster than the previous methods, going through the thirty-plus pounds of engineering documentation, or finding a domain expert out on the floor that you can work with, but who might be tied up with someone else, or away on vacation."

Which reminds him of something one of the domain experts, Craig Diltz, had told him. Palese asked the technician what the expert system had done for him personally. Diltz gave him the usual IBM answer: career enhancement, productivity. Palese pushed a little harder. Diltz thought about it for a few moments and then said, well, thanks to the expert system, he could now sleep at night. As one of the leading experts, he was always getting called; the phone would wake his wife and children. Now everybody slept peacefully.

Palese points out the difference between the conventional accumulations of expertise (in manuals and human heads) and an electronic accumulation. "Human knowledge is somewhat perishable. People leave their jobs, transfer, take early retirement, get promoted, whatever. With the knowledge captured electronically, it's permanent. That 3380 product has very complex engineering and the knowledge is hard to document and transfer, and the process itself makes diagnosing a problem slow and unpredictable. The rules are an excellent form of documentation, especially engineering documentation. With the expert system, we know once we have the knowledge captured, it's easy to transfer. We've demonstrated that we can do that very well. San Jose is the primary manufacturing center for this device, but we have sister facilities in Japan, Germany, and Brazil. We shipped our knowledge bases to them and we've instilled our methodologies in their organizations."

On the technical side, DEFT is a rule-based expert system written using IBM's ESE tool. Its knowledge base consists of about two thousand diagnostic IF-THEN rules. One of the rules is:

IF   the testcase failure is not CFTSA(E)
and there are multiple failures
and multiple devices are failing
and the failures are on A1 controller
and multiple parts are failing

THEN the cause of the failure is
A1M2 DHPLO (VFO) card with 60% probability
or A1X2 DDC/DXB card with 20% probability
or A1N2 SERDES/CLOCK card with 10% probability.

Ensure all R/W cables are seated properly. Rerun failing test-case. Note: For better diagnosis of this condition it might be necessary to troubleshoot devices independently.

Palese concedes that in theory they could have built DEFT using ordinary programming methods. But it would have taken far more time, and an expert system is the only thing that permits program change as the business changes—"and sometimes that seems on a daily basis. You can meet business demands with an expert system that you just can't meet with a linear-type program."

This is a good opportunity to compare expert systems with conventional systems. Suppose the rules were written as if-then conditional statements in one of the common computer languages. Then decisions about which rule to execute next, what to do when more than one rule can be executed, and so on (what's called execution control in conventional programs, and inference control in expert systems) must be interleaved with the statements. When changes need to be made, the programmer must worry not only about the new knowledge but also about the embedded control statements. This makes modifying programs a very complex and error-prone task. Expert systems separate the knowledge and the control, making knowledge-base maintenance and control changes independent of each other. Using an expert system shell such as ESE (with which DEFT is built), the control structure is part of the shell, and all the system builder has to think about is providing and updating the domain-specific rules. This is ideal for domain experts with no programming background, and we will see it again and again in these case studies.

In August 1986 Herb Schorr gave the keynote speech at the annual meeting of the American Association for Artificial Intelligence. He surveyed IBM's work in applied AI and used DEFT as an example to illustrate early application and payoff. Schorr said that savings from using DEFT amounted to five million dollars per year, a figure also cited by people at IBM San Jose. By 1988, DEFT was in use in Brazil and Japan as well, and savings rose to $12 million per year.

The knowledge bases have been transferred to many different IBM divisions and sites with quite different missions, such as field divisions. They've found them useful in doing their own tasks, and in some cases have shipped knowledge back to San Jose to help manufacturing refine the system.

The next step will be to put a tool like this out in customer sites to help solve disk failure problems customers experience.

But if things have been good for the developers and users, there have been certain other IBM groups, particularly in management information systems (MIS), who've resisted the whole idea. For one thing, they accused Palese of reporting rosier numbers than he has any right to report. ("Well, we didn't sandbag anything. It's all real.") Then came accusations that DEFT would badly affect their mainframe system performance—expert systems have the reputation, rightly or wrongly, of demanding lots of computing cycles. ("We say to the MIS people, you're providing a service, it's productivity that counts, getting the job done. But truthfully we know that the impact on the system is trivial. It's just a delaying tactic. Once we were accused of making a machine perform poorly. It turned out to be another problem. But the idea of artificial intelligence—people think of science fiction as soon as they hear it. The Star Trek machine is gonna consume all the electrons in the world!")

Rufus White, the manager of CIM (Computer Integrated

Manufacturing) Project Office, adds: "What we're really getting is a rejection of change. They're saying, I've always been this way, I'm a traditionalist."

Productivity enhancement, savings from salvaged parts, dynamic documentation and communication (as opposed to the static documentation of handbooks and manuals), reduced training time, and better training; it all adds up. But perhaps the most penetrating insight comes from a former manager who moved on from San Jose to Poughkeepsie. He came back and tried the expert system, loved it, and turned to Palese and O'Neal: "You don't know what you have here. Clearly we can engineer the best product in the world, but any of our competition can reverse-engineer it in a matter of months, and come out with a copy. But what they don't have is our *knowledge*. Our knowledge is going to be our competitive edge in the future—not how you build the project or what goes into it, but our knowledge about the whole system. That's what you have here."

Endicott: Winning a Skirmish
with the Bureaucracy

Some people might be amused that the largest computer manufacturer in the world has developed an expert system to help get around the bureaucracy. Some might argue that rather than build expert systems as guides, the bureaucracy should be eliminated altogether. But IBM is nothing if not realistic, and in the real world, where auditing and tax laws and other statutory obligations are here to stay, it's better to light a candle than curse the darkness.

CASES, for Capital ASset Expert System, simplifies the very confusing and complex problems of the business procedures—the paperwork—surrounding company-owned physical assets, from drill presses to oscilloscopes, from custom-designed manufacturing machinery to off-the-shelf doohickeys. It tells engineers and managers how to go about the paperwork for getting such assets, or transferring them between local owners or to other IBM sites; it advises them on the procedures (including but not limited to paperwork) for temporary storage, disposal and scrapping, relocation outside IBM, cancellation of orders, and the like. In short, it has the modest aim of guiding a person through the dungeons and dragons of one branch of the huge bureaucracy.

Though Cases deals specifically with the procedures and paperwork surrounding IBM's equipment, it stands as an example of a whole new way of dealing with the adjunct tasks every knowledge worker faces on the job. Every business has such procedures and thus faces an often hidden but nevertheless real—and sometimes painful—cost when highly trained experts must turn away from their "real" jobs to attend to those procedures. Though Cases happens to deal with company-owned physical assets, any knowledge worker could name a dozen such procedures that take up time, generate frustration, and yet must be followed. In Chapter 9 we'll see another example of the same thing at Texas Instruments, where an expert system helps professionals justify capital expenditures. IBM considers Cases a paradigm, a model, whose spirit has begun to inspire a number of similar aids for knowledge workers.

Cases was developed by a group led by a young staff programmer named Joseph Caldwell, who works out of IBM Endicott's information-systems plant productivity center. He laughs as he remembers showing up at a meeting of IBM expert systems people in Palo Alto and feeling a little bit sheepish, because everybody had such earthshaking schemes to introduce expert systems into the manufacturing world, solving complicated technological problems, whereas all his system did was, well, help a person fill out the right forms.

"When everybody was going around the room telling what their grand applications were, we felt like we shouldn't be there," says Caldwell, who has the penetrating earnestness of a Jesuit postulant. "But when people heard what we were up to, they said, Wow! Why do we have to think about these huge, complex problems? This technology can be applied to simple things, inefficiencies in business processes. They're things people don't know how to do, don't *want* to know how to do. The cost is buried and never shows up, yet it costs." Then he pauses. "Just as a little plug for ourselves, our application was one of the few that actually got finished."

To understand the scope of Cases, consider IBM's Endicott site: 12,000 employees in a development laboratory and two manufacturing plants for various IBM products. Caldwell himself belongs to an information systems group whose mission is to keep abreast, even ahead, of new technologies in information systems. Cases was commissioned from his group by the equipment control people at Endicott, who knew they had a problem and were tired of trying to solve it the old-fashioned way.

The problems with traditional business procedures, the paperwork surrounding internal company functions, are obvious. The sheer number and complexity of them are overwhelming, and they often require multiple references to other processes and information sources. Complicated exceptions are always raising questions about which procedures apply and which don't, and the procedures themselves are almost always written and updated by different people, which leads to differences in terminology and style.

Employees who face these procedures soon rise to a state of high irritation—it isn't part of their "real" job, they reason, so why should they even have to be bothered with this bureaucratic nonsense? They're engineers, managers, not clerks. And even the best-willed employee finds that he doesn't do these things often enough to remember from one time to the next how to do them.

To make matters worse, the procedures are always changing. Since most of them, at least those that concern capital assets, are dictated by federal tax laws and not, as is widely believed, by demons in the company bureaucracy, procedures change as the tax laws and other circumstances change. But those changes aren't always immediately reflected in printed forms and manuals. The experts themselves aren't always adequately informed. And as for the printed forms, most of them are generalized with the stated and surely noble aim of cutting down on paperwork, but in fact they're normally geared toward the worst case, often creating unnecessary work for people with ordinary needs.

The knowledge about how to fill out these many forms, which signatures are necessary, and other information that must be acquired, resides in thick business procedures manuals and in the heads of a small group of people. "So you often have the ludicrous picture of an expensive engineer standing in line for an hour to get advice from a clerk," Caldwell says. "It's a terrible waste of time and manpower. And it's a cost that you'll probably never see showing up anywhere, yet you know it's got to be killing you." Each party to the transaction sees the other as an adversary, instead of somebody who's just trying to do his job.

Since Endicott has three different major entities, two plants and a laboratory, three IBM subcultures coexist there, and it isn't unknown for control officers in each to give advice that conflicts. In fact, although the knowledge is supposed to reside in the heads of the equipment control group, even those people are specialists: the disposal specialist certainly doesn't know what the intersite transfer specialist knows, and neither of them knows much about temporary storage.

"The truth is, getting some sort of coherent answer to your particular problem is just plain hard," Caldwell says.

Plenty of IBM engineers and managers have taken the expedient route of simply filling out the forms any old way and submitting them in the hopes that the equipment control staff will take over and fill them out correctly. But this, as often as not, leads to more wasted time on returns and reworking, not to mention frustration on both sides.

A final expedient is simply to give up. Caldwell gives an example: "Let's say I'm an engineer charged with the 'ownership' of a piece of equipment, a drill press. The auditors' books show Joe Caldwell owns that drill press. At physical inventory time, the auditors come around and say, Okay, Caldwell, where's your drill press? I'd say, I don't know. I gave it to somebody. I don't remember where it went. That requires even more busywork, human chasing-down. The auditor says, Come on, remember, who was it you gave it to? I say, Oh yeah, try so-and-so. They go to him, and he's passed it on; his form got bounced out because it had the wrong owner on it to begin with, he wasn't really the owner. It just keeps going on and on." This leads to a condition called unlocated assets. IBM, surely one of the world's better managed firms, had a recent audit that showed approximately $20 million worth of assets were "unlocated."

"This takes half a percent out of everything that everybody does every day," says Bob Bachman, from IBM's central expert systems group in Harrison. "There's nobody with his name on this department—there's no department. So there's no one to stand up and say, I see this problem and I'll fund an expert system for it. Instead you need an information systems group with a history of introducing innovations, and a general manager on the site who's willing to take a chance on things. That's many critical factors to fall into place, and it isn't easy."

But those critical factors fell into place at Endicott, and Cases was built by Caldwell's group, using an IBM expert systems shell. They chose the shell because it had to be very clear to everybody what the rules said and why they were in the system. It also had to be very easy for the financial people to update—you can't call in a systems programmer every time the company or the government varies its requirements.

Cases is a one-on-one consultative dialogue between a human who wants to do something with a piece of equipment and a system that tells him how to do the proper paperwork. Most of the dialogues take only five to ten minutes, and the whole thing runs on existing terminals around the Endicott site. The system asks for information from the human only if it's pertinent to the particular situation (if it's a new acquisition the system won't ask questions pertaining to disposal), and only if it can't be found any other way— in other words, Cases can access external data files and can infer things from information it already knows (given a person's name it won't ask his or her office address, telephone number, supervisor's name, and so on). Like all expert systems it contains knowledge, in this case knowledge about many forms and different form-processing procedures, expressed in IF-THEN rules. It also offers explanations if wanted. In practice, most people using the system don't care why, they just want to know what to do.

The system provides a cohesive course of action customized to the individual situation: it tells the person what forms must be filled out and how; what signatures are required (often the actual names); where to send the forms (the actual addresses); offers precautions, warnings, tips, or advice; specifies other departments and locations that must be notified; and gives other pertinent information. Unlike the human equipment-control experts, who work a normal 9-to-5 weekday, Cases is available twenty-four hours a day, seven days a week, a special benefit to the second and third shifts that run at Endicott.

The system has been in use since the middle of 1986, and has brought about a noticeable reduction in routine "How do I . . . ?" calls and drop-ins at the finance office, in signature authorization problems, in noncompliance with procedures, in missing or incomplete information on forms, and in follow-ups. It has also produced—dear to the heart of any bureaucrat—neater forms with less crossing out and arrows to the margins. Its users are very happy with it.

But one question that might occur to any reasonable person is, If an expert system can tell you which forms should be filled out for a given transaction, and how, why doesn't it just do the job itself? Why should a person still have to fill out paper forms, no matter how much easier the job may now be? The answer to that question is complicated, hinging on legal and company requirements for paper documents with inked signatures. But it also has to do with people who "own" the various forms, who've fallen in love with them and can't bear to give them up. Caldwell sees his system as a precursor to the paperless office, but many strategic decisions must be made about just which paper will eventually be eliminated. When those decisions are made, Cases will be ready to expand its capability.

"It's staging for a potential explosion of productivity," Bob Bachman says. "Whatever the benefits of this are, you can get an order-of-magnitude productivity increase in the next stage. But without this, you couldn't get to that. It's going to take some people about fifteen minutes to understand this. Others will never understand. We'll just have to wait till they, uh, go on to other opportunities."

Bachman is particularly concerned with evaluating the

worth of any knowledge to be automated. "Process knowledge is especially valuable," he says, "and Joe's application is a kind of showcase of process knowledge expertise. We're looking to that application as a pilot for ways to put some forebrain into the office. You've got the arms and legs, and the business process analysis is the brain function of it all. Expert systems are a technology to put those two together."

Bachman has been concerned with the flagging productivity of office work, despite the automated tools. "Even if expert systems didn't do much for anybody else, in the office they'll be a huge boost, because of the enormous benefits associated with office productivity. Up to now that yield isn't coming forth."

Partly that's because there isn't any sound way yet to measure office productivity. For example, of eight hundred potential Cases users at Endicott, nobody knows how many people have used the system at least once. Caldwell didn't put in a tracking function because the equipment control people, who commissioned the system, weren't particularly concerned with that. But in addition, "To take statistics after a system is put in would imply that you had some statistics to bump them up against, to show whether you were making an improvement. Those people had no statistics about how many forms were coming in wrong. They just knew it was a big problem for them."

Bachman sees all this as another dimension to the problem of seeding expert systems around a corporation. It's his group's task to cheerlead and encourage from headquarters at Harrison; is he really going to insist that functions be added that the local sponsor isn't interested in? There's no easy answer to that question.

But some numbers exist. Cases took less than one and a half person-years to develop, and cost less than $100,000. It will save IBM $1.5 million a year if it only saves an hour per year for each of the manufacturing engineers, a very modest estimate. And Cases will have future improvements: more financial expertise; a tie-in to paperless forms, electronic signatures, asset control, and logistics applications. Meanwhile, because the idea of Cases is so easily understood, and its benefits so obvious, it has acted as a catalyst at IBM, sparking ideas and projects in other IBM business areas, and among IBM customers.

The FMC Corporation: Hands-On, Hard-Hat, and Hot

FMC is an international conglomerate with manufacturing and mining facilities all over the world and 1986 sales of $3.1 billion.

Great mountains of phosphorus-bearing ore, delivered by rail from an FMC mine, sit beside a giant heavy-chemicals plant outside Pocatello, Idaho. Like an insect, a bulldozer crawls over those mountains, redistributing the ore to give it some consistency of quality.

Within the plant are great furnaces—three, maybe four stories high. Phosphorus is being made in those giant furnaces: phosphorus for fertilizers, for industrial uses, for detergents and water softeners, for military smoke screens and ordinary pesticides. In its pure state, it's a dangerous product. A worker says that when you accidentally pick some up on your clothing, you probably won't know about it until the water in it evaporates; then the pure phosphorus ignites, setting your pants on fire. A furnace explosion can be catastrophic.

This is hands-on, hard-hat America. But with its dust, its vibrations, its possibly dangerous chemicals, this hardly seems the best place to introduce a high-tech expert system. Dust has shorted out other computers in the plant and even set them on fire. But FMC, highly committed as a corporation to placing expert systems throughout its sites, refused to be deterred. For one thing, the problems were simply too big to ignore. At a strategic level, FMC had determined it would be a low-cost phosphorus producer. Low-cost production requires experts, but along with other U.S. chemical industries, FMC has a mature work force: many experts are near retirement or have already retired. FMC uses an expert system to substitute for those disappearing human experts.

At a phosphorus plant, the furnace expert must manage the mixture of silica, coke, and shale that goes into the furnace, aiming to extract the maximum amount of phosphorus and lose the least in waste products. This optimal performance can be achieved only if the reaction zone is maintained in the middle of the furnace interior. If the zone drifts downward, excessive phosphorus flows out in the slag; if it drifts upward, the combustion can react with the refracted surface of the furnace, which will mean replacing the furnace. In extreme conditions, a furnace top can blow off, which means operations must be shut down while the furnace is replaced. The furnace expert can recognize those dangerous situations early and take steps to avoid them.

All this is a dynamic, relatively unstable process, and experts know very well the five or six things that can easily go wrong; they also know how to avoid or solve those problems. However, their diagnoses are made in a very indirect fashion, for nobody can peep into the furnace to see if the reaction zone is too low or too high; they can only observe temperature points and some qualitative information—ease of flow out to the slag pit, the appearance of coke nodules in the slag—check some sensors, and from all that make an informed guess, based on a lifetime's experience.

Pocatello's furnace expert is Gordon Scherbel, a heavyset, middle-aged man with many years of hands-on, hard-hat experience. His typical day is spent walking around the plant to get a current view of conditions, gathering data from several scattered sources so he can decide whether to change the mixture inside a furnace to prevent waste, the premature erosion of the furnace, or, worst of all, a catastrophic explosion. He'll offer advice to operators and foremen based on his best judgments.

But available information is often scattered in different places and incomplete. Sometimes foremen must make decisions on their own. Not all foremen have equal access to information. Sometimes action is taken that only affects local problems; sometimes two foremen will take two quite different actions in the same circumstances. Experienced foremen are also disappearing into retirement, but their expert judgments and best guesses have never been recorded. Even if knowledge has been recorded in any conventional way, it is difficult to consult on the spot. In summary, the unreliability of information makes it difficult to judge and interpret data in a proper context. The problems are complex, and the expertise is varied and inconsistent.

A few years ago, when FMC began its expert system work, it decided to develop its own software shell—one that would benefit a broad class of applications having to do with process control. The shell was developed in collaboration with specialists from Teknowledge, a firm that FMC considered so significant to its future that it bought a 10 percent interest in it. Urged on by a farsighted CEO, Robert H. Malott (who by chance fell into fascinated conversation on an airplane with Peter Hart, an early expert systems developer in Silicon Valley), FMC established its own in-house AI expertise, and identified important generic problems across the entire company that might lend themselves to solution by expert systems methods.

The phosphorus burden problem belongs to one of those generic categories: the general problem of managing processes that are (1) changing over time, (2) where the environment is dynamic, and where (3) managing the process can be either by an open loop (needing a human to take action), or a closed loop (where action is taken without human intervention). In the phosphorus plant, of course, the problem is to manage the flow of silica, coke, and shale through the furnace, aiming at maximum phosphorus, minimum waste, and optimal furnace use and life.

And so an expert system was developed, codifying the expertise of the about-to-retire Gordon Scherbel.

The expert system (its computer encased in special housing to protect it from the harsh conditions of the Pocatello plant) continuously acquires and monitors relevant data to identify or predict situations that require control action; it alerts plant operators when exceptional situations are identified; it determines the nature and cause of those exceptional situations, plans corrective actions, and advises operators. The advice results from applying rules about a number of different aspects of the process. Following are two examples:

IF the reaction zone in the furnace is low
and it is not caused by the purge of coke
and it is not caused by an increase in the burden ratio
and P205 content of the slag is high
and the temperature of the slag is hot

THEN it is definite that the process is in an undercoking state.

IF the slag from the east tap has average temperature
and the slag does not contain coke
and the ferrophos tap does not contain coke

THEN it is definite that the east tap is cold.

The phosphorus burden advisor runs in open-loop mode, meaning that recommendations are presented to the operator for final decisions about how to respond. The prototype has been operational for the purposes of evaluation, operator training, and further knowledge engineering. The system will become fully operational in 1989.

Perry Thorndyke, who heads FMC's AI group, observes that the corporation has had several experts like the phosphorus furnace specialist. The expert system was designed to capture the best of their expertise, thus smoothing operations at the highest levels of expertise. "Some have already retired, and the expert in question here may retire soon, so management was concerned that we'd have to capture his knowledge or it would be lost with him. And you know, large amounts of money are involved in losing material off the bottom of the furnace. Reducing that loss only a tenth of a percent saves half a million dollars a year!" (Even Thorndyke concedes that that is a very conservative figure. More realistic estimates are that the expert system will save between $800,000 and $3.2 million per year based on running four furnaces. Also calculated in that saving is reduced capital expenditures as a result of keeping the reaction zone steadily in the center of the furnace. You don't have to replace the furnace as often with the expert system.)

FMC is a splendid example of an old firm (it was founded in 1928 to sell agricultural equipment to a valley then known for its fruit, not its silicon) that has seen the future and intends to be there, and be there profitably. Its AI group, housed at the Santa Clara, California, Central Engineering Laboratories, was formed because the company saw such a variety of opportunities to apply the technology—to expand or enhance existing product lines, to start entirely new product lines (for example, an expert system for crop management that complements the company's traditional sales in agricultural chemicals), and, most important, for internal uses, such as the system described here.

FMC's move into artificial intelligence was ardently supported by Ray Tower, the president and COD. "Are you *sure* that's enough money?" he asked an astonished Perry Thorndyke when Thorndyke, the new head of the AI group, went to Chicago to present his first technology plans and (he thought) an aggressive budget. "Come back for more if it isn't." Thorndyke still remembers how well-prepared Malott and Tower were in the fundamentals of AI: The briefing Thorndyke had intended to give seemed superfluous.

By mid-1987 the AI group had grown to some forty AI professionals, 80 percent of whom had advanced degrees, half of those Ph.D.s.

The AI group concentrates assiduously on serving its customers, FMC's business units, where initiatives for expert systems can come from either side so long as they fit the company's strategic long-term goals. As a matter of course, the business units pay for any work the AI group does for them, based on the firm belief that technology transfer works best when users buy in with real money. Technology development works best that way, too, since it stays close to customer needs.

The internal shell FMC and Teknowledge have developed for monitoring continuous processes has been disseminated throughout the AI group so that applications programmers, more numerous than AI specialists, can develop expert systems without help from the central AI group. It is, for example, being used by a group involved in military applications to build an expert system that plans the locations of howitzers in "shoot-and-scoot" operations—a maneuver in which howitzers are moved from place to place to avoid being located and to confuse the enemy. The potential returns on proposed AI projects are evaluated just like those of any other corporate project. In addition, many of FMC's systems are "defensive,"protecting the knowledge the firm already has—the essence, it believes, of its competitive advantage in the world market now and in the future.

Toyota:
If It's Broke, How to Fix It

The automobile, the mechanical mare of modern man, has become a high-tech machine. Run by onboard computers, the electronic conveniences that please the consumer, and the electronic control systems for efficient engines, transmissions, and brakes, have brought about a crisis of maintenance. High-tech cars are being fixed by low-tech mechanics.

The New York Times (April 16, 1988) wrote about the crisis this way:

> About 60 million cars with on-board computers have been sold in the past six years, and these high-tech vehicles are causing a major shakeout in the $112 billion car-repair and collision-repair industries, which are being forced to become computer literate or go out of business. . . .
>
> The service industry is . . . hampered by a shortage of mechanics. . . .
>
> "You would have to say that the crisis has arrived," said Lucille Treganowan, chairman of the Transmission and Driveline Institute of the Automotive Parts Rebuilders Association. "The lack of training in the industry is a severe problem now," she said, "but it's awfully hard to figure out which is the worst problem: the changes in technology that require more training and diagnostic equipment; or the difficulty in getting young people interested in auto mechanics; . . ."

The *Times* goes on to report that 40 percent of the cost of car repair goes for unnecessary procedures or parts. The report continues:

. . . too little time is spent diagnosing problems, and technicians are not skilled. . . . Recruiting and training mechanics is the biggest headache. The trade has a poor image and the pay is low. . . . "The average age of the technician is over 40 and, as such, it's a problem of old dogs not too interested in learning new tricks," said George W. Merwin, executive vice president of the Automotive Service Association. . . .

What does all this mean for the consumer? The frustration and expense involved in keeping a car on the road will increase, automotive experts say, until the service industry catches up with the new technology.

The opportunity for a major assault on this problem using expert system technology was seen by car manufacturers in the USA, Europe, and Japan. General Motors and Ford made equity investments in three start-up firms in the embryonic expert systems industry. Both companies developed engine diagnosis expert systems (GM's is called "Charley" in GM's entertaining TV ads) that have received limited deployment. Renault, on the other hand, has widely deployed to its service shops an expert system for diagnosing problems with automatic transmissions.

Both the crisis and the opportunity were seen early by the Toyota Motor Corporation. At its central research and development laboratories in a suburb of Nagoya, Japan, an expert system called Atrex has been developed to advise technicians on automobile diagnosis and repair.

The system isn't intended for direct use by the mechanics at a local dealer's repair shop. When an ailing Toyota is brought into the shop, the mechanics there are expected to do their best to diagnose and repair the problem. But if they're stumped, they can telephone one of Toyota's five Central Service Technology locations around Japan, where they can speak to specialized, high-level technicians and get advice. The specialists themselves are getting advice from Atrex, the expert system.

The knowledge in Atrex comes from both engine designers and members of the Toyota technical staff who normally answer questions from mechanics. At the beginning, Atrex concentrated on the electronic components of one particular

Toyota engine model, but the system was later expanded to include three other engine types.

Atrex works very much like a medical diagnosis expert system—preliminary information is entered, the "patient history," and then the symptoms. Information from diagnostic instruments is considered, and other germane details, such as outside temperature when the problem occurs, and so on. Atrex even asks about things humans can see and report but instruments can't—whether smoke is coming out of the exhaust, for instance. The system also inquires what has already been done by the shop and with what result.

As the system continues its diagnosis, its questions get more detailed, someimes entailing several phone calls as the serviceman tries out the system's suggestions. When the diagnosis is finally accomplished, the system explains its reasoning, and all is printed out for the record.

Toyota's strategy is somewhat different from the strategies of other automobile companies such as General Motors or Renault, which are installing expert systems on workstations in local shops for individual mechanics to use. Toyota says it believes in making cars that are reliable at the time they're built—it doesn't believe in relying on expensive equipment for diagnosing in the field, nor in equipping Toyota autos with large numbers of expensive sensors inside their engines. Instead, Toyota has chosen to invest in high-tech equipment on the production line, thereby improving the initial quality of cars. Since fewer reliability problems show up later, expense is also minimized that way. Further, some in the Toyota organization worry that a workstation in a local repair shop might put confidential knowledge at risk of being stolen.

For the customer, Atrex represents a remarkable improvement in service. Problems that used to take two or three days to solve are now solved in two or three hours. Simpler problems that used to take a few hours now take five minutes. For Toyota, this translates into a productivity gain for its mechanics of about a factor of ten.

Toyota and its customers both share in another gain from the system, improved quality: what Toyota calls "overlooked mistakes" are avoided, since being a machine, the system is more thorough than even the best human expert usually is.

The system has also cut Toyota's internal costs. Three of its troubleshooting experts in each of five different locations, fifteen people overall, have been freed for other tasks. Finally, since warranties in Japan are for two years, and statistics show that most problems appear in the first two years of a Toyota's life, the cost of replacement parts, which is borne by the company, has dropped.

Toyota, General Motors, Ford, Renault, BMW, and Mercedes are all moving to exploit one of the major dimensions of gain from the use of expert systems: capturing, improving, and distributing inexpensively the scarce and critical expertise that is so difficult to teach. Increased reliability of cars, the resulting increased customer satisfaction, and a major reduction in labor, training, and parts are the demonstrable results. If computers are to run our cars, let computers figure out why the cars won't run!

The British National Health Service

Internal cost savings and product quality control aren't solely concerns of industrial manufacturers. Consider Britain's National Health Service. Like many government agencies all around the world, the National Health is faced with rising costs and clear signs that service isn't all it could be. Quite unlike most government agencies, the National Health is trying to do something about it.

A few years ago, when the Thatcher government declared that solutions to the National Health's glaring problems would have to be found in better management because no more money was available, Parliament began the reform by mandating the collection of enormous amounts of performance data. The intention was to see where money was being spent, and if it was being spent wisely.

National Health's most obvious symptom was the long waiting times for treatment—waits for surgery might be measured in years. But nobody seemed to know what caused those waits. Was it operating room time, or doctors, or the central management of admissions, or some other unknown problem? In a given hospital, the actual throughput of patients might be a function of how difficult the diagnostic mix is, or how long patients stay, or how fast the caseload is turned over. Each of these factors is important, and linked in complex ways to the others.

But which indicators should be watched, and which affected others? Does high infant mortality in Glasgow reflect low baby-care staffing levels? Was it helpful to know the numbers of pacemakers installed in Devon as compared to Liverpool, if the populations were very different? Could the home nursing service of Edinburgh be usefully compared to home nursing in Birmingham? Were the residents of the pretty village of Port Isaac claiming more than their share of cardiac bypasses?

To confuse matters further, the system is relatively decentralized. There are fourteen regions and 190 legally independent authorities. Management clearly needed to be sharpened and accountability increased.

The trick was to measure performance. In 1984 eight committees of experts, consisting of professionals—doctors, nurses, other health-care professionals and analysts—met to define the key indicators of medical-care performance. They reported their findings later that year, and outlined the key performance indicators, eventually numbering 450. Six months or so later, statistics on those 450 indicators from the entire country had been accumulated as a tool for management review.

But, alas, the committees weren't specific about how those indicators were to be interpreted. "The job of making sense of it is pretty complex," Tom Bowen of the Department of Health and Social Security would concede with some British understatement. Here was the perfect data-processing product: numbers by the thousands, but in their mass almost useless. How was meaning to be found in all that? How could weak spots in the system be discovered, and managers informed of them? A staff of six operations researchers at the Central Office in London tried to formulate a procedure for analysis that could make sense of the data.

These operations researchers spotted the opportunity to

build and deploy an expert system for the analysis, and called on the consulting firm of Coopers and Lybrand for help. "It wasn't a case of automating an existing function; the function couldn't be performed manually," says Charles Church of Coopers and Lybrand. "When the data specialists looked at the difficulties, they said, Well, here's something which can't really be done sensibly. Let's use expert systems to do it."

Luckily certain "islands" of knowledge had already been encoded, and certain logical relationships linking those islands had also been established. For example, the length of time a patient with a femur fracture stayed in the hospital might relate to nursing care, but might also relate to local rehabilitation services. But the complexities of cross-checking and cross-referencing were still overwhelming: numbers couldn't really express medical judgments. With the islands of knowledge as guides, the knowledge engineers, overseen by Coopers and Lybrand, went back to the key members of the original eight committees and started asking questions. How was this finding to be interpreted? What did that indicate? In your best judgment, what should be made of this statistic?

What eventually emerged was the DHSS Performance Analyst (DHSS-PA), an expert system with some 11,200 rules— one of the biggest in existence. It was developed over a period of less than four months in 1986 using a British expert system shell called Crystal, the product of a small firm called Intelligent Environments. Encoded in the system is the judgmental wisdom of those key medical committee members regarding the evaluation of quality medical care. Using the DHSS-PA system, evaluations of medical care that used to take six human experts two hours to do now take nine minutes on an IBM-PC, a spectacular eighty-times productivity gain.

Interestingly, the users of this expert evaluation aren't solely the analysts at the Central Office in London. Instead, the system, distributed on floppy disks, is purchased out of local funds by the regional and district health authorities to help them assess themselves. The deployment strategy was based on the view that if the analyses and evaluations were done centrally in London the regional and district sites wouldn't pay much attention.

The U.K.'s chief medical officer objected to the number of value judgments the early versions of the system made. He didn't want the system to say things were "good" or "bad" when the data were only indicative; such judgments couldn't be made until the problem was examined in detail. Thus the system doesn't draw the final conclusion. That's left to the professionals using the system. Sometimes it simply points out various pieces of information from which humans can then draw their own conclusions.

Distributed as it is on microcomputer diskettes, the expert system is so flexible it can easily be extended so that regional and local offices can add their own rules applicable to their own locations. That facility for local change is essential; the system wouldn't have found acceptance otherwise.

"The fact that people can go straight in and say, I don't think about it like that, I have a slightly different interpretation; I want to put in this information which is available to me as well, means that the system itself is viable, and people understand what it's doing," says Church. However, knowledge base development and maintenance are problems that require real expertise: Coopers and Lybrand continue to offer advice on those to the local regions and districts. This isn't for profit so much as an investment toward the scores of other opportunities for expert systems they see in the health service.

The National Health Service expert system is a management tool, doing a job of collating and interpreting data that have never been collated before, all with the aim of serving the public and spending its monies more effectively. In theory, many government agencies might be able to use such a system, but will they? There's no incentive to innovate in government, Bowen says regretfully, and Church adds that as a rule, government agencies aren't task-oriented or concerned about managing things well. Right now, they all collect vast amounts of information, just as the National Health has done, but they're overwhelmed by the job of interpreting it. It's as if government agencies have their sensory system working, Church says, but the wherewithal to interpret that sensory data is missing. That interpretation, he believes, is one of the big opportunities expert systems present for government agencies.

Chapter 5

Quality and Consistency in Decision Making

HERE ARE FOUR MEMBERS of the service sector, which economists tell us employs more of us than any other sector in the developed world. Each of these organizations faces a similar business problem: a complicated decision, based on a very complex set of rules, must be made by company representatives when dealing with customers.

This chapter features the extraordinary and innovative success of American Express, where an expert system facilitates a routine but demanding task of human judgment—authorizing charges. The payoff is in the tens of millions of dollars every year. Productivity savings are considerable; losses avoided through bad debt and fraud are huge.

Other stories concern Nippon Life Insurance, one of the largest insurance companies in the world, whose employees must make decisions involving complex corporate criteria on disease and actuarial data; the British social security system, which has something of the same problem; and Japan's Sanwa Bank, which provides portfolio management service for its customers. Each organization has many employees who must deal with millions of customers. The right decision—every time—is crucial.

American Express:
How to Make the Right Decisions Fast

Recently, a New York–based collector of rare books unexpectedly found a valuable first edition in Paris. Since he hadn't planned to shop for anything so pricey, he was short of cash. Luckily, the dealer accepted his American Express card, and the traveler took his treasure home to his library.

The book buyer was taking advantage of one of the most important features of an American Express credit card, the absence of a preset spending limit. If an irresistible purchase comes along, as it did in Paris, the card holder need not worry he'll be denied credit.

That is, he can use the card as long as he remains creditworthy. American Express expects its customers to pay their bills in full within thirty days. But people travel, sometimes for weeks at a time; what if, once in a while, you don't get home and pay the bills? Will you then face instant mortification at a foreign department store, or even the corner service station? Will American Express, which earned more than a billion dollars in 1986, cut you off without mercy for accidentally overlooking the July statement?

How decisions are made about creditworthiness is hardly simple. The computer first analyzes a charge statistically, and can deal with about 80 percent of the charges automatically. But when a transaction falls outside certain patterns established by a cardholder, the computer shifts the decision to a human authorizer at one of over twenty different sites around the world, who decides within seventy seconds whether approval will be granted.

A few years ago, when Robert Flast was appointed vice president of transaction services at American Express's Travel Related Services (one of the several interlocking firms that comprise the American Express Company), he became responsible for the point-of-sale network, 400,000 shops and restaurants worldwide where charges are made, transmitted to American Express, and authorizations are obtained.

Ordinarily, a point-of-sale terminal takes the amount of a purchase, entered by the sales clerk, reads the magnetic strip on the credit card, and sends all this information over telephone lines to one of two operating centers in Phoenix, Arizona, which serves the Western Hemisphere, or Brighton, England, which serves Europe, Asia, the Middle East, and Africa. (Phoenix also serves as backup for the Brighton center.) At Phoenix or Brighton, the statistical analysis takes place; from there approval returns to the point-of-sale terminals. In the case of questionable decisions, the transaction is shifted to the human authorizers at one of the authorizing centers to decide.

The authorizers at the Fort Lauderdale center are together in a large bright room, with a map of the United States on the wall they face. Each sits at a computer terminal where every few minutes a questionable transaction is presented to him or her to decide. The authorizer now has seventy seconds to consult an individual's credit record (which may be called out of as many as thirteen different data bases), perhaps have a conversation with the customer or the merchant, and decide whether to approve the transaction by applying to the customer's record a body of knowledge and policy rules derived from all the experience American Express has built up over the years.

The knowledge and rules are codified in the authorizers' training manual, a book some four or five inches thick. Each authorizer handles about 26 such transactions an hour, or 150 a day. Transactions, of course, go on twenty-four hours a day, seven days a week—and, companywide, American Express employs three hundred authorizers to handle over a million transactions a month.

Authorizing is a difficult, exacting job that takes place under considerable stress. As one authorizer explains, she doesn't want to offend the customer if indeed he or she is creditworthy, and doesn't want to delay him in such a way that he might use a rival company's card instead. She's also mindful that American Express makes no money from transactions that don't occur. But she doesn't want to approve a transaction that will turn out uncollectible or fraudulent.

Authorizers must sometimes endure abuse from customers; their every decision is collected and analyzed by the company, and their advancement depends on how well they do their job. This is no place for dithering. And authorizers are human. Yet despite the stress, they exhibit a refreshing eagerness to do right by both the company and its customers.

Bob Flast spent the first few months on the job in the fall of 1984 interviewing people around the firm and asking what they thought he should be paying attention to. He remembers collecting maybe seventy ideas, and somewhere on the list was the idea of using artificial intelligence, applying it to the firm's existing Credit Authorization System (CAS), which was based on rules derived from American Express statistics about purchases and purchasers.

Flast didn't know anything about artificial intelligence, but he read up on it and quickly realized that if automation of the credit authorization system were to be extended, it would move into the turf of the human credit authorizers. Supposing some of what the authorizers did could be captured in an expert system to streamline the function and ease their jobs—was that the right first choice of an expert system for American Express? Did it have enough impact, was it visible enough to be worth the effort?

Flast agrees with the view that if expert systems are going to be useful in a firm, it's best to offer those of high impact and great value first. "At American Express, that's particularly true," he says. "A skunkworks approach wouldn't have worked here at all. In fact, one could argue that it had failed, because many people were playing with inexpensive expert system shells, but nothing was happening, nothing was moving forward."

Just as Flast was making his survey, it happened that Louis Gerstner, the president of American Express and CEO of the Travel Related Services Company, met with his senior management council in Rome and told them that he was concerned American Express wasn't doing enough of the sort of risky development associated with R&D. With so many bona fide, short-term, high-payback opportunities, Gerstner said, the firm tended to use its operating budgets to fund those. Therefore the risky, long-term projects were winding up low on the list.

"He was right," Flast says. "If you look at the kinds of things we did, they were always shaving another minute off the time it took to get the mail out the door, so money would come back in the door."

Gerstner announced he was putting up a $5 million challenge fund and invited the various staffs to propose projects to compete for that money. Let's see, he said, if we can't kick some projects out of the closet, and do some risky but important things.

Flast thought an expert system to help the authorizers make their decisions was just the sort of risky project Gerstner might have in mind. If successful, such a system would benefit the company in many ways. These were: a reduction in losses from bad debt and fraud; more approvals for creditworthy customers in marginal situations; faster service time for customers and merchants; consistency of decision making; control over the rising costs of operating expenses for the authorizations; and a faster "learning curve" from novice to expert for new authorizers. With a Prolog shell (like other expert system shells it contains an inference engine and knowledge representation scheme, but in a logic language), Flast sat down and coded a few rule-based examples using rules from the authorizers' training manual as a demonstration, put together some charts, and made a presentation to the executive committee of his own business unit.

Flast is a husky, dark-haired man with slightly parted teeth and generously distributed eyebrows. He has a quick, analytic mind, and gives the impression of great energy carefully deployed. The committee was delighted with the tangibility of what he showed them, and approved sending it on to the higher-ups. Eventually, eighty-five projects were competing for funds, and of those, five were approved. Among the five was the Authorizer's Assistant (AA).

With the funds assured, Flast decided that actually building the AA was going to require outside help from a vendor. Trying to do it internally would take too long, have too many unmanageable risks. He gathered together an informal advisory committee of about ten people who might have an interest in the project—people from Fort Lauderdale, people from telecommunications, from systems, and people who were known AI enthusiasts around the company. They advised Flast on the request for proposals, which was subsequently sent out to fourteen companies that offer expert systems services. In addition to its stated system requirements, the request included an invitation to visit the Fort Lauderdale center to see firsthand how authorizers actually worked. Eight vendors accepted the invitation for May of 1985.

As Fort Lauderdale management showed the potential vendors around the center and explained where credit authorization fit into larger systems, Flast and his team (which included his ad hoc advisory committee) put a number of questions to the vendors. Did the Authorizer's Assistant seem like a suitable application? Could it be done in a finite period of time, with finite dollars? If the answer was yes to all those, could a system be built that would interface with the IBM mainframes, maintain the high throughput, support the authorizer in both the gathering and the evaluating of data, and make a recommendation within seventy seconds?

In addition to all that, Flast wanted a system that would be sufficiently self-monitoring and self-logging so that over time heretofore hidden patterns could be detected and automatically rewritten as procedures. For instance, the new system might report: "In the last 6 months, this pattern has presented itself 70,000 times. The system approved 99.9% of those charges and the authorizer concurred." Finally, Flast hoped for real technology transfer; that is, he wanted a system that might be generalized into other applications. The vendors nosed around the center and asked their own questions.

Aside from the considerable difficulties of capturing the authorizer's expertise, the job offered some other vexing technical problems. The IBM mainframes at the operating centers run under a system descended from the airline reservation systems of some years ago, designed for real-time, high-throughput, high-availability applications. However, while that system can handle the high volume of transactions necessary, it isn't a data base system. American Express must keep data in a different system from its transactions, which raises serious information storage and retrieval problems. Adding to all this an expert system, which would run on a Lisp machine, was going to complicate matters even more.

Finally, American Express imposes a software freeze every year, beginning in November and extending through the holiday season, because the volume of transactions then is so high that untried software simply cannot be risked. A prospective schedule for building an expert system would have to take that into account: American Express wanted its AA project to begin in the fall of that year, 1985, and be finished by October 1986, before the systemwide holiday freeze took effect.

Of the eight vendors who visited Fort Lauderdale that May, five submitted proposals that fell into two categories: one was custom expert systems development—a system built specifically for the authorization problem—and the other kind was tool-based, built with commercial expert system shells. Flast and his group pondered both carefully, and at last decided that while the custom expert systems would probably function well, they offered little hope for technology transfer, whereas a tool-based system would leave a tool behind for further exploitation.

"It would have been nice if we'd thought about that originally, because we would have solicited fewer proposals, but that's part of the learning process, and it wasn't clear until we saw the proposals that *that* was the tradeoff. At that point, we put the custom proposals aside and focused on the tool-based proposals."

In differentiating between the proposals, Flast and his group looked at obvious things: money and time. But they also looked at the degree of commitment the vendor was making. "Some vendors said, We'll build a prototype in six months, eight months, twelve months, for X dollars. Then we'll figure out whether we can go beyond that, and there's nothing we can say about how much time that might take, or how much that might cost. So all we knew was that we'd have a prototype in some period of time."

But Inference Corporation of Los Angeles declared it would build a prototype AA in four months, and the whole thing in just over a year, all for a given sum. That kind of precision appealed to American Express, and they decided to talk seriously to Inference. Flast checked with Inference's board of directors, and its scientific and technical advisory board on the company's future plans, and checked with some of Inference's current customers. Four months of very intense negotiations began, with performance guarantees, escape clauses, and financial conditions added and subtracted. The initial fee went up two and a half times, was at last brought down to within 40 percent of its original amount.

"By October of 1985 we were able to surround a seventy-page proposal with an eighty-page contract," Flast laughs. "It's a very good document for future use elsewhere in the company." The contract set the schedule: The project would begin in November 1985, the prototype to be delivered on April 1, 1986. A pilot system would be developed in the next five-month period, extending the breadth of knowledge and developing the communications interface with the mainframe. Then would come a two- to three-month tuning, ending approximately at the end of 1986.

In August of 1985, as negotiations were proceeding with Inference, Flast had been asked for a formal budget, with software, hardware, and personnel costs. He put it together and submitted it to the treasurer's office, where it more or less silently disappeared. When the eighty-page contract with Inference was finally concluded, Flast put his name on it, his boss signed it, and the knowledge engineers from Inference arrived in Fort Lauderdale on schedule, November 1985.

Therefore it came as something of a disagreeable surprise when, in Janury 1986, Bob Flast received a letter from American Express's corporate vice president of finance saying that the budget submitted in August had been rejected; that in fact, if he wanted this project to go forward, it could only do so under extremely tight guidelines. Specifically, for the Authorizer's Assistant, Flast could only have 60 percent of the money he'd put forward in that detailed budget.

"I said to myself, This is ridiculous, absolutely flat-out ridiculous. These people have no concept of reality here. The time to say this is *before* you sign a contract for a million dollars, not three months afterward, let alone six months after you've been given permission to proceed. Well, it was a horrendous administrative nightmare in the background, because what it caused me to do was go scramble for the remaining funds that were necessary." Flast found himself pitching to the heads of other companies within American Express to make up the difference.

What had happened? American Express was feeling straitened ("a bad year here is still very enviable") and belts were being tightened. "You can get dragged into those gears of the bureaucracy and then you have to start scrambling like crazy to protect the initiative. That's one of the challenges of a project that extends over the kind of time we're talking about. All kinds of surprises can come up—they can come up from Inference, from Fort Lauderdale, from changes in management. This was just another unpredictable complication that emerged from the finance community. But it didn't stop us. We'd signed a contract, we were going to go forward, just had to scramble for funds. Just a surprise."

The first of several.

Setbacks and Derring-Do

At a time when he was only reading books about expert systems, it had occurred to Bob Flast that not only would he have technical problems implementing any artificial intelligence application, but the whole idea would be countercultural to American Express's management information systems group.

There were, first of all, the technical problems. Any expert system and its special-purpose Lisp machine would have to deal with the two systems already running on American Express's mainframes, the fast transaction system and the data base systems. "We decided early on that we wanted a co-processor type of architecture, where essentially the expert system would be running concurrently with our current authorization system. So if this funny new technology in any way, shape, or form, was acting up, we could shut it off and default to our existing method of handling the business. Nothing could jeopardize that," Flast recalls.

The next critical issue was latching the expert system, running on the Lisp machine, to the existing authorization system. As Flast began to think about it, he realized that one important reason American Express has human authorizers is because they act as a link between the fast-running transaction system and the slow-running data base, which otherwise don't connect. The transaction system, for which Flast was responsible and on which the statistical authorization system ran, doesn't store and retrieve data easily—its primary purpose is to get the transaction through. So American Express has different systems for data base applications—for recording and retrieving card transactions, billings, correspondences, and so on. Some transaction problems could easily be solved by getting, for example, billing information, but that can't be done directly, and a human authorizer is needed as an intermediary.

Flast knew very well that the right architecture for linking an expert system to the existing system was one where the expert system went directly to the data base for data it needed, and went directly to the transaction system for data it needed from that, acted on the data, then gave back its answer to the transaction system, just like the human authorizers. But he also knew that if he were to try to get this ideal system accepted as a common priority, not just within his own organization but for other organizations in American Express, such as telecommunications and data base, the expert systems project would never, ever be completed. Organizational boundaries would see to that.

"So rather than try to negotiate the optimal systems solution early on, I said to the systems people: We don't know what the authorizers actually extract from the data on these screens. We're learning that in knowledge engineering, as we observe them and interview them on the job. Therefore we can't specify to you today a single data base transaction that you could build that would get us the relevant data. We need to do a lot more knowledge engineering and we need to do it with a current environment, that is, information on the screens, not from the data bases. We want to see the data the way an authorizer sees, not the way it's represented in a data base."

Flast would emulate within the transaction system what an authorizer does when accessing the data base, down to the details of the keystrokes, then retrieve the screen, pick out the relevant data elements, convert them into a form the expert system could use, and ship them on to the Lisp machine. It was cumbersome, but he could use his own resources, not be dependent on anyone else. And it was suboptimal. But Flast figured he'd deal with the issue of optimality later on. "It's internal. It has nothing to do with the expert system, how we get package data across incompatible environments. In the interests of bringing this project home in a reasonable amount of time and minimizing my risk of having to depend on these other relationships entirely, I assumed that responsibility."

Even with the concessions, and even though the access from the transaction system to the data base system emulated the actions of the human authorizers, problems crept in. Errors and extra overhead would appear in the data base systems and the systems programmers got testy. They would show the error logs to Flast and his group: do you realize what you're doing to us? Matters weren't helped by the fact that, unbeknownst to Flast's organization, the Southern Regional Data Center (the Fort Lauderdale center) was in the middle of splitting its data base into two different host computers.

And then, three weeks before the prototype Authorizer's Assistant was due to be fielded, Flast discovered through a series of aborts and errors that the data base machine he was building a link to wasn't the machine where the needed data resided. There was such poor communication among the various systems groups that all the months the prototype had been undergoing development, nobody had known. Inference people had been systematically extending the AA's knowledge base, and systems programmers had been building the bridge to the data base—only it was the wrong one.

Flast felt terrible, very discouraged. "You could say that we should have strived for getting consensus from the other people in the systems community, but the reality of that is it wasn't achievable then." So they set out to do six months of work in the three weeks remaining of the schedule, building a direct access to the right machine. Meanwhile, the skeptics were saying, See? We told you so. We told you it wasn't gonna work.

"I had to manage that, too, and the best way was quietly, not to deal with it, but pursue what we knew was going to work. The question was, could we get it up in time?" (Before American Express's annual software freeze, when the company forbids all systems changes because holiday volume is so high and software changes then would risk downtime at one of the company's most critical periods.) "We'd targeted the end of October to give ourselves two weeks of leeway. We consumed that two weeks without any question, and, in fact, extended the start of the freeze by a week closer to the holiday season. Even at the eleventh hour, we were close but not close enough, so we had to shut the effort down on November 20, a tremendous disappointment to everybody— shut it down until after the freeze, when we could resume trying to get a production-level system up and running. We continued to test and debug and do a lot of things in the test environment, but we couldn't fool with the production environment for six weeks."

At that point, an entrepreneurial systems group in American Express's New York offices came to Flast and said, Look, for $78,000 we can have a functional alternative up for you by December 22. It was a quick fix strictly for demonstration purposes. "I said, 'You've got it. I mean, you've got $78,000 or $150,000, I don't care what it costs, but that's something I want to do.' Obviously I wanted to do it for more symbolic reasons than anything else, because I knew it would deal with the naysayers who were now becoming fairly loud. I also wanted a very powerful motivator for the systems community to do all the testing and debugging that could possibly be done during the holiday software freeze, so that come January, when the freeze was over, it wouldn't be back in a test-and-reiterate mode; it'd be done."

And that's what happened. On December 22 in Fort Lauderdale, the demonstration took place: real transactions handled by real authorizers—slowly, but in real time, as they occurred, with the expert system providing authentic, appropriate advice for each transaction: "credit on this transaction is recommended," "credit on this transaction is not recommended," with explanations if the authorizer wished them.

The demonstration finally succeeded in doing what nothing else could: it galvanized the MIS community. There it was, real. Flast had pushed it through, got around another obstacle, another hurdle, and now the MIS people realized they had to join in, not be seen as the project killers, the fossils. The first thing they did was move the annual end of the freeze from January 16 back to January 6. On January 7 they even offered a better solution than the quick fix. It still wasn't the best solution, but it worked better. Flast is convinced, however, that if the quick fix hadn't been put together, he and his people might still be saying, Well, another day now, another day . . .

Flast himself had been in charge of a systems organization during the early part of the project (midway through, he was promoted up to vice president for technology) and he'd been able to motivate some very bright people and then commit them to the AA project. "I'm not trying to be immodest, but if you've got somebody who really believes in expert systems and happens to control an MIS resource, you've got a big, big win on your hands. Failing that, you've got a big problem on your hands, which is what happened later in the year."

Flast had been promoted, and the man now holding his old job controlled the same MIS resources Flast had been able to commit to the AA. He telephoned Flast in January, a few days after the new system had been successfully installed in Florida and told him Sorry, but the shop was going to have to stop work on the AA—there were more important things to do, and the resources to continue on the AA just didn't exist.

Flast was furious. Aloud he calculated the man-months available in the organization, argued rationally that work on the AA could indeed continue; but his successor was adamant. No more work on the AA. Flast pointed out that a contract existed with Inference; certain commitments had to be met, and if they weren't, a large sum of money would simply be wasted. There were budgets in the operating centers that were predicated on the AA being in place by a certain time. If work on the AA stopped, then the operating centers would soon be over budget. On he argued.

"You just array all the facts. Is it emotional? Yes, it's emotional, but you try to defuse that by focusing on the facts of the case." It wasn't anything more than a manager setting his own priorities, even as Flast had set his when he'd had the same job. However, the new man had Flast to contend with, who was fighting for something he believed in deeply, and who saw his task as reordering his successor's priorities, showing that the AA would be more important than other competing projects.

And he could make the case. Efficiency and quality, competence. Efficiency is easy to measure. "It's obviously there. I mean, without question there are seconds shaved off transactions, many seconds; in the neighborhood of 25 percent or more of the time that authorizers spend will disappear. We can have fewer authorizers handling the same volume of work, or we can handle increasing volumes without ramping up the number of authorizers needed to handle that. That is impressive, but by itself it may not be enough to justify the costs of rolling this thing out."

In other words, how fast a decision to authorize credit is made isn't nearly as important as how well it's made. "In this case, effectiveness is what matters. The opportunities for credit and fraud loss avoidance are enormous. We don't talk about our numbers, but the industry reports hundreds of millions of dollars of exposure. Just very, very small improvements in that have tremendous consequences."

Flast would later muse on the whole problem of traditional MIS people and their conservatism. One solution, he suggests, is to make artificial intelligence so visible a goal among top management that the MIS people have no choice but to go along. The AA made it into American Express's annual report, and was a cover story on the magazine *High Technology*.

"The MIS people wanted measurable efficiency. But that wasn't the big, big win with this system, although it turns out that's actually going to make it. But there's no way you could know that at the start. I've heard senior systems and operations guys say publicly that even if the system doesn't have an economic payback, we might want to complete this project for other reasons strategically. Implicit in these statements was an expectation that it isn't going to pay back. When they started to see the numbers come back from Fort Lauderdale, in terms of sheer time reduction that authorizers spend on transactions with the new system versus the old, they're suddenly believers—in the pure nuts-and-bolts efficiency sense, which is great, because then anything else is gravy. But my point is, the gravy dwarfs the efficiency opportunity by many, many dollars."

MIS people weren't the only benighted ones. Operations people raised lots of questions. The person who supplied the expert knowledge for the expert system, Laurel Miller, had to contend with her opposites in the other three operating centers who were mighty unconvinced and argued that the AA wasn't working on a representative knowledge base. It was a direct challenge to Miller and her team's expertise.

Acting on analysis of the facts, Flast invited them to sit down with the cases themselves and say how they'd have handled the problem, case by case. "Fact-based analysis goes a long way in this company," Flast says, "because Lou Gerstner, our president, and a number of other senior managers were with McKinsey, and there's a tradition there of dealing with things in a rational way."

But when sweet reason didn't work, Flast would have to go to the executive levels above and simply point out that irrational obstacles were being put in the way of the AA, which was compromising the consistency with which customers were being treated by American Express. That got fast action.

Flast likes to use the phrase *killer technology*, which comes from the McKinsey consultants (who in turn borrowed the phrase from its creator, the vice president for research at

Bell Labs, Arno Penzias). A killer technology is one that "kills" the technology it replaces. AI is seen as a killer technology because it will eventually kill conventional interactive software implementations.

Soon, Flast says, American Express will move from back office to front office applications, exposing customers to the expertise and knowledge of American Express's best employees without the buffer of the employee and the cost that goes along with that employee. "That's where I see the next big win," Flast says, "in sales and service."

In the Trenches

The Fort Lauderdale center, officially the Southern Regional Operations Center, became the pilot site for American Express's first expert system mainly because the senior vice president of the southern region, Terry Smith, had stood up and asked for it when Bob Flast announced the project. Smith was eager to commit whatever resources were necessary.

Among the resources was Laurel Miller. When the expert systems vendors were invited to Fort Lauderdale in May 1985, one of the American Express people welcoming them was a tall, auburn-haired woman with intense blue eyes who can put away an entire pot of coffee in half a day without realizing it. Laurel Miller had come to American Express with an unusual background.

"I graduated from the University of Illinois in biology, and I was a registered, licensed medical technologist. But I soon realized that eventually I wanted to be more than just the supervisor of a hospital lab. So while I worked at Presbyterian–St. Luke's in Chicago, I took courses toward my M.B.A. I thought about hospital administration then, and I said, Nah, I wanted something else, more business-oriented."

In November 1982 Miller began at American Express as a management intern, a six-month program for M.B.A.s that acculturates them to American Express. Miller then spent nine months supervising a credit authorization system relay area, where transactions are received from the point-of-sale terminals and 800 numbers, and was then moved to the Fort Lauderdale authorization site, where decisions are actually made. She spent sixteen months as a supervisor in authorizations until May 1985, when she was promoted to manager of the CAS relay, where she had done her first stint as supervisor.

"So I was in that capacity for about a month when I was invited to a meeting where somebody said, Let's sit down and talk, and by the way, Laurel, you're going to be hosting a bidder's meeting for this project that's an expert system, and you'll meet the prospective vendors. I said fine. I had a cursory knowledge of expert systems just from being in the hospital—reading about medical expert systems, MYCIN and such. But since June of 1985 I've been intimately associated with this project."

Laurel Miller was to be the expert for the Authorizer's Assistant. She had a small staff of authorizers working with her, but the main responsibility for explaining and clarifying the authorizer's tasks was hers.

"Time it took," she says, "lots of time. I had no idea it would require so much time. I thought I'd be an expert for the two weeks these knowledge engineers came to Fort Lauderdale, and then they'd leave, right? They left, but they took my phone number with them." From contact person at American Express for Inference her job expanded to managing the project; eventually she racked up some 90,000 miles on her frequent flier program (which she took as a vacation in Australia a year and a half later).

By then she'd earned that vacation. She was to spend six weeks in Los Angeles at Inference during the first September and October of the project, and at least a week there each month for the next year. Simultaneously she had full-time responsibilities at Fort Lauderdale. But her passion became the AA, to make it the very best it could possibly be.

In the beginning it might have seemed a relatively simple thing to articulate how authorizers analyzed the data of a cardmember's credit record when faced with a decision about a given transaction. A simple rule might say:

IF   a card has been reported lost or stolen
and a member presents a card
and the member can establish his identity

THEN approve the transaction.
(because the member may have subsequently found the card)

Miller would describe to the knowledge engineers what might happen, and they'd go off and cast that into a program, which would then be run against some 650 test cases that had been pulled out of the day-to-day transactions of the center.

Authorizers begin with a fundamental question: Why did I get this referral? Is it for reasons of fraud, or credit reasons? They quickly study the account data, calling, for instance, on a monitoring program that forecasts possible late payments and analyzes other patterns. Perhaps there's an issue of fraud; a cardmember seems suddenly to be using a card more than he's ever used it. Step by step, but in a matter of seconds, the authorizer calls up information from as many as sixteen screens, doing a full analysis of the account to make the decision to authorize or not.

During knowledge engineering, Miller and her staff not only explained these things, but Miller also found herself asking for what-if scenarios (suppose this account was sixty-five days past due instead of thirty-two), and all this knowledge was duly set down in the form of elaborate IF-THEN rules. For example, *if* customer identification has not been made, *and* fewer than three charges appear on the account, *then* pattern analysis is required, *and* if the amount of the charge is in pattern, *then* the velocity [frequency of card use] is within the pattern; therefore credit is recommended. Or, *if* the fraud check based on pattern analysis is strong, *and* the merchant is not a restaurant, *and* the velocity is high, *and* the dollar amount is in or out of pattern, *then* the fraud indication is strong.

Obviously, the rules for credit authorization are judgmental, not numerically precise, and different authorizers handle the same case differently. The system was run continuously against the performance of human authorizers in the test cases, and modified as discrepancies came up. As the system was demonstrated at various stages to different segments of the company, it also emerged that the vice president for credit, say, had somewhat different criteria for granting credit than the vice president for sales, or even an on-the-job authorizer. All this had to be reconciled and encoded.

Of the experience, Miller would later say: "Knowledge engineering is a difficult task, but being engineered is probably equally difficult. The idea of sitting down and talking about what you do and how you do it is difficult. You, the authorizers, you, Laurel, anybody who participated in one of those sessions thought differently about the job and exactly what they did, 'cause you have to talk about things that come as second nature, and that isn't always easy, to talk about the things you do because your gut tells you to. I can appreciate the engineers trying to communicate in my language—which they had to, because I couldn't be expected to communicate in theirs. They had super minds to assimilate all that information. They didn't exactly have to learn how to be authorizers, but they had to pick up on all the terminology, and follow the thought patterns, and then go emulate it."

She laughs, recalling how after a while, the knowledge engineers began to talk as if they *could* be authorizers, and the bona fide authorizers would challenge them, Go ahead, try to do my job. "We could do that in this environment, because they're under supervision; they could be controlled." But they weren't too good at it.

"My people not only have to resolve transactions, but they have to talk on the telephone," Miller says, pointing out that Credit Authorization is the only place in American Express that deals directly with both merchants who are customers, and cardmembers who are customers. The decision to bring one of the customers to the phone is very delicate: American Express wants to protect itself, at the same time it provides customer service. "It's very important for the authorizer to make the customer feel comfortable, so not only are they monitoring activity on the account and watching the screens as they flip by, but they need to provide service and be very sensitive to a situation." It was here the knowledge engineers ran into trouble. "Knowledge engineers perhaps aren't as good at talking to real people as they are to each other, or to an expert. So they found that actually doing the job wasn't nearly as easy as watching over somebody's shoulder."

Nobody had ever measured both the qualitative and quantitative effectiveness of authorizers, Flast would say. Their judgmental performance was subjectively evaluated on a daily and weekly basis, and their efficiency was measured continuously, but until a computer program was presented that could operationally define what authorization is all about, based on the performance of the best authorizers, nobody had ever successfully determined how much credit loss and fraud were avoided by the best authorizers compared to the average.

With the AA, the first screen an authorizer gets with a referral is called the *main screen*, an assimilation of eight screens of raw data, re-formatted so that the eyes flow over it easily. On that screen is advice and a recommendation: Recommend credit be extended, but inform customer this is last time until balance outstanding is paid off. Or: Recommend credit be extended; customer shows evidence of traveling, which may be why balance is outstanding. If the authorizer disagrees, explanations for the system's recommendation are available; the final decision is always the authorizer's. "It's the upfront, preliminary critique of the account that's done for the authorizers," Miller says. "But they still own that decision. They see a recommendation they can choose to agree with or not."

The AA has made some big differences in time per decision. Recently, American Express compiled the numbers. "Since we don't talk openly about authorizer performance, I'll present these findings in relative, as opposed to absolute, terms," Flast says. "From an efficiency perspective, the AA will autonomously handle between 20 and 35 percent of the current traffic, and contribute to a 20 percent reduction in the handling time for transactions that go to authorizers. These productivity data alone produce an internal rate of return [IRR] significantly greater than the company's hurdle rate." The newspaper *Computerworld* estimated the IRR in the range of 45 percent to 67 percent.

In fact, American Express foresees no layoffs; the volume of its transactions is increasing so quickly that the company simply looks forward to greater productivity from the same number of authorizers.

But to repeat, both Flast and Miller have been at pains to point out that important as these savings are, they aren't the reason the AA was undertaken, or where its greatest significance lies. The greatest opportunity lies in improving customer service while reducing losses—usually antagonistic goals.

"If you feel that authorization itself has value in the credit stream of American Express, and you buy the fact that the experts do it better, then you must accept the fact that if their skills are emulated, you'll pick up benefit that way," Miller says.

Flast says, "From an effectiveness perspective, the AA results in more approved transactions by reducing the decline rate approximately one third. That's good news from a service perspective, but what about loss control? For the approved transactions, where a small fraction today wind up in trouble ninety days later, AA advice will result in a 50 percent reduction of that fraction. For the declined transactions, AA advice results in identifying double the number of cases destined to wind up in collections than the current manual procedures. *The losses avoided through this improved screening are in excess of five times the size of the productivity savings.*"

How much will a fully deployed AA save American Express per year? Though the company will not divulge this number, it can be estimated from the quoted performance statistics. From the number of authorizers employed, a guess as to the range of their salaries, and some arithmetic with the quoted performance statistics, one can estimate an annual savings of $27 million, a remarkable return on investment.

No wonder Flast was so exasperated by the seconds-saved-per-authorizer mentality of some of the skeptics.

Consistent application of rules not only realizes savings, it pays in customer satisfaction. Customers want to be treated consistently, whether they're dealing with the authorizer Harold or the authorizer Betty, whether that authorizer is in New York or Greensboro.

Senior managers appreciate consistency, too. Edwin Cooperman, president of the consumer card group, has said he doesn't care about AA's payback in terms of efficiency. Instead he cares about the consistency and effectiveness of decision making it brings, the opportunity to meter, play with the controls, and know that, instantaneously, changes he wants to make will become part of the process, as opposed to sending out an update to policy #372 that gets inserted into page 530 of the training manual.

Miller believes the AA has been well received by the authorizers themselves. The enormous complications of deciding whether an account is current or past due (yes, this check pays off this balance, but it was later returned, and now here's a new check entered for later charges; is it good?) plus the tension of the unexpected make the assimilation done by the AA a welcome help. "You never know what's going to happen next," Miller says. "It could be a $50 restaurant charge. It could be a $55,000 shop purchase." Moreover, the authorizers have had a chance to participate in system design; they too "own" it, and have had a say in the information the system presents to them, and how.

As for Miller herself, though her tone is always subdued, her phrases laconic, clearly she's an enthusiast. She admits to being more emotional about the AA than other people are. "I'm possessive of it. I spent a lot of time on it. I can't help but think about it and worry about what's happening in L.A., what's happening in Phoenix. So whether it's because I live it, or whatever, I am emotional about it. I deal with the problems, and I deal with the successes." One pleasant personal success is this: when Laurel Miller came back from her Australian vacation, she was promoted once more, this time to director of authorizations and card issuance at Fort Lauderdale.

As for the authorizers themselves, they've seen the hours Miller has worked; they've worked hours on the AA themselves. So although Miller sees motivating her workers as a manager's task, she observes that motivation doesn't just come from her, it also comes from the authorizers them-selves, who feel ownership and involvement.

But as the AA's development was under way, problems inevitably arose. Each department and sector had its own perspective, and wanted to see that reflected in the AA's rules. The people concerned with sales, for example, might be far more willing to extend credit under risky circumstan-ces than the people concerned with company finance, for though they were each aware of the rules, they saw them from a different point of view. In August 1986 the directors of the other authorization centers were invited to Los An-geles for a demonstration of the system. The explicit nature of the rules made everybody step up to his convictions, and a certain amount of tension ensued. Flast says: "They were less interested when they thought it was speculative, but when it was actually in front of their faces, a real system, they got more serious."

But the solution to those disputes was to test against the cases, make people say what they'd do explicitly. "That's the nice thing about expert systems: They're fixable, and in a more transparent, tangible way than any other piece of software you've ever been exposed to. We'll fix it today and you'll have it this afternoon to exercise against the testbed."

Flast was trained in psychology and mathematics, and his first professional job was working on tests and measure-ments for job performance. "It gave me a good appreciation for how difficult it is to measure human ability in a com-mercial setting, as opposed to standardized intelligence tests. So I come to all this with a particular set of biases and experiences, asking questions about human performance, and realize that it isn't easy. And the funny thing is that because we're dealing with a machine model of behavior, we're asking a different set of questions than we're accus-tomed to asking about the people we're modeling. We have higher expectations for the machine than for the people whose behavior it's modeling. I find that interesting—and difficult. I have to stop and think about that occasionally. The good news is that if the machine model starts to force the question of job performance being asked more, and if somehow the mechanization of some of this decision making requires us to answer that question, that won't be all bad. It's hard to do, which is why we've avoided doing it, but it can eventually be done. I love a quote that was on the wall of Thomas Edison's library, from Sir Joshua Reynolds: 'There's no expedient to which a man will not resort to avoid the real labor of thinking.' "

Flast has mulled these issues over a lot recently. "Two years ago I was of the impression that what the world would evolve to is smart machines. Now I'm convinced, more than ever, that the world needs smarter people *and* smarter machines. AI, interestingly enough, is the join that makes smarter people and smarter machines possible."

Nippon Life Insurance Company

Nippon Life is Japan's largest life insurance company, with total assets of some $70 billion. Its head offices are in Tokyo and Osaka, with 121 branches throughout Japan, and it has an active overseas network with branches in Australia, North America, Europe, and elsewhere in Asia. For nearly a hundred years it has strived to offer every customer the best possible service, at the same time it maximizes its life insurance sales and its asset management. But like all large financial organizations today, its interests are international. It takes advantage of and suffers from, the same pains of deregulation, competition, cross-border asset flow, and aging population that others like it face.

Nippon Life is not only Japan's largest insurance company, but ranks first worldwide in terms of new life insurance business. The company receives 2.7 million applications a year for life insurance from people who have been visited by sales representatives. Normally, the decision whether to offer a life insurance contract begins by processing the information that the customer has provided on the medical application form.

Of the 2.7 million applications, 1.2 million can be approved on the basis of the initial customer application, and no follow-up medical exam is necessary. But for 1.5 million, a further medical exam is required. About 700,000 of those turn out to be easy cases, yes or no. At this stage, evaluations are made by conventional computer means, similar in nature to the statistical analysis used during the first phase of credit authorization at American Express. But 800,000 cases are difficult, and the results of each of those exams must be evaluated by a team of two experts, one a physician and the other a life insurance specialist. Neither one alone has the expertise to make decisions about the severity of a disease, or its debilitating effects for insurance purposes; both specialists are stretched to their utmost to decide whether the application should be accepted, and if so, what the terms of the insurance contract should be, including the outpayment and premiums.

This decision-making process is exacting, time-consuming, expensive, and plagued by inconsistency. Forty such life insurance specialists work at Nippon Life, and each one has needed between five and six years of training to attain real expert status (this, of course, is beyond any formal education).

One reason attaining expertise takes so long can be explained by the company's Manual of Disease and Insurance—a compendium of all the insurance-related medical knowledge that the company uses in making its decisions, with medical data and mortality statistics related to given diseases, a manual many inches thick. This manual is supposed to guide every decision made by a Nippon Life specialist, and to some extent it does, but like the credit authorizers' handbook at American Express, some experts use the manual better than others. And also like the credit authorizers, the medical and life insurance specialists have parallel goals: they want to do the best for the company, and they want to do the best for the customer by giving him a fair premium schedule.

A few years ago, Nippon Life was approached by Computer Services Kaisha (CSK), the company that subcontracts to run the insurance company's considerable data-processing installation. Senior data-processing officials were informed about the expert system technology. CSK is also a software distributor, and distributes KEE, IntelliCorp's expert system shell, in Japan. CSK provided a seminar for the senior data-processing people at Nippon Life, who were immediately enthusiastic and bought the shell plus a Lisp machine. Everyone was hopeful that the job of deciding the 800,000 difficult cases each year could not only be eased by an expert system but could be improved, since all forty specialists, senior and junior underwriters alike, would be working at the same high level of expertise and applying the same rules consistently.

Between May and June of 1986, with the help of CSK, the Nippon Life data-processing people built a prototype for an expert system that would assist the two-man teams that labored over the 800,000 difficult cases each year. The prototype of course was limited; it handled only diabetes cases. But results with the prototype were so encouraging that the company decided to move into a full system, adding fourteen more diseases to the knowledge base, which now covers 90 percent of the 800,000 difficult cases. The remaining 10 percent are handled manually, without assistance from the expert system.

The expert system evaluates the data provided by the customer and his physician, and responds with a statement about the probability of death during the ensuing period. The probability is expressed as a certain number of insurance points over a nominal zero level, assessing risk for that particular case. Second, it gives the price of that policy and any special terms that should be indicated for the case. As an example, for certain cancer patients and certain premiums, there might be no insurance payout from the beginning of the contract until five years later. If the patient is still alive after five years, some normal insurance payout on the face of the contract becomes applicable. When the system recommends against writing an insurance policy, it states why and shows the chain of reasoning that led to its recommendation. With assistance from the expert system, an underwriting case that used to take a few hours to resolve is now done in a few minutes, for an average productivity gain of fifty to a hundred!

Nippon Life's goals are clear. It wants to cut the number

of experts it employs in the decision-making process, and it wants to speed up the training of new experts so that novices soon begin to make decisions as soundly as veterans do. It expects to save some $650,000 per year by cutting out these jobs (a number that doesn't quite correspond to salaries eliminated, because though jobs will change, nobody will be laid off). The company also wants to acquire a dynamic book of its century's worth of expertise, one that is full, complete, instantly accessible, and easily amended. Nippon Life will not disclose what gains it expects to realize through consistent top-quality decision making.

In employment-safe Japan, the experts welcome the system eagerly. Referring to the huge manual is tedious, cumbersome, and time-consuming. The experts themselves rate the system as "perfect" in producing the correct acceptances and rejections of insurance, and in assessing the correct basis points of the risk above normal, and in the insurance terms.

Nippon Life's annual report presents familiar rhetoric about continuing to offer the best service and still maximize assets in "this changing climate," but the difference is that Nippon Life's management strongly believes what it says and is acting upon it. Expert systems are now being designed to assess different kinds of financial investments that the company must make all over the world. Nippon Life Insurance runs one of the largest conventional IBM mainframe data-processing installations in Japan. Their advisory system for life insurance applications runs on microcomputers that are tied directly to the mainframe complex. But in this company the decision to use expert systems technology was made by the head of the MIS/DP organization, so the turf battles frequently seen in large companies simply did not arise. MIS owned the idea, and they're excited by the opportunity. They say they aren't interested, pro or con, in its artificial intelligence lineage. They simply want to get an important job done. No fights, no delays, no inertia. At Nippon Life, unlike so many other companies, the MIS people are the heroes.

The British Pension Advisor

Britain's social security system, the symbol of a society's efforts to be humane, has grown in patchwork fashion over many years. Each patch represents new opportunities or insights about how a well-meaning society can benefit its oldest members. Unfortunately, that very patchwork nature makes interpreting the rules and regulations an inhumane nightmare. Pensioners in precisely the same circumstances can end up with very different pensions just because one clerk has interpreted the rules differently from another.

The Social Security Department (DHSS) offers a Retirement Pension Forecasting Service to its citizens. It is set up to handle two kinds of questions: Am I entitled to a pension at retirement age? If so, how much? But citizens routinely ask more complicated questions, and the DHSS would like to be able to answer these in a way that is both timely and correct.

Let's say a citizen writes to the social security offices with a problem: "I am fifty-five years old. I was widowed two years ago and went back to work. This year I got ill and couldn't make my full contribution. Now that I'm back at work, how much voluntary contribution do I need to make to bring my contributions in line again? How long do I have to make this extra contribution? I should add that I was unemployed between 1948 and 1964 rearing my children [which counts in Britain's system]; does my late husband's contribution raise my retirement pension?"

Somewhere in the maze of social security rules and regulations, an answer exists, but the social security people are very hard put indeed to find it. They genuinely want to help people, but the complexity of the patchwork system of rules and regulations works against their well-meant efforts. The problem gets more intractable as the number of requests for pension forecasts rises steadily. In the 1986–87 year, 260,000 requests were received. A response to a request takes an average three months for a citizen to receive, and about one out of five of the responses is incorrect.

The DHSS approached the consulting firm Arthur Andersen (see Chapter 9) for a solution, and AA's London office recommended developing an expert system. Knowledge engineers from Arthur Andersen built a prototype expert system in four months that had 330 rules and ran on a microcomputer. The full system was then commissioned, and put into use in April of 1988. It handles a remarkable variety of questions and circumstances related to a citizen's Basic Pension and Additional Pension, including such things as deferred and early retirement, wages changing at either a certain rate or a set amount, payment of arrears, contributions that cease, overseas insurance, married women's election, and many more.

When a citizen query arrives, the citizen's record is retrieved from the electronic files of social security and printed out. From that printout, an office worker at the pension board can set to work with the expert system and answer that query in minutes. It may seem awkward to take a two-step route, mainframe to microcomputer, but this solves the difficult human problem of having to persuade the management information systems people that an expert system should be attached to their mainframes.

Operating at a centralized Newcastle facility, the system will save the DHSS £870,000 (about $1.5 million) per year. But the cost saving is not the primary goal. Service is. Citizens will be assured that they can get prompt, consistent, and correct answers from their pension administrators about their particular situation. Pensioners around the world might well envy them.

Sanwa Bank

In Japanese, *zaisan* means "financial assets," and the word on everybody's relatively prosperous tongue in Tokyo these days is the catchy mixed-language *zaitech*, or "financial engineering." In world markets, the Japanese financially engineer their assets with the treasury bonds, real estate and equity holdings of other nations, particularly those of the United States; but, on a much simpler level, ordinary Tokyo-ites are talking *zaitech*, too—it even appears as a slogan for ads in the subway, selling three-piece suits as "*zaitech* wear."

Tokyo's Sanwa Bank ranks among the top ten largest in the world, with offices in the center of the Tokyo financial district in a monumental building overlooking the Imperial Palace. Not surprisingly, Sanwa understands Japanese *zaitech* fever.

Sanwa has many different kinds of clients, but one set it particularly caters to is composed of wealthy individuals who have between a third to two thirds of a million dollars to invest, usually in a personal portfolio which must be man-aged—engineered, if you will—with great care to achieve maximum return within the goals stipulated by the individ-ual—that is, he might be willing to run some risk because he's interested in high growth, or he wants very little risk because he's saving to give his son a house in the suburbs, and so on. These customers are so valued that officers from the bank make house calls on them to help them with their banking needs.

Formerly, the calling officer would note the client's indi-vidual goals and preferences, and then return to his branch, where he would consult three portfolio mix specialists in the main branch. These specialists would then select a rec-ommended portfolio manually, perhaps a mix of tax-free instruments, mortgage securities, gold accounts, and gov-ernment bonds. The Sanwa Bank decided to automate that selection process as their first answer to a larger, more im-portant problem that had puzzled senior bank officers.

They knew very well that routine data processing, the work of clerks, had been automated for the past twenty years. But decision making, the kind of difficult responsibility that falls to portfolio managers, was still done the old-fashioned way. Shoji Sakamoto, an enthusiastic manager of the computer systems department in Sanwa's main office, began looking into systems to support decision making in the banks. Spurred by a cover story in *Business Week*, he traveled to the United States to explore what was happening with expert systems in financial and insurance companies. What he saw gave him direction.

The result was an expert system called "Best Mix." By early 1987 it was available at six branches and will be made available to the many other branch offices when knowledge updates related to the new Japanese tax law are made. Given a customer's circumstances and goals, the system selects instruments from six different categories of investments. It not only takes into account the customer's preferences, but it knows about tax regulations (e.g., the government restricts how much of a couple's assets can be invested in tax-free vehicles) and the relative advantages of a choice among more than a hundred different discounted government bonds (each with a different term), the yield on time deposits, certain kinds of securities, mortgage or gold, and so forth.

Best Mix runs on an IBM mainframe and was developed with the use of an expert system shell called "Brains," which is a reworking of an expert system shell developed at Rutgers University in the 1970s. The bank was aided in the development by Toyo Information Systems, an affiliate firm. It's a relatively simple system, with only 130 rules. It picks up fifty-three different variables, like customer data, and is capable of selecting one or more, a best mix, from fifteen different types of bank products. Changing interest rates and maturities are easily inserted daily, as well as a list of "favorite" bonds human experts pick each day.

The system was developed between October 1985 and April 1986; a prototype was evaluated that summer, and the full system was put into use in September 1986. It fused the knowledge of two of the portfolio experts at the main branch. In the course of building the system, they discovered some contradictions in the way each of them worked, and in extreme cases, the managing director had to resolve the conflict, especially as related to policy decisions in investment strategies.

Of course Best Mix was a maiden effort in expert systems for Sanwa Bank, which they expected to learn from for future systems. But the bank also undertook the project for short-term, practical goals, aiming to reduce the time it takes to produce these portfolios for wealthy customers, and taking advantage of the built-in explanation facilities of expert systems—the system provides automatic explanations of why it recommends particular mixes—a real competitive advantage for the bank. Normally it takes from one to two hours to produce such a portfolio mix by hand, and the expert system has reduced that time to five minutes, including the time it takes to input the customer model.

But other advantages have accrued. The system works so fast that simulations can be run—customers can be offered certain what-if alternative scenarios. The portfolio officer can experiment in what the Japanese call "the space around the rules," which doesn't result in a large gain, but might be an improvement of a tenth of a percent, significant to a customer who's investing a large sum of money.

On average, one of these portfolios is done in each branch every day. At that rate, time savings isn't a startling payoff. But Sanwa isn't looking for that kind of payoff so much as it intends to enhance its reputation as a forward-looking *zaitech* institution, a place in which any prudent Japanese would choose to have his money managed, since all Japanese believe that high-tech or computer processing is more reliable than people; high technology means a better product. And sure enough, Sakamoto notes that in the month just after the service was introduced, and people read about it in newspaper ads, deposits at the Sanwa Bank increased. This secondary benefit was as important to the bank as the primary mainstream service enhancement benefit.

Best Mix is a beginning effort. Now the bank has moved on to three other consultation systems it prefers to keep confidential, each a significant part of financial engineering.

Chapter 6

Technology Insertion: Hard Work, Vision, and Luck

A NEW TECHNOLOGY is something like an undocumented alien: no matter how worthy, the forces keeping it an outsider are stronger than those that can ease it into full citizenship. Even documentation—facts and figures—isn't enough to assure its acceptance. People who cherish reason (and in AI who doesn't?) might be under the impression that a simple demonstration of the facts—a ten-times speedup of some important task, or saving a goodly sum of money, or the chance to do a job that simply wasn't possible before—would make expert systems self-selling. That hasn't been the case. An aggregation of circumstances must work together to bring about the successful insertion into a going concern of a new technology like this.

The Champion. Surely the fundamental requisite is a champion, an individual or a small group with unwavering vision, the willingness to take risks, to push on in the face of obstacles. These are the people who take the first steps of educating themselves, of identifying an appropriate task for expert systems application: one that's useful, cost-effective, and likely to have a visible impact on the corporation, a task that fits the corporation's strategic goals.

Northrop Aircraft's Ken Lindsay and Bob Joy not only saw

124 · *The Rise of the Expert Company*

that expert systems would solve their problem of automating manufacturing process planning, they then tirelessly mounted their traveling Apple-on-a-dolly Ken and Bob Show for anybody who'd pay attention. They didn't let anything stop them, not their boss's displeasure (recall how they pretended to be doing what they were told and went ahead and did what they thought was right instead) nor the tightly woven red-tape barriers erected by the Northrop MIS people. American Express's Bob Flast had to battle nearly everybody in sight, including his own successor, to get American Express's groundbreaking expert system going. Though the message of each story is slightly different, in every place expert systems have been established we encounter energetic, often charismatic, champions. A determined human being with a vision both mighty and precise is essential.

Selling.   And the champion must sell. He must talk until he doesn't think he can talk once more—Du Pont's Ed Mahler estimates he's given his introductory expert system speech hundreds of times. Led by George Heilmeier, the Texas Instruments artificial intelligence business effort went divisionwide, companywide, nationwide, then worldwide via satellite with their extraordinary "AI Blitz."

Bending the rules.   A champion must sometimes bend the rules to serve his vision. Digital's Dennis O'Connor filched his initial investment in expert systems from a more conventional budget item he declines to name to this day. The Fujitsu middle manager who was afraid the marketing people would tell him what he didn't want to hear simply went ahead without asking and ordered Fujitsu's Lisp mainframe processor into production. Westinghouse's team of Bob Osborne and his boss John Traexler turned a twenty-five-year work relationship of trust into a vehicle for bringing expert systems to their Westinghouse group despite the cries of unfairness from engineers who offered surer bets to support.

Learning.   A serious effort to learn is essential at the personal level. Near retirement, Navistar's John Bowyer, busy head of the management information systems group, insisted on learning about this strange technology for himself instead of delegating the problem to his subordinates, and was thus able to argue for Navistar's giant commitment to expert systems. Canon Camera's optics physicist Toshiaki Asano was actually on the systematic lookout for a new technology to help his lens designers when he taught himself about expert systems. And Motoo Matsuda, a young engineer at Kajima Construction, listened seriously to his friends outside the company and then introduced the technology to his friends within the company.

Scaling the MIS barrier. Champions are supposed to overcome obstacles, but why are obstacles so often found in those divisions variously known as management information systems, electronic data processing, or administrative data processing? The anger and bitterness of our interviewees at the inertia, conservatism, and obstructionist attitude of these conventional data-processing managers came up so often that it emerged as a major theme. We considered separating it out and writing a special chapter, complete with battle plan.

Typically, the MIS departments manage corporate computing and the huge sums of money spent on computing equipment and applications. Further, they have been doing so for a long time and have built up strong power bases within companies. When some of our interviewees reviewed early drafts of material on their companies for factual accuracy, a depressing pattern emerged. Though the recorded transcripts of their interviews contained bitter comments on their frustration, they asked us to delete quotations. "You can't imagine what kind of retribution they'll take," one high-level executive wrote in the margin of a draft of a story that detailed the MIS obstinacy at his company. "Please delete this section," another wrote, "life won't be worth living if you don't."

Respecting their wishes, we deleted the quotations in context but decided to exhibit appropriately sanitized versions of the original manuscript.

"It took six months to get a Lisp machine because the MIS people demanded to know what on earth [the group] would use such a machine for. When explanations were proferred, MIS countered that any new computer purchased would have to meet the requirements all computers met at [the company], which is, it would have to be able to communicate with a set of protocols on the IBM mainframe known as SNA [System Network Architecture]. It made no difference that the Lisp machine would be stand-alone and would never need to talk to an IBM mainframe: rules were rules, and nobody was about to bend them for this artificial intelligence stuff. In an exercise of mind-boggling vacuity, somebody took a few months and wrote the SNA protocol programs for the Lisp machine. The revenge of the MIS, the group would call it later."

And another said: "The MIS people resisted the whole idea. They accused me of badly affecting their mainframe performance. Truthfully we know that the impact on the system is trivial. It's just a delaying tactic. Once we were accused of making a machine perform poorly, and I said, Look, you tell me who's logged on that's using expert systems. And the MIS people did a search and nobody was. Then how's that causing the problem? Tell me how that's happening? And they ran off to the corner, embarrassed. It turned out to be another problem, but the idea of artificial intelligence—people think of science fiction as soon as they hear it."

Educating the company—and beyond. Education, informal as well as formal, is as vital at the company level as it is at the personal level. But it only succeeds when the local corporate culture is well understood. Consider some case studies.

Digital Equipment Corporation's AI groups have technology transfer as their explicit aim ("We want to get this technology into the hands of everybody around DEC who's had problems because we've been starting to see that this stuff really works"). Since DEC has had more experience than any other firm in inserting this technology, the company has much to teach others.

In the early days, the firm offered a conventional course in building expert systems, with Lisp and prototyping, but while some interesting things were done, the approach was on the whole disappointing. It failed to take into account the resistance many people feel to a new technology, the not-invented-here syndrome, the possible psychological threats new technology posed.

Nowadays at DEC, the effort to insert an expert system begins with securing a high-level commitment from the management of a given business unit. DEC's AI groups have spent much time with managers, engaged in what has turned out to be mutual education, for while the AI people were busy convincing various high-level managers that AI really worked, and moreover, wasn't going to break anything, they were learning the virtues of incremental, rather than revolutionary, change in a business that needs to make a continuing profit. Thus one important rule of thumb is not to replace existing systems but to make them smarter. A top-level management committee oversees to make sure that any system fits into long-term business strategies.

But besides upper management and expert systems technologists, a third group has to be considered. "The management of the technology transfer into the end user group is critical," Dennis O'Connor has written. "Preparation is key. One critical lesson is to start small, build incremental prototypes that service a real need in your corporate business. Make sure you have identified a real, but bounded, problem."

Thus, once the high-level commitment is secured, the AI people move immediately to the users, involving them from the start in the design of any system. This is known around DEC as the "buy-in": it makes sure that everybody understands why this is being done, why it's important to them personally and to the firm as a whole. The prototype is demonstrated early in order to decide if it's the best solution. "It helps to have lots of patience and persistence," O'Connor observes, "and be willing to fail forward, gracefully, toward success."

Would-be knowledge engineers at DEC are admitted to an apprenticeship program that takes from nine months to a year, working with the central AI group to learn the techniques. Well over two hundred people have gone through that course, and another thirty-five to forty have gone on for another year at universities. A new and very popular course of study has been introduced that lasts four to five months.

But by now, AI saturates the air at DEC: engineers are so eager to learn it that a few barriers must be raised. If a DEC person wants to take the AI course, his or her manager has to have a plan for how the technology will be applied. Otherwise, the firm fears, there would be too many trying to get into the course, and the firm can't afford to solve problems that aren't important. Though **IBM** seems to be infinitely wealthy, it has the same problem: its small and lithe AI group in Harrison, New York, makes sure that any substantial expert system effort anywhere in IBM worldwide fits with long-term company strategy.

Schlumberger offers an interesting contrast to DEC. In 1978, Michel Gouilloud, the director of the company's Schlumberger-Doll Research Laboratories in Ridgefield, Connecticut, sponsored a conference to discover how AI might be applied to Schlumberger's industrial problems. Gouilloud fits the mold of the champion: restless, energetic, persevering, and deeply aware of new technologies and their potential impacts. Gouilloud enthusiastically supported the first commercial application of AI, the Dipmeter Advisor, which codified the thirty-five years of experience of a superb analyst named J. A. (Al) Gilreath, whose interpretations of specialized scientific oil well data were widely acknowledged to be part science and part black art, but surely the best in the business.

Early versions were developed in Ridgefield. In 1980 a prototype emerged which was sent to Schlumberger's engineering lab in Houston to be made into something that could be used in the field office, this after some delays caused by changing the computer on which the system runs.

Thus the Dipmeter Advisor had user pull from the field engineers (especially Gilreath and his assistant David Hammock, who improved the knowledge base) and it had developer push from Ridgefield's Reid Smith (now director of Schlumberger's Palo Alto research lab). It even had top-level push from Gouilloud. But between the Ridgefield labs push and the field pull lay the Houston Engineering Center, whose task was to turn the system into a product suitable for the conditions under which it would have to operate.

Unfortunately, no AI champion existed in Houston. The Dipmeter Advisor languished there, and occasional grumblings were heard from the Houston computing traditionalists that while Ridgefield had reaped all the glory for development (in 1982 there were practically no other industrial expert systems and the Dipmeter Advisor got much publicity) Houston was going to get all the blame when the product didn't work in the field.

In the course of a company reorganization, the Dipmeter Advisor was moved to Paris. Bob Langley, a geologist from Houston, and Bob Young, a computer scientist from Ridgefield, went along to see if they could finally make a product out of it they could sell.

In the end, it was Hammock and Young who finally saw that things were done right. Another three years and one organization later, responsibility for the Dipmeter Advisor moved to a new center in Austin, and only a last-minute decision by David Hammock to postpone going back to school and to further develop the Dipmeter Advisor saved it once more from the shelf.

Why had Schlumberger, which has computer scientists, but not a management information systems barrier, taken so long to make a commercial product of its first expert system? Why, when so many people wanted expert systems to saturate the firm, hadn't they?

The answer lay deep in Schlumberger's view of itself and its goals, which were shifting even as the fortunes shifted of the oil fields it served. Schlumberger had always been a data-collection and measurement-tools company, not a data-interpretation company. Nearly ten years after Michel Gouilloud's first insights about AI applications for his firm, expert systems and other AI techniques have finally taken hold at Schlumberger, as evidenced by the design of the computing environment in the firm's new Field Log Interpretation Centers, the important interpretive outposts all over the world, and the company's new well-logging trucks, which will all have advanced AI software. The Dipmeter Advisor has finally begun to be used, as well as other expert systems we describe in Chapter 8, titled "Preserving, Selling, and Using Expertise."

A much more successful case of technology insertion can be seen at **Texas Instruments**, which began with a consciousness-raising program called the AI Blitz, designed to bring attention to the new technology and its possibilities. The Blitz got under way even before TI had anything it could point to as an example of a homegrown system. The AI group lectured indefatigably; it built, it convinced, until finally there was enough positive feedback so that a push was no longer required: suddenly there was company pull. The TI Satellite Symposiums, which were started as a means of simply educating outsiders to the possibilities of AI, and perhaps generating some business for TI's own AI consulting groups, helped convince others *in* TI that this was important. Now TI offers its employees a wide array of formal courses, too, and sends them to universities for further training.

In a different way from Texas Instruments, Japan's **Mitsui Group** also goes beyond the companywide. The Mitsui Group is one of the large Japanese trading companies that act as loosely linked multicorporate conglomerates. (Hitachi and Mitsubishi are others familiar to Westerners.) The Mitsui Group consists of twenty-five companies with more or less closely knit relationships, and though it's helpful to use intercompany products and services, it isn't mandatory. Toyota might take advantage of Mitsui Bank's credit, but on the other hand, it uses non-Univac products at its central research laboratories.

In 1968, a new company called the Mitsui Knowledge Industry Company Ltd. (MKI) was formed to continually update and educate the employees of the Mitsui Group about new ideas in software and information systems areas. (MKI also does a variety of developmental and contract work for the Mitsui Group, and for outsiders as well.) It has fallen to MKI to propagate expert systems and knowledge engineering throughout the Mitsui Group, and MKI does so by means of regular conferences and study groups. The study groups draw from different, often competing, firms, but this seems to be no special problem in Japan, as it might be elsewhere.

One general problem the study groups have tackled is building an expert system for personnel inventory, matching people and their skills with new tasks. While this project intends to provide experience in building expert systems, MKI also wants to develop the best method for this kind of application, and a shell that others can use. Competing study groups are taking two different approaches, using two different kinds of expert system tools, because another purpose of the educational effort is training in the best kind of tool for a given application.

Du Pont, however, believes that the best transfer agent for this new technology is the interested user himself. Thus AI technology insertion takes place at Du Pont in a series of steps. The first—and the most effective continuing step—is information passed along the old-boy networks: word of mouth, a friend telling a friend. The next step is a management-awareness lecture given by the head of the AI group *by invitation* to a Du Pont business unit. If the management-awareness lecture provokes interest, alternatives follow: The curious can take an introductory course consisting of a few hours, or they can go to Wilmington for a more elaborate two-day course. Another alternative is for the interested person to work independently with the expert system shell Du Pont itself has developed, or with one of the commercial shells it has licensed, with occasional advice from the Wilmington AI hotline, or even a quick visit, a "jump-start," from the Wilmington experts. Some take advantage of all these possibilities. But if the entry barrier is low, so is the investment, and if one individual's interest should wither, it's obviously no great loss.

Sometimes user pull helps insert the technology. A man-machine interface research team at **Mitsubishi Electric Company** in Kamakura, outside Tokyo, had been mildly interested in expert systems technology, but got actively engaged when a group of engineers from the Nagasaki plant came to Kamakura and asked for a system to help with estimating costs of building electric motors.

At **3M**, Tim McCullough, who has championed a number of expert systems, says: "If any technology significantly complex cannot be distinguished from magic, and to appreciate magic you must have faith that the performer can do wondrous things, then to have your audience appreciate AI technology you must first develop faith, not understanding." The new technology must be explained in terms of the corporation's own perceived needs. "Sell yourself," says McCullough. "A CEO may not fully grasp the technology, but is likely a good judge of character."

A case in point: When **FMC** decided to move into a large-scale commitment to expert systems, including an equity position in the AI startup Teknowledge, at least one member of the board listened to the arguments, shook his head, and said, "I don't understand all this. But I've worked with the man who's making this presentation and I trust him. I'll vote for it."

The university connection. Nearly everybody into expert systems early has had strong ties with university researchers. DEC's vice president for research, Samuel Fuller, had been a faculty member at Carnegie-Mellon before coming to DEC, and along with Gordon Bell, then DEC's vice president for engineering (and himself a former professor at CMU) knew all about AI research at CMU. The large Japanese firms systematically send their brightest young researchers to graduate school in the United States, believing, as DEC does, that knowledge travels best in human heads. Fujitsu's Takeo Uehara came upon expert systems at one of the meetings of an industrial affiliates program at Stanford, of which Fujitsu is a member. Du Pont and Australia's Lend Lease Corporation both have—or had, until those men got seduced into exclusive relationships with expert systems—ministers without portfolio whose job was to scout the universities for any new technologies with long-term possibilities. Bruce Johnson, who headed Arthur Andersen's AI group, assiduously nurtures his university ties, as does Du Pont's Ed Mahler.

Luck. Whether you believe nature favors the prepared mind, or whether you think luck is just dumb, if FMC's CEO

Robert Malott hadn't been sitting on a plane next to an expert systems pioneer, Peter Hart, and got into conversation with him, FMC might eventually have moved into expert systems, but not with the panache and deep commitment it has.

If Ross Quinlan, himself an AI pioneer, hadn't married the daughter of the chairman of Australia's Lend Lease Corporation, and then talked up expert systems at a cocktail party so that minister without portfolio and technology sleuth Alan Stretton went off to see for himself and was further persuaded by dropping in on an old friend at Stanford who just happened to be playing around with expert systems, Lend Lease might still have gotten into the technology eventually, but surely not so soon or so significantly.

A champion who sells and sells and sells, and doesn't flinch at bending the rules; individual initiative plus corporate education; warm university relations; end user commitment, ownership, buy-in; and finally, luck. This is how the technology has been inserted.

Chapter 7

Making Waves at Du Pont

THIS CHAPTER is about one company that stands alone in many ways. Du Pont is, in the words of Ed Mahler, the ebullient manager of the company's artificial intelligence program, "the U.S. economy less fast food, defense, and banking." It's big, diversified, and does things its own way. One of its own ways is to eschew the make-a-big-splash expert system, the boulder, and instead cast pebbles into the pond, small systems whose ripples move out everywhere. But just to be on the safe side, Du Pont houses a loyal opposition, too, a group that's trying to shake loose that big boulder—or, to use the metaphor around Du Pont, bag the elephant while the company still feasts on rabbits.

Note how Du Pont engineers usually build their own systems to leverage their own jobs. It's as if an assembly line worker built his own personalized robot. It works. The average engineer spends a man-month on the task, and the company sees an average payback of $100,000 per year. Multiply that by the two hundred expert systems presently in use, the hundreds under development at Du Pont, and the thousands to come, and you're beginning, as the saying goes, to talk real money.

From Pirate Ship to Business Unit

The Du Pont Company seems to be everywhere—everywhere in the world, and everywhere in products and research. Chemistry, of course: Eleuthere I. du Pont de Nemours, a French immigrant to the United States who'd once worked at the French royal powderworks, made his fortune in high-quality gunpowder during the War of 1812. But he also owned woolen mills, and ardently pursued farming. All these have shaped the modern Du Pont Company's interests, which range over fibers (found in everything from apparel to communication satellites), agricultural and industrial chemicals, biomedical products, industrial and consumer products, polymer products, coal, and petroleum (from exploration to transportation and marketing). To put it in numbers, Du Pont has seventeen hundred products, and some of the products have up to ten thousand subtypes. Sensitive to its early military successes, the seventh largest corporation in the United States does no military contracting.

Though Du Pont is a very loose confederation of many business units of varying sizes, the corporation has a continuing research-and-development program with broad objectives of growth, expanding product lines, economy, and efficiency. Supporting these broad R&D objectives is a program of basic research, and groups in the life sciences and electronics now account for over half that program.

Ed Mahler, a chemical engineering Ph.D. out of the University of Texas who's been with Du Pont for more than seventeen years, working his way through plant work to manufacturing, and later to corporate planning, became Du Pont's roving ambassador for far-out ideas. When he discovered expert systems, he decided they were so much fun he'd pursue them exclusively. Now his job is to champion expert systems throughout Du Pont.

Mahler is *sui generis*, one part Texas good ol' boy, one part shrewd businessman, one part ebullient philosopher-poet, one part wild man; West Texas in every inflection. His cowboy boots are notorious. In the spring of 1987, Mahler had been invited to lecture at the Harvard Business School. One of his colleagues hinted that *perhaps* the cobraskin boots weren't the most appropriate footgear for a lecture at Harvard. "I told him: I got boots, I got sneakers, I got barefoot. Take your choice."

In late 1984 Ed Mahler began paying attention to expert systems. For any new business, he believes, three things must be established: first, the opportunity, or the market; second, the production capability; and third, the human resources. What was the opportunity or market for expert systems at Du Pont? Did Du Pont have the means to produce expert systems? What kinds of people did such a task require, and were they at Du Pont?

To answer these questions, in the spring of 1985 Mahler began inviting in vendors—small startups and big-time companies—to pitch AI to Du Pont. "Well, we had 'em all in, you know? And every one of them says: Forsake all others, we're the one. And furthermore, you're going to have to undergo a cultural revolution." That meant forget Fortran, forget Cobol; forward-thinking programmers would have to learn Lisp, maybe Prolog. "It meant $300,000 to buy a workstation, primary software, a year of training to make things really fly. Oh, and one guy isn't going to do anything all by himself, so you need a group of between six and ten. You're talking about an entry barrier of $3 million." Texas-fashion, Mahler permitted himself an exaggeration factor of three, but he had a point to make.

For a company like Du Pont, where did the opportunity in AI lie? So far as Mahler could see, it was in in-house applications: Du Pont certainly wasn't interested in selling AI technology, any more than it sold any other kinds of software.

And what about resources? "At Du Pont we had less than five Lisp people in the whole company. We had three thousand programmers that could code Fortran and Cobol, and fifteen thousand Lotus users—they could use a computer, but they couldn't write a line of code."

Five years down the road, no matter what Du Pont did in AI, it was going to have fewer programmers, five hundred fewer maybe; and more applications people, about 30,000 Lotus-users. Mahler believed Du Pont ought somehow to use that big and quickly growing chunk of people—that would be the ideal case. And while he was thinking about ideal cases he wanted somehow to use the existing hardware as well. In short, Mahler wanted an incremental approach to expert systems, and he wanted to lower the entry barrier. Three million dollars was simply too high.

But in the summer of 1985 it wasn't at all clear that any technology existed to satisfy those conditions. The AI vendors were saying that to have AI you had to undergo the cultural revolution, cultivate Lisp fluency, then find the big applications. But Du Pont's structure didn't lend itself to that at all: its corporate knowledge was dispersed all over the place in more than 120 plants scattered all over the world. And what about after some expert systems were built: how would they be maintained, kept current? It was discouraging.

In a perfect world, users would build their own little systems that they themselves could maintain. But that required a tool with a built-in knowledge engineering capability simple enough for any engineer to use, a Lotus 1-2-3 of expert systems applications software.

"So that's where we were, struggling with it. I saw the first expert system shells, and God, they were terrible! But you could look through them and see the promise of an applications tool that could be widely disseminated." The main problem with the first shells, Mahler thought, was that they were visually cluttered, and more important, intellectually cluttered by far more operations than anybody starting out to build a first expert system would need.

Mahler admits they still didn't know what the opportunity was. But he was convinced they were on the right track; AI was going to be big and important somehow. He thought some experimentation might uncover the opportunities, and so he rounded up a few other visionaries to help him out. "It was a true pirate ship operation, ad hoc, and I funded it out of my office automation budget, which we overspent by a factor of four. I went at personal risk to do it."

Personal risk? Du Pont wouldn't fire him—or the group's co-founder, David Pensak, from central research and development, who was sharing the risk by committing resources to something that couldn't logically be called central research—but careers would be finished. No advancement. "And since I didn't have any budget for people, one of the requirements was that these people who joined me share the vision, and that they be so committed they could convince their boss that he should pay for them to work for me."

The original task force was a group of old friends, plant managers or directors who'd come up through the company together; what Mahler calls his old-boy network. "I'd call 'em up and say, Hey look, let's get crazy together—I want to run an experiment and I need somebody to run the experiment with me. I need you to risk a man-month. They were all willing." The task force began to form: Pensak, from central research and development, who had a background in biology but who'd been actively pursuing research in computing, particularly graphics; specialists from marketing research and communications research. Eventually some six departments were involved, each with very different skills, and each with access to other old-boy networks: the process control network, the marketing network, the manufacturing network, the MIS network, the research network. Access to those other networks leveraged the work of the original group.

Networking is a marvelous way to do business because there's no greater quality control check in a company, Mahler says. "If you're not supplying value, you're not going to get recommended, because hey, these are their friends." Moreover, the task force brought a multitude of views. "When you've got marketing control expertise with process control expertise, it's sort of like managing a circus, but it's marvelous. You get great creative ideas and open discussion. I think that's important." Eventually, old-boy networks, not exhortation or education, would begin and sustain the spread of expert systems through Du Pont.

About this time, Mahler's boss, Raymond Cairns, the vice president for information systems, got involved. "We could see Ed was beginning to bring it together, and so my boss, Al McLaughlin, the senior vice president for technology, and I decided to consolidate all this and treat it like an embryo business unit." Mahler wanted to give up his roving ambassadorship for far-out ideas and concentrate on expert systems, so they thought up an innocuous title for him, Program Manager—Artificial Intelligence, and Mahler was in business.

"Since December 1985 the marketing I have done within the company is, I've answered the phone," Mahler says. "Now I've given hundreds of speeches, okay? But they were triggered by the old-boy network. When I do work for another business unit at Du Pont, I send them an invoice: here's how much I did for you, here's how much it cost. Send me this amount of money, or send me a one-page letter telling me how it stunk and I'll swallow the costs, I'll do better next time. That's a great marketing tool, because I've yet to get a single letter." He stops, then laughs: "Probably because it's easier to send me the check than write the letter, but the marketing concept is sound nevertheless!"

Meanwhile, more commercial AI tools were becoming available, but none of them were suitable for what Mahler wanted to do. Not only did Mahler and his embryo business unit want a tool easy enough for the Lotus users to deal with, they also believed it ought to run on existing machines. Du Pont uses Vax minicomputers for domestic manufacturing computers; its marketing and business computers are IBM; and its international computers for both marketing and manufacturing are Hewlett-Packard.

Since there was no suitable expert system shell on the market, they built one instead. It was designed by a Du Pont engineer named Lester Shipman, and is known as the Tool Kit. It requires no programming knowledge, it has embedded graphics and statistics, and is easy enough to use so that it can be taught in a two-day course (along with the use of two commercially available shells and some elementary knowledge engineering) and then people can go back to their own laboratory, plant, or office and build a system for themselves. "It's a marvelous package," Mahler says, "probably one of the best on the market—except it's not on the market."

Will it be? Mahler hedges. He's not in the software business. Tool Kit is maintained for internal use, but to have to maintain it for outsiders . . . he makes a face. And then from a business point of view, there's much value in Du Pont having it when the rest of the world doesn't. (Some seven hundred copies of it had been distributed around Du Pont by mid-1987, as well as seven hundred copies of a commercial product called Insight.)

What has emerged at Du Pont is a small support group of twelve or so charged with the task of catalyzing the application of artificial intelligence techniques, particularly expert systems, broadly and effectively through Du Pont. Half the group is permanent, half the group is on loan from other parts of the company—another way of nourishing the old-boy network, and similar in size and responsibilities to IBM's AI group.

However, Du Pont's group adheres to the old-boy system as a way of getting things done. The AI old-boy network (a third of which is female) started out as Mahler's pals, the people who were willing to get crazy with him. Then a second layer was added, about fifty site coordinators at the various plants and departmental locations. A third layer consists of the hundreds of people trained in the two-day course, going up at the rate of fifty per week, all linked by electronic bulletin boards. They aren't full-time knowledge engineers. Du Pont's attitude has been to proffer expert systems as one more tool for its workers, like electronic spreadsheets, electronic mail, electronic filing.

The care and feeding of old-boy networks (and they exist everywhere, not just in AI) accords with something fundamental in the Du Pont corporate culture: the company believes it should use its corporate size to strategic advantage. It tries to avoid inventing the wheel in six different places by fostering exchange among the old-boy networks and by trying to break down the not-invented-here syndrome.

So nowadays, if Du Pont users can't build an expert system for themselves simply by sitting down at their own plant or office with a piece of software they've bought at cost from Mahler's AI group, they have the option of attending a two-day course in Wilmington that costs $500. Students in the course aren't required to know programming, because the Tool Kit requires no programming in the ordinary sense. In addition, the students learn to use other shells, Insight and First-Class, and they learn some elementary knowledge engineering. Another option is the jump-start, where members of Mahler's group will come and consult for a day or two, no more, to get a system started. Mahler considers the jump-start a learning experience for his own group: it shows them what they need to teach in the course. Telephone support is also available. The course, the consulting, and the telephone support are all handled by Mahler's twelve-person Artificial Intelligence Program group, each one of whom must take a turn at doing every task—teaching, consulting, and answering the telephone help line.

"We teach. We jump-start. We'll give support. We'll do corporate licensing of commercial shells to lower the entry cost, which is part of the staff's sharing the risk with the operations units. I've gone out to the plants and given the speech a hundred times which, in essence, says the corporation thinks this is so important they're willing to share the risk with you. And they've done these sorts of things to enable you to get started. And here's the kinds of opportunities we see."

Mahler's management-awareness speech, as he calls it, is usually the first step when a Du Pont site is considering artificial intelligence, and that speech itself is usually by invitation. Then comes a four-hour course for managers and engineers, the people who'll be managing expert systems as distinct from the people who'll actually be building and using them. That introductory four hours includes, among other things, tapes from the Texas Instruments satellite symposiums on expert systems, including the footage where Mahler himself appears. Next comes the two-day training course, and thereafter the help line, manned by people who can do everything from tell a caller when the next classes are scheduled to how to jump-start a system.

"When we started out with fifty people trained, we got twenty-five calls a week. With thousands of people trained we still get twenty-five calls a week. It's an interesting phenomenon there, which I don't understand. Half the calls are first contact; they've heard about the course through the old-boy network; the rest are jump-start requests." Mahler calculates that of the fifty Du Pont people trained per week, twenty go through the two-day classes. Of those twenty, perhaps five have a system up in field-test in a month; another ten will have a system up after two months. "And so we're right on the edge of a geometric explosion—we trained four hundred people in the fourth quarter of 1986 alone. By the end of 1987 I expect we'll have fifteen hundred people trained and able to build expert systems. By the year 2000? Maybe four thousand people." The group also assesses new software and programming tools and offers advice to anybody at Du Pont who's thinking of purchasing them.

By mid-1988, more than two hundred systems were in routine use, with six hundred under development or in field test. The AI group sees applications everywhere it looks. "At this point, we feel like we're taking water out of the ocean. We have no idea where the end is."

The success rate on new applications is 90 percent. "Nine out of every ten projects we start are finished and turn commercial."

What Are the Payoffs?

But back in 1985, if the technology was beginning to fit the resource base at last—foolproof expert-system software for the Lotus-users—the question of opportunity still remained. Were expert systems really worth pursuing? The pirate ship task force undertook some experiments—in support, in manufacturing, in marketing—all aimed at establishing the opportunity.

In mid-1987, when only seventy systems were in use, Mahler reported: "What we found is amazing. We found just incredible opportunity. And now we have about a seven-times return on total cash invested," Mahler asserts. This factor of seven is calculated by placing all cash expenditures in the denominator—salaries, benefits, training, software costs, allocated hardware costs, "everything we could round up we put there—and we have averaged over the seventy expert systems in routine use seven times return on our money. An aggregate numerator divided by an aggregate denominator. So 700 percent annual return on cash. That certainly beats CDs!" But at Du Pont the learning curve was steep, and by the end of 1987 Mahler reported to the newspaper *Computerworld* a return on software and labor costs of 1500 percent and an aggregate savings of $10 million. He added: "That is nothing compared with next year [1988] . . . Now we are ready." Indeed, by 1988 two hundred systems were in use.

There's really no such thing as an average system at Du Pont, but typically, a system requires a man-month of effort to build and yields $100,000 savings per year. Mahler says possibly another man-month might go into maintenance after the system is installed. These are pennies in the Du Pont context, but Mahler argues that return on investment is what matters. "If a guy spends half a day to save two hours per week of a technician's time, on a ratio basis that's a marvelous return. And I think that's the point. If you go out and fundamentally change the character of the way you do business, you let the pennies turn into dollars."

As a rule, payoff from expert systems can be measured in several ways. At Du Pont, most of the payoff has come from the replication of expertise, which either frees experts to do the most difficult jobs or moves processes down from the responsibility of experts into the hands of nonexperts. Another source of payoff has been improved quality, and still another, consistency in decision making.

An example of freeing the expert to attend to the most difficult problems is what Du Pont calls its "principal consultant apprentice" expert systems. Du Pont ultimately hopes to build some three hundred of these. The best in-house consultants at Du Pont are always very busy, and when field engineers call them for help with a problem, there's often a three-day delay before they can be reached. It emerges that some 80 percent of the problems these human consultants face can be solved over the phone, once they hear the specifics. The principal consultant apprentice expert systems are aimed at handling this 80 percent of end-user problems. The systems can be accessed remotely by the end user. After the user tells an expert system what problems he is having, it would provide a solution after querying the user for all the relevant information.

Slurry flow diagnostics, for example, are nearly always the same. Slurry, a liquid with solids suspended in it, often plugs pipes it flows through. The expert system will tell a caller—at least 80 percent of the time—how to unplug that pipe, usually by examining the particular slurry in question and suggesting new designs for the pipe and pumping system. This frees the human expert to concentrate on the 20 percent of the problems only he can answer.

The other kind of expertise replication, which moves expert operations downward toward the nonexpert, is illustrated by the expert system that finds unwanted water in the slurry process at a large manufacturing plant. The plant is on the Gulf Coast, and is roughly the size of a football field, five stories high and full of processing equipment, all baking under the southern sun. Under such conditions, slurry can plug up pipes very quickly.

Typically, when a plug occurs, an operator will hook up a water hose to a drain valve and leave it there to flush out the plug and get things moving again. Once a plug is dissolved, the water hose should, in principle, be removed, but operators can't always remember where in the huge factory they left hoses, and it's uneconomical to have a person wander through this enormous plant looking for inadvertent water sources. But at the end of the process, the water that was used to unplug the slurry must be boiled out of the product, and such water removal is an enormous energy waste. Deciding whether inadvertent water is in the system, and if so where it's coming from, used to require an engineer to do four hours a day of calculating interlocking material balances, energy balances, and thermodynamics. An expert system now does this, guiding not the engineers but the operators, who themselves couldn't do such calculations, toward where the problem might be, stopping it at the source instead of fixing the problem expensively at the end of the process.

The sales tax advisor serves as an example of consistency achieved by using an expert system. As a rule, Du Pont must pay sales taxes on materials that are used on plant equipment or in the office, but not on materials that will be made into a product and shipped from the factory. Unsurprisingly, there are some very gray areas here, and one person may decide to pay a tax and another may conclude that it is not necessary. At one particular plant, Du Pont discovered it was overpaying some $2 million a year on sales taxes and put in a system that reads stores' records and decides what is liable for tax and what isn't. Not all states have the same sales tax rules, so Du Pont is building a master system where a state's particular rules can be entered; the system can take it from there, not only saving where savings are possible, but also bringing consistency across the corporation to the sales tax problem.

Finally, expert systems are considered a form of technology documentation at Du Pont, another way of preserving corporate expertise. "Know-how in a videotape is like know-how in a book. It's passive. The know-how preserved in expert systems is action-oriented," Mahler says, "and such systems could eventually be networked into larger systems."

Only Three Problems, Really: Diagnostics, Selection, and Planning

At Du Pont, local knowledge is everything. In a plant that makes X-ray film, the technology hasn't changed much in twenty years. Two production lines run side by side, one ten years older than the other. The newer one is two feet wider and runs twice as fast. The expertise for making quality products and solving problems is localized even down to the line: the expert on line five doesn't do a very good job with problems on line three. If this is true for expertise in one manufacturing situation, it is all the more true from one plant to the next.

Did these hundreds of problems in so many localities have anything in common?

Mahler leans back, cobraskin-boot-clad feet on the table, and ruminates. "In the year and a half we've been in business, I've only seen three problems—man, they've been dressed up in every color suit imaginable, but there's only three. It took a long time to understand that. And once you understand that, it helps you building your applications tool: you don't have to build a tool to solve a hundred different problems; there's only three. They are"—he counts off on his fingers—"diagnostic problems, selection problems, and planning problems."

Diagnostics appear everywhere, across functions. In marketing, for example, the diagnostic problems appear mainly in technical services, which Du Pont maintains as a part of its marketing effort. Du Pont is primarily a wholesaler, selling to a middleman who operates on a product, adds value, and retails it. Du Pont sells functionality, but sometimes a customer gets the right thing and it doesn't work. Why not? That's a diagnostic problem for technical services.

In manufacturing, process diagnostics dominate Du Pont's problems: For example, the yield is bad, why? Not only why, but what's the remedy? Or a turbine might be jumping two feet off the floor: Why? And what to do after it's shut off? As a matter of fact, Du Pont recently built an expert system fault diagnoser for its DEC 11/70 computers. "The diagnostics of that are difficult because the machine is terribly confused," Mahler laughs, "and when the chip melts, it's melted its brains. We had a guy down at the Sabine River works in Orange, Texas, who was really good at diagnosis, so we had him head the team that did the diagnostic system. The mechanics love it; now they fix it right the first time. Tremendous savings because before, they did the moron's approach to auto repair: Open the hood and start changing parts until it works. You'd end up with this whole stack of boards on the floor, and only one was bad, but you didn't know which one."

Encouraged by that, the team built other equipment diagnosers, and then decided everything should be tied together in a grand maintenance diagnostician.

And yet as much time, trouble, and money as the computer diagnostic systems save, Du Pont has been unable to propagate them very far beyond the Sabine River plant. Not-invented-here. No buy-in. It's a common problem and takes subtle psychology to overcome. Mahler is depending on his newest old-boy network, the AI network, to propagate it, because it would be wasteful to duplicate the effort elsewhere.

An important system that was built early—"my first child," says Mahler—went a long way toward establishing the legitimacy of AI at Du Pont. The problem was purging a complex distillation column of impurities, where the product was chemicals for making solid-state electronics and had to be 99.99 percent pure. The distillation column had to be watched constantly, and complex purges decided on the spot. The problem had been around for ten years, and Du Pont had used it as an exercise for engineers who were moving into management. "We'd have young engineers with a bad case of smart-ass, and they'd need a little humbling, so we'd give them this problem and tell them to solve it. After two or three months, they'd be sufficiently humble and then we'd send them on their management careers."

A man-month of effort transferred the knowlege out of the head of the only engineer who could do the job and into an expert system, known as Mike-in-the-Box, which meant that, for the first time, the engineer's expertise was available twenty-four hours a day, and the operator was out of the hot seat. Operating acceptance has been very high, and there has been a clear $100,000 savings per year.

After diagnosis, the second generic problem Mahler sees at Du Pont is selection. Suppose there are six hundred kinds of neoprene, each of them functionally a little different. A customer has a set of functional needs, and the sales rep is trying to sell him the right neoprene to fit those needs. The sales rep could call the laboratory, or technical services, or take out an enormous book and thumb through it—but isn't there a better way to help the sales rep face-to-face with the customer? Can't he be helped first to discard all but the legal candidates, the candidates that satisfy the functionality, and second, to optimize among those? "That problem shows up again and again," Mahler says. "You don't see it at first, but when you unravel it, that's what it is."

Another early system was aimed at helping customers select plastic wrapping needed for certain kinds of packaging. One of Du Pont's competitors had an enviable share of the market, and Du Pont wanted to shift those proportions. Thus the sales rep's job was to convince a customer to switch from the competitor's product to Du Pont's. Choosing plastic wrap for packaging is extremely complex, depending on whether the bottom of the package will be heat-sealed, whether the surface should be slip or nonslip, whether the object to be packaged has sharp edges, and so forth. Moreover, there are some twenty-five grades of wrap, and perhaps fifty kinds of operating machinery the wrap might have to be used with.

"Even if you could train the distributor to know all that, he couldn't remember until he got out the door," Mahler says. "So we built this system to put in his hands so he can go out there and say, Hey, let me show you . . . and then it does a one-on-one comparison: here's Du Pont and here's what you're using now and look how great Du Pont is."

Another expert system of the selection genre works splendidly but isn't used, and the reasons for that are interesting. When a chemical spill takes place outside a plant—for example, because of a truck accident or train wreck—the first people on the site are frequently volunteer fire fighters from a local company. There are 900,000 fire fighters spread out all over the United States, and a third of them are replaced each year. The problem is to get them to do the right thing in a chemical spill, as opposed to the wrong thing, which may make the spill worse. Since there are some two hundred different chemicals they might have to deal with, it gets very complicated. The federal government proposed to train each fire fighter to deal with each of these chemicals.

"It's an impossible problem," Mahler says. "You can't train them an hour on each chemical, not with the 300,000 turnover and the geographical spread. And as a manufacturer of many of these chemicals, Du Pont's share of the bill for that training was going to be $30 million. What a way to throw away $30 million! So we began building expert systems. We built one for sulfuric acid, and one for an agricultural poison, and we built for the general classes of chemicals. And we had it all built, all very thorough, and visualized cellular phones on fire trucks and log-in terminals, and so forth. And then the problem of ownership came up. The guy who was sponsoring it in the government got transferred, and no one really stepped up to own it. We couldn't get it sold. I went down and showed it to the people who man the hotlines at the National Transportation Safety Board, who tell fire fighters how to respond. They said they wouldn't have any use for something like that. And then I talked to their supervisor, and he said it was just great, he'd get rid of those guys. But it didn't happen; the system never got off the mark. The system is technologically sound, but it's dormant because it doesn't have an owner. You never know. These dormant things sometimes wake up. Last week we had a consultant in who looks like he's going to be an owner, so we'll probably sell it to him."

The third generic problem is planning and scheduling, which usually show up in manufacturing. Scheduling—how to make something when you want to make it because you need it then—is no problem if a year's worth of inventory is on hand. But there are problems in scheduling: machinery sometimes breaks, or you have competing demands for facilities. "We make A, B, and C in the same continuous flow reactor, and they differ only in type, so my big problem is minimizing my transitions, A to B, B to C, yet meeting my production demand, given that every time a transition occurs materials are thrown away. Minimize the transitions and make what you have to, but you're limited by storage and you've got this demand, according to marketing."

It took two months for Mahler and his group to find out what the real problem in scheduling and production was. As he says now, it's so simple he should have thought of it in the first two minutes, but he didn't. It was human stress. He finally got at it by putting the following to managers he spoke to: Forget about how I'm going to do it, but I'm going to build you the perfect planner and scheduler, a black box. What symptoms will go away when you have it?

Everybody agreed inventory would be reduced—a little—and that would be a one-time event. But their eyes glowed when they talked about eliminating the weekly scheduling meeting. "That's cutthroat stuff, they told me; we have maintenance there, we have production, we have technical there;

everybody has different objectives, and we just finally hammer out a compromise when everybody gets tired. I say, okay, well, how many people? Six. How long do they meet for? Usually about an hour. The economics of that are *nothing*! But it's a very high-stress thing."

Many companies have problems with idle equipment waiting for material, but as a rule that's not a problem at Du Pont, whose equipment is running most of the time. Mahler and his group wanted to deliver the equivalent of round-the-clock engineering help to the plants, and had a chance to try out the idea with a site that was undergoing reduction from five plants there to one, from 700 people to 130. "The seniority rollback was going to leave operators who didn't know what they were doing, in essence. And they wanted to *insure* they'd get into trouble by moving out all the technical people. Now there's a formula for a wreck fixing to happen. So we jumped in with the technical people while they were still there, we had a year, and said, Let's build assistants to operations in the boxes. We thought there'd be twenty, fifty systems. We didn't know how many there'd be. We built four and got ninety-five percent of the squeal of the hog. These expert systems for operations assistance run, they're marvelous, and they're accepted by production."

People Are Everything

There's another situation that makes small systems compelling at Du Pont. The same corporate streamlining that affected most American firms in the early 1980s has reduced staff at Du Pont by 30 percent since 1981, but that represents a loss of perhaps 70 percent in experience, since much of that reduction was through early retirement. A few hundred of those early retirees are being brought back to have their expertise captured in expert systems that will help do the jobs they used to do themselves.

For example, one retired expert was brought back to help diagnose problems in the fiber-dyeing process. Du Pont creates thread (or staple, a component of fiber) which is sold to a mill that makes fabrics. The fabric is then dyed, but properties of the fabric (actually at the molecular level and not in the weave itself) can create problems, such as blotching or streaking. Though it is often the customer's fault for having failed to do something correctly in the dyeing process, Du Pont has nevertheless sent this human expert to the mills to diagnose problems; to ascertain, say, whether the fabric was run through the dye bath fast enough, or whether the bath was the right temperature. He was called back from retirement as a consultant to put his expertise into what has emerged as a three-hundred-rule system which Du Pont hopes ordinary sales reps can use.

And how do the people at Du Pont feel about expert systems? Retirees who've been called back in as consultants love the idea that their knowledge will be captured and propagated beyond them, what AI people like to call "the immortality syndrome." Du Pont, for its part, is acquiring a continuity of experience that would otherwise be impossible to attain.

But for those who haven't retired, who are at an early or midcareer stage, the story is more complex. "We try to sell these systems as apprentices," Mahler says. "The human issues around job jeopardy, we haven't seen much of that."

Thus the primary issue in the adoption and use of expert systems at Du Pont isn't technology, it's ownership, or what Digital Equipment Corporation calls buy-in. "If you don't have the user believing from the first that it's his, there'll be twenty reasons why it gets put on the bottom of the list, and they'll all be good reasons. We put a lot of energy into that; that's how my group acts." Ownership, the AI group believes, is the key to success. Thus the best situation is where the domain expert is the knowledge engineer, where he interviews himself. That isn't always possible, so next best is to have a local support person work with the domain expert, local in the work group.

At Du Pont the small systems act as assistants, doing 80 percent of the work of experts. Mahler believes that to get them up to 90 percent would probably require perhaps twice the effort of the first 80 percent, which is why Du Pont prefers to think of its systems as partners for experts, rather than experts themselves. Still, Mahler sees that the system designers, their "owners," are often infatuated by the technology and can hardly resist adding the next few layers of expertise, even when it isn't cost-effective. It's management's role to move people on from that.

Another strong belief in Du Pont's corporate culture is that staff groups, such as Mahler's AI program, are to be enablers, that is, to support operations groups and share their risks, but always as nonintrusive helpers. "Let's translate that into kid talk," Mahler says. "Only go to parties that you're invited to, and you won't be thrown out near as much. Our group lives—and dies—by word of mouth. We let the interlacing old-boy networks create our opportunities. Now, early on, I pushed a little. But that was an amazingly little push, in the perspective of what we have today: I went out and pushed eight friends."

Again, the AI group's business mission, which everybody believes and lives, is to catalyze the implementation of artificial intelligence, particularly expert systems, broadly and effectively through Du Pont. Mahler isn't interested in running an internal job-shop, putting together systems to order. "We will not catch a fish for somebody, we'll teach him how to fish. I do not believe you can be true to yourself if you're in the teaching-people-to-fish business, as I am, and also running a fish market."

For operations units that ask to have jobs done for them, Mahler gives them a list of outside firms that will serve, but he feels strongly—and Ray Cairns agrees—that the AI group should remain small and catalytic. A few units took him up on the list of outside knowledge engineering firms and report, on the whole, unsatisfactory experience. "We have one or two things that worked out okay, and we have ten that worked out not okay."

If a fundamental rule of introducing expert systems into your firm is to buy the best equipment and the best help available, why hasn't it worked that way at Du Pont? "We tried to establish a few relationships so that when we had an elephant we'd have some measure of who was a good elephant hunter. I tend to come across very hard as the PC guy; it turns out I'm spending a lot more in total on the big-end tools than I am on PCs—with a hell of a lot less payoff, I might add—but anyway, we've gone through them."

Mahler believes he knows why outside knowledge engineers have a hard time at Du Pont. Although they come well equipped with knowledge engineering skills, they don't—they can't—know specific jargon, and this generates mistrust among highly trained technologists and scientists who rely on jargon to quickly identify the ins from the outs, the knowledgeable from the ignorant. "And evidently you go to arrogance school to become a knowledge engineer," Mahler adds, grinning. "It must be part of the training program. If you're an outsider to an old-boy network and you're arrogant, you're not going to be very effective."

Modest local systems provide uninviting economic returns for outside firms. You can't support a knowledge-engineering firm unless you're working on bigger problems than Du Pont generally is trying to solve. As for the big problems, Mahler says he's brought in the elephant finders "who were also hunters and slayers, okay? And skinners. They came in—I remember the meeting vividly—they sat down and said, Okay, what problems do you want us to solve?"

And so Mahler and Du Pont turn conventional AI wisdom on its head, going it alone without help from AI experts, and choosing to do many small systems instead of attacking the problem that's going to make the big difference. It can be argued that by choosing the strategy of small applications, the very large ones right at the heart of the company's mission, such as DEC pursues, will be overlooked or even foregone.

"We believe our strategy is the finding mechanism for the larger system," Mahler says. "Look, we find a problem. Either it's small, and we make money in a month, or it's a *big* problem, and you've done the work you'd have had to do to justify solving the problem anyway. Finding the big problems by sending out a letter saying show me your big ones doesn't work: what we get back is nothing. We tried that. So we said, Okay, while we're looking around for the big ones, we're going to pick up all these nuts on the ground."

Du Pont is unusual, Mahler points out. "You've got to think of Du Pont as the U.S. economy subtracting out defense contracts, fast food, and banking. We've got all this very dispersed knowledge in a very loose federation of companies. The reason small expert systems work is because our knowledge is dispersed—we aren't like Boeing with its 747 or DEC and its Vax computers—so it just comes back to understanding yourself, what your business is."

Not everybody at Du Pont agrees with Mahler on the small-systems-versus-big issue. David Pensak, who'd been a co-founder of the AI task force, considers himself the loyal opposition on that score. "PCs are fine for getting started, but you can't think of them as a real tool. In a woodshop, if everything you've got looks like a coping saw and a hammer, what you'll build will look like a birdhouse no matter how clever you are. The complaint is often raised that the big tools are much harder to use, they take more time to get trained on, you can't pick up a language like Lisp in fifteen minutes. But if you're going to use big woodworking machinery, you don't learn how to use a five-horse jointer in five minutes either.

"You must take the time to learn how to use your tools properly. And the big tools give you more opportunity for thinking about your problem without having to worry about the constraints of MS-DOS and 640K bytes, or fighting with the machine. I'm in favor of working with tools that will give us more freedom to explore and hypothesize, because very simply, a lot of the American economy is in trouble right now because we took a very conservative posture. Now we're trying to play catch-up. Now, I don't think we're going to be able to catch up by the traditional methods of sitting there and trying to replicate what everybody else is doing. We're trying to design tools and techniques that will let us play leapfrog over what everybody else is doing, and hopefully, we'll finesse our way through it. If we succeed, great." But Pensak's considerable research is for the future, while Mahler concentrates on the present.

"We meet once a quarter with Dave and his group to try to find the elephant so that Dave can work on it. And he's been looking hard for the elephant. He's got some good general research topics that he's working on, which might pay off handsomely. But it just isn't clear what things we ought to do that would be the home run. My problem is finding the home run. Because we have plenty of people that would know how to hit it."

What about scaling up from the one-person-month, one-hundred-thousand-dollar systemlets? What about a two-person-year, two-million-dollar expert system?

Mahler shakes his head. "I have had my checkbook open, ready to sign. The facts are, people cannot identify such a problem here. It's one of two things with such big problems: either people have nibbled away at them with classical systems, or they don't recognize that they're doable at all. That's another possibility, that they just can't conceive it can be done. But we've got tremendously creative people around here. And we can't find the buffalo. That's what we call them: you know, if the leading edge is elephants, and we're killing rabbits, where are the buffalo? We just can't seem to find them. And we're making a conscious effort."

Mahler says he doesn't tell people to think small—he tells them to start on the problem that's their itch. "We've given advanced knowledge-engineering courses, but it still hasn't produced a long list of candidates for big systems." The limits lie in ideas, not resources. "Everyone says, well, you're missing the boat. You can't get on the boat if you can't find it!"

Pensak's argument is, of course, the birdhouse argument, that people's ambitions are shaped by their tools, and he goes on to say that more resources should be spent in developing skills for three years from now.

Mahler concedes Pensak's point, but counters with a business argument: "Do I give up an almost certain ten times return on my money for this? If there were a lot of documentation out in the world that said build a big one and you'll get twenty times on your money, I'd probably be pushing harder that way. I'm hedging my bets. I've got a several-million-dollar effort looking for buffalo, if you add it up across the whole company. I think that's enough. But that's a big worry; somehow you're jeopardizing the future by running around picking up the little stuff."

Mahler believes that within five years there'll be some big expert systems at Du Pont, but meanwhile he's happy with having lowered the entry barrier and got people started.

Mahler and Pensak wind up an interview together stressing an unusual point: they've never seen any project at Du Pont where people were having so much fun. Nobody can quite understand why AI turns so many on as it does, why it transforms people who were once mediocre into outstanding performers, voluntarily working extra hours and keeping killing travel schedules, and having the time of their lives. But it does.

And Du Pont only stands to gain. As engineers build their own small expert systems, the pebbles in the pond, the company realizes a spectacular return on investment. Its precious corporate expertise, that might have departed in the heads of experienced retirees, is being permanently captured and is accessible to workers who weren't trained to do jobs they can do now, with expert system assistance. At Du Pont, even these small expert systems—a reflection of Du Pont's distributed, highly local knowledge—are making an impact on sales, on manufacturing, on business procedures. And by nurturing its own corps of AI researchers, Du Pont stands to realize further gains when the boulder splashes into the pond beside the pebbles.

Chapter 8

Preserving, Using, and Selling Expertise

EVERY FIRM sooner or later discovers that what makes the difference between itself and its competitors is its expertise. Doing it better is humanly exhilarating—and often profitable besides. As a rule, the expertise that makes this difference is built up over many years. We might compare it to the maturation of an artist: We all cheer the promising artist, but the promise we hope to see fulfilled is, after all, mastery.

Here are some stories of the masters of their crafts, whose expertise has been captured in software, expert systems. These masters happen to be housed in businesses—a Japanese steel mill, an Australian heavy construction company, an international oil-field services company, and an American electrical equipment manufacturer. Their mastery is essential to the organizations they serve. For the organization, preserving that individual mastery for daily use has vital implications that go beyond the tenures of the masters themselves. In some cases, it doesn't just enhance business but turns out to be a service that can be sold, an entirely new form of business.

Nippon-Kokan Steel:
God in the Works*

They call him "god." Like one of the ancients, he has a domain: not revelry or mercy, but the fifth blast furnace at the Nippon-Kokan Fukuyama Ironworks in Japan's Hiroshima prefecture, one of the largest furnaces in the world. "God" learned his trade, troubleshooting the giant blast furnace, in the days when operators had to stand before an open furnace door, judging the quality of molten iron by its appearance and adjusting the furnace accordingly; when instantaneous good judgment was a life-or-death matter.

Kazumasa Wakimoto of the Fukuyama pig iron department explains bluntly that blast furnaces are like human beings: They eat at the top and they excrete at the bottom. Their meal of iron ore gradually descends into the furnace pit, where the temperature reaches some 2,300° Celsius, heated by coke gases burning below. The dissolved iron ore, now chemically transformed by carbon and carbon monoxide into pig iron, gathers at the lowest part of the furnace. As coke (as fuel) and limestone (as an additive) are introduced, multiple layers of pig iron are produced over several hours. If the iron ore flow moves in an orderly way, steel is produced from the furnace bottom.

But sometimes crises occur. For example, if the descending flow doesn't move, or moves too quickly, the problem is called "slide." Slide occurs for several possible reasons— damage to the furnace wall has produced an uneven flow of air in the combustion process, or powdered ore has clumped on the furnace wall and then dropped all at once. The operator wants to avoid slides because large clumps of inadequately dissolved raw material falling into the molten iron will lower its temperature and thus its quality. Slides vary from furnace to furnace, and can happen as often as once an hour if it's an unlucky day. Wakimoto likens the

* Adapted from *Artificial Intelligence Journal*, No. 6, a Japanese magazine published by UPU Publishing, Tokyo, Japan.

clumping powdered ore to cholesterol, which has to be removed.

A second crisis, far more fearsome than the first, is "channeling," where a hot blast of gases rises from the bottom of the furnace and explodes in the descending raw material. This will disable the furnace, and may even force a shutdown, a process so complicated that it can ruin the furnace forever, particularly if the shutdown lasts for more than ten days. That shutdown not only endangers the life of the furnace, it also affects the rest of the company's production. The task of the operator is to catch abnormalities and fix them so slide and channeling do not occur.

Within the furnace, thousands of sensors ("like hairpins on a geisha") are continuously monitoring the steel-making process. But, interpreting the sensor data—whether everything is normal or some crisis is in the making—requires expertise. If all goes normally, nowadays no further human intervention is necessary. But if an abnormality occurs, only human experience can anticipate, interpret, and remedy to prevent these two crises. It takes between fifteen and twenty years to train an experienced furnace operator, and "God" is no exception; the only difference is, he's the best. A combination of events led the Nippon-Kokan management to consider capturing "God" in an expert system. In part, they wanted to have his expertise, the very best, at every furnace, not just his own. They also wanted to be readier for the frequent changes in process and the furnace remodeling that new steel-making techniques continually demand.

Nippon-Kokan also faces some delicate economic questions. Japanese output of crude steel has dropped over the past few years to less than 100 million tons, and will slowly continue to drop to below 80 million tons in the near future as less developed nations do the job cheaper. Thus it's unfair and costly to put workers through a fifteen- to twenty-year training program for jobs that might someday disappear. Nevertheless, Japan will meanwhile continue to manufacture steel, and if new operators can't—or shouldn't—be trained, the knowledge of the experts who are slowly retiring must be preserved.

Nippon-Kokan's upper management turned to its main-frame vendor, Fujitsu, for help. Fujitsu has made a big com-mitment to artificial intelligence; it has a large staff of knowledge engineers, and manufactures the most successful Lisp machine in Japan, FACOM-alpha, which works as a back-end processor attached to its mainframes, and which runs an expert system shell called EShell. (EShell also runs on Fujitsu mainframes.) A team of knowledge engineers from Fujitsu and steel experts from Nippon-Kokan got to-gether in January 1985 to put together an expert system that would detect abnormalities that lead to slides and channeling and to advise on how to deal with the abnormal situations. The expert system would get the sensor data directly and would process them every two minutes—it would be on-line in real time.

A month later knowledge engineering got under way in earnest. The team faced the usual problems: how to evoke knowledge from "God" (and a number of demigods) that even he didn't know he had and how to represent relative and subjective knowledge so that it could be processed by a computer. As they began to build the knowledge base, they realized how arbitrary and biased experts are, and how their opinions differ from one another. An ability to reason with uncertain knowledge ("With 90 percent certainty, the problem is X") was introduced to deal with ambiguous or probabilistic information, which improved the system's cred-ibility. Design and testing took most of 1986.

Finally, in February 1987, the fifth furnace was refired (it had been dormant since 1983 and was now to replace a furnace that was being phased out) and its expert system came alive with it, the first on-line real-time expert system in Japan. The system proved to have an 85 percent reliability rate relative to "God's" for predicting furnace abnormalities, a rate that delights the managers but which will still be improved. At the moment the system only forecasts abnor-malities; soon it will be able to advise an operator on rem-edies as well. Eventually blast furnaces will be operated unmanned. Interestingly, the knowledge engineers were having a difficult time testing and tuning the knowledge about channeling problems. The preconditions for channeling are usually multiple slides, and because of the effectiveness of the expert system to monitor the slide problem the furnace has been very stable since the inaugural fire-up and has had only a few episodes of channeling problems.

When the blast furnace expert system was publicized in Japan, it made a considerable stir. Inquiries came from abroad, where operator competence is low, causing speculation that Nippon-Kokan might market the god-system as a product. On this the company is so far noncommital. Meanwhile, other Japanese blast furnace companies felt obliged to reveal that they too had AI plans afoot. For example, Nippon Steel Corp., with Hitachi Ltd., had built a similar system to monitor the operation of their blast furnaces. They report that in 93 percent of the test cases the expert system produced superior results—as good or better corrective actions than human experts—*and* the decisions for actions were produced faster (this according to the *Proceedings of the AI87 Conference* in Japan).

In the planning report that launched the Japanese government's Fifth Generation Project, the Japanese envisioned the creation of a new "knowledge industry." In an oft-cited section, the planners pointed to Japan's lack of natural resources, but observed that it had an abundance of resources in the "knowledge and skill of the Japanese people." This could be not only used but sold.

The traditional steel industry in Japan, as we have said, is in decline. The business of selling turnkey steel mills to developing nations is just emerging. As steel exports decline, the steel companies like Nippon-Kokan expect to sell their expertise to those countries that can make steel profitably. The expert system of the knowledge of the furnace god is an attempt to package their expertise for later sale. It's a dramatic vision of the export-oriented mercantile mind.

The Lend Lease Corporation
of Australia

The Lend Lease Corporation of Australia is the largest construction company in that booming land, and it reaches out beyond Australia to the bustling lands of the Pacific Basin, building, developing, and managing commercial property all over the South Pacific. In addition, Lend Lease (whose name has nothing to do with the British-American World War II program of that name) provides a variety of financial and insurance services connected with property development.

But the corporation's heart is construction. Lend Lease has a wholly owned subsidiary called Civil and Civic Property which builds *big* buildings: office towers and parks, industrial complexes, mammoth shopping centers and sports stadiums. In 1987 its volume was approximately A$700 million.

A few years ago, Lend Lease appointed one of its top executives, Alan Stretton, to be a roving ambassador of new technologies. "I don't have any particular brief except to maintain a broad watch," he explains. In the course of a 1983 cocktail party conversation, an AI pioneer named Ross Quinlan, who just happens to be the son-in-law of Lend Lease's chairman of the board, mentioned to Civil and Civic Property's CEO that somebody really ought to take a look at expert systems. As a result, Stretton took a look.

"At that stage, the literature didn't turn me on much. Maybe I didn't get very good literature. There wasn't all that much around. But when I visited the U.S.A. in mid-1984, I went to the World Future Society Conference, where I'm a member. Out of that came the very key fact that expert systems were up and running, and accelerating at an enormous pace. It so happened that immediately after that, I called in at Stanford University, to see my old friend Ray Levitt, a civil engineering professor, and he said, 'Hey Alan, guess what I'm working on—expert systems.' I couldn't believe it."

When Stretton returned to Australia, he confirmed with

the Civil and Civic's CEO that expert systems were what Lend Lease should be doing. The question was what the first application should be. Stretton felt he knew.

When Lend Lease first talks to a customer about a large project, it feels it must have a very good idea of what that project is going to cost and how long construction will take. "That first time, we really have committed ourselves, because you can't realistically go back and say, Oh, whoops, we've made a mistake, it's going to cost you an extra ten million and take X amount longer—particularly in this day and age when time is money, and particularly with the interest rates in our country."

The initial estimate is often made on virtually no information, just a dream in somebody's eye which may be transformed into a few odd sketches on a bit of paper somewhere. "Remember, one way or another, we're always in competition. So that time estimate has to be what we call a 'typed time.' But it must be achievable. From our point of view, we must be able to do it in that time." Unfortunately, Stretton observes, Australians are often overoptimistic with their estimates of building times.

One study of the whole construction industry found that on average, actual construction times have exceeded the original contract times by 47 percent and much of that excess was due to unrealistically short original estimates. Since the study was of buildings that were already fully designed and documented before the estimates were made, how much worse would the estimates have been if they'd been based on only sketch-plan information?

Lend Lease's Civil and Civic Property did an internal analysis that showed its construction times averaged two thirds better than those that appeared in the study, a large factor in customer confidence; but the actual estimation has remained a problem.

Making time estimates involves two kinds of expertise. One envisages how the design is going to develop, and therefore what the final shape might be, including many of the details, services as well as finishing. The second kind of expertise is knowing how things are built, and what kind of resources and restrictions may exist. All this requires experience and intelligence. Lend Lease has experts who have one kind of knowledge or the other, but only one man—Geoff Stevens—excels at both kinds.

But Stevens can't do everything. First, he can only do a small fraction of the work Lend Lease would like him to do; and second, he's sixty years old, eligible to retire whenever he wishes. Stevens is so valuable to the firm that when it came time to try to pick his brains for an expert system, the knowledge engineers couldn't get ten minutes alone with him in four months' time.

Meanwhile, as a large and valued Digital Equipment Company customer, Lend Lease began talks with DEC about expert systems. DEC was very enthusiastic, and proposed to co-sponsor such a system, happy to use Lend Lease as an Australian showcase. Both corporations saw this expert system as an investment in their respective futures, and treated it as long-term research and development.

Stretton recommended to the chairman that Geoff Stevens be pulled out of day-to-day work to have his knowledge captured without interruptions for an expert system. After consulting with his board, the chairman agreed to this unusual procedure, potentially a very costly one to the company, given Stevens's value, but again, a long-term investment.

Once he got started, Stevens was unstoppable. "One of the interesting things about Geoff, which I gather is unusual, is that he's been able to do most of his own knowledge engineering. He's one of these people who's able to work out in detail how he's come up with these heuristics, their basis." The "book of rules" is called "Geoff's Book," and consists of thousands of rules for time estimation.

Stevens worked with two DEC knowledge engineers. The original idea was that he would go to Hudson, Massachusetts, where DEC has its AI installation, or they would visit Australia, and Stretton himself, having made the match, would step aside. But the huge distance between Hudson and Sydney—geographic, cultural, and professional—exacerbated communication problems, and Stretton stepped back in as full-time project manager.

Matters then moved along briskly. Over the course of a

year, Stevens and Stretton would travel to Massachusetts every other month, and the knowledge engineers would go to Sydney in alternate months. Meanwhile, the electronic mail flew back and forth. At the end of September 1987 the prototype was delivered, and field testing began prior to full field use.

Predicte, as it's called, is an expert system for estimating time of construction. It determines what contractors call the indicative construction time for a multistory building before any design development takes place beyond the initial concept stage. It analyzes and compares indicative times for alternative concepts before anybody becomes too committed, and it organizes the knowledge—in Geoff's Book—for easy access by others. It does so in detail: five months of excavation and foundation, X days for lowest structure, X days for upper structure, and so forth. It searches for opportunities to reduce time in those various stages, and permits the user to do what-if scenarios. It uses graphics extensively, sketching on the screen so that the users can see exactly what is being considered.

Thus the system asks questions about the project, the design, and the site; anticipates the developing design; decides on likely construction methods and sequence; assesses the resources available to do the work; works out how long the project is likely to take, and answers questions about how its results were arrived at. Human cost estimators can use Predicte's time estimates to make much more accurate estimates of the construction cost at an early stage.

For Lend Lease, the value is long-range. "We're really well known for long-range thinking," Stretton says. "As a leading company, you better be up front in all the key areas of your business. It's as simple as that." The company perceived that artificial intelligence, expert systems in particular, was likely to be the most important of the information technologies, and furthermore decided that the best way to learn about it was to participate in it. Predicte is only Lend Lease's first expert system, the beginning of what Stretton believes is a new dimension in planning and operating in the construction industry.

Schlumberger

The multinational Schlumberger Ltd., French in origin but headquartered in the United States, is often cited as one of the world's best managed companies. It has carved out a profitable niche for itself by logging, or collecting, data about the geology and hydrocarbons in a deep hole so that oil companies know what to expect as they prepare the hole for oil recovery. To accomplish this logging, Schlumberger drops measurement tools, contained in a heavy metal tube a few inches in diameter, thousands of feet into the earth's crust.

Inside the tool, custom-designed transformers feed low-frequency power to the sensors that reach out through openings in the tube wall and probe layers of earth and rock as the tool is slowly pulled back up. The sensors send information—quite literally the lay of the land—back to surface computers that dutifully record and interpret the data, so that geologists and oil people can make sensible decisions.

In 1978, Michel Gouilloud, then director of Schlumberger-Doll Research in Ridgefield, Connecticut, held a conference to discuss the question of how artificial intelligence could be useful to Schlumberger. The result was the first commercial expert system, the Dipmeter Advisor, that codified the thirty-five years of expertise of J. A. Gilreath, an expert so valued for his skill at interpreting the data coming up from below ground that some oil companies actually kept an office waiting for Al Gilreath's occasional visits.

In the heady days of post–oil shock search, there weren't enough Gilreaths to go around. As it turned out, Gilreath's codified expertise would eventually be sold by his firm like yardage—expertise at fifty cents the foot of logged bore hole, an average length of two thousand feet. Schlumberger's adventures with expert systems were described in Chapter 6 on technology insertion; suffice it to say here that, after some difficulties, the idea these days has really taken hold inside Schlumberger.

Consider, for example, the transformer design problem. Packed sometimes half a dozen in a single tool, it isn't just that the transformers must be miniature. They must be robust as well. Anything can happen down in a hole; the heat and the moisture and the shocks are punishing. Yet if any part of a tool fails, large amounts of money can be wasted.

Since nearly every job is different, every tool and its innards must be custom designed. The engineers can get into that, playing with exotic metals, drill-bit stresses, sensors that nearly defy the laws of physics. But transformers? Nobody has thought about transformers since college; at the very idea, torpor overcomes a modern engineer. Designing a downhole transformer is as tedious as listening to an explanation of the Law of Large Numbers.

When even the technicians started complaining that they didn't want to be stuck with the design job either, somebody looked around the shop to see who else might be good at dull, exacting, complicated design. The computer smiled back, born to handle jobs like that. Of course an engineer could pull off a shelf a handbook that gave him all the formulas, hack out a little code, and get a perfect, mathematically verified, Platonic ideal of a transformer design.

The only problem was that the Platonic transformer doesn't work inside a *real* tool, dropping through the reality of the earth's crust, with slush and mud and shale and sand and solid rock hitting, heating, choking, and otherwise abusing it. To get a workable design for a real transformer, you must adjust the ideal design—tweak it, the engineers say, adding bits of black magic, fixes, Band-Aids, hand waving, and whatnot.

So at Houston Downhole Sensors, they listened hopefully when a young manager, a native of India, trim and impeccably dressed, came by and said maybe design-tweaking for a transformer could be done by computer; he'd give it some thought. He was Arun Jain, manager of the Applied AI Projects in Technology at Houston, and he'd come to Schlumberger with a Ph.D. in operations research, accustomed to thinking about linear programming techniques, putting industrial processes into nice, neat formulas. The idea of programming heuristics, rules of thumb, that might work and might not, instead of surefire formulas, was a confusing thing to get his head into, but if he'd wanted to do plain-vanilla linear programming, he could have gone to work anywhere. In fact, he'd chosen Schlumberger because everybody knew they were the first firm ever to adopt artificial intelligence techniques at their laboratories. Jain had thought he could get some on-the-job training.

When the transformer design problem came up, he sat down with his boss, Robin Kerr, director of information technology at Houston Downhole, who agreed that maybe you could put together an expert system to tweak the design for a downhole transformer. If you could, it would be useful: Nobody wanted the job anyway. Kerr also had some reservations about the company's reliance upon vendors and thought it ought to be producing in-house designs.

To be sure, the job of transformer design was being done after a fashion: an engineer would tell a technician in general terms what he wanted; the technician would start with an old design, then get out his paper, pencil, and calculator and add and subtract, sketch and erase, depending on a particular job. That design would next be sent out to a vendor for prototyping. But it was a trial-and-error process normally taking three or so tries, and by the time each version was designed, a prototype built and tested (and inevitably found wanting), two months had gone by. Thus it wasn't at all unusual for it to take six months to get the final design and prototype built.

Jain gathered together a team of transformer experts: one of the technicians, who had years of practical experience and whose retirement had brought on the crisis in the first place; a design engineer who knew the theory of transformers, or where to get his hands on it, and who had overall design experience; and a smart college student to program the whole thing up as a summer project. In the three-month summer of 1986 the team produced an expert system for designing low-frequency downhole transformers, in a bit longer than it would usually take to design and debug a single instance of a transformer.

Using the expert system, a design that would have taken a week is now produced in twenty to forty minutes, a hundredfold productivity enhancement. But more important, the design is optimal. For the first time, engineers are able to talk about functional tradeoffs: if I'm willing to give here, can I get more there? People who couldn't hear the word *transformer* without yawning are suddenly in front of a screen playing what-if games with transformer design. In 1987 the expert system was expanded to include two other kinds of transformers.

As delighted as everyone is with the system, Robin Kerr believes its greatest utility is in the changes it's brought about in design philosophy at Houston. "We used to design simplistically—an engineer and his crew would build whatever they needed, starting from scratch every time. Now we're thinking about standardizations—standard chassis, standard power supply, standard downhole microprocessors. That will save us even more." The system has not only saved time and money but has begun to save parts as well. And finally, the program is building up a knowledge base of transformer design, a corporate data base for the special, outside-the-textbooks world that Schlumberger operates in.

Westinghouse:
The Steam Turbine Generator Expert System

When a distinguished old manufacturer adds a profitable new business—servicing its old equipment—customers benefit too: everybody wins. For many years this Westinghouse division has manufactured multimegawatt steam turbine generators and parts for its public utilities customers around the world. In such a generator, high-pressure steam drives blades connected to a turbine shaft, and that rotary motion is converted by a generator into electric current. Though the steam must enter the turbine at extremely high pressures, and the turbine is very hot, this is an old, tried-and-true technology, not so much high-tech as brute-tech. It appeals to public utilities for its reliability, and also because their business is very often governed so exactingly by statute that any innovation would require a change in a local public law.

But its very tried-and-trueness makes it boring to bright young engineers. The interesting problems in steam turbine technology were figured out years ago, and although the maintenance and diagnosis of problems is a richly complicated process, and a turbine failure is extremely expensive— a single day's of outage of one machine can cost a public utility between half a million and a million dollars—by the mid-1970s it was becoming clear that something would have to replace the diagnostics engineers who were staying away from steam turbine generators in droves.

As if this weren't headache enough, by the year 2000 it's reliably estimated that more than half of all the electrical generation in the United States will come from equipment over twenty years old (worldwide, this will also be true, but to a somewhat lesser extent). All this aged equipment will have remained in place for economic reasons. That is, before the 1974 energy crisis, power usage increased on the average of 7 percent per year, and utility companies bought generators based on that steady growth. But when the energy crisis hit, growth stopped for ten years. No growth meant no reason to buy new generators. Now growth has begun again, at about 3 percent annually, but meanwhile the old equipment remains and must be maintained.

Finally, public utilities commissions in the United States have lately looked askance at capital equipment purchase: they'd rather see profits returned to customers in the form of lower rates, and have the old equipment fixed instead of replaced.

All these circumstances have meant a dramatic change for this Westinghouse division: between 1980 and 1985, service shifted from 30 percent to 60 percent of its business, turning it from a sales into a service organization.

In the mid-1970s, Robert Osborne, a Westinghouse research engineer who began his career in process control and is now manager of diagnostics, monitoring, and AI development at Steam Turbine Generator Products in Orlando, Florida could see the problems looming: the disappearing engineers, the aging equipment, the economic stresses customers were undergoing. It might be worthwhile, he thought, to find a software solution to the problems of diagnosis and maintenance of these large machines. He first explored some statistical methods. They worked well when data from a small number of sensors were involved, but as the number of sensors increased, the complexities of the combinatorial explosion became unmanageable.

As Osborne explains it, a monitor is a piece of equipment that measures variables—pressures, temperatures, flows, loads—and can display, store, and in this case, transmit them to the Orlando Diagnostics Center. But diagnostics, the ability to show the condition of the equipment—a bearing is failing, a conductor is broken—requires interpreting the data sent by the monitor and is a judgmental process.

Thus it was in the late 1970s that he turned to expert systems as a possible solution. Expert systems were hardly known beyond a few aficionados when, in 1979, Osborne invited knowledge engineers from Carnegie-Mellon University in to build a demonstration system and an expert system shell that would permit Westinghouse to use it to build other systems. (Westinghouse and CMU had virtually co-founded CMU's Robotics Institute and had long-standing relations.) The entire effort would eventually grow into a service the company now sells, a series of diagnostics expert systems for the major parts of steam turbine generators. These services are twenty-four-hour, on-line diagnostics controlled by a new AI Diagnostics Center in Orlando.

But at the beginning it required the unquestioning support of John Traexler, the division's technical director, for Osborne to move beyond speculative hope. Osborne didn't know what an expert system would cost, or whether it would pay off for the company; he simply had a hunch that it was in the right direction. Traexler laughs now about the agitation it caused among Osborne's fellow engineers. "I took heat from Bob's peers—why was I giving him money for this thing, and none to them? But they wouldn't do something that wasn't mainstream." The division had recently moved from Philadelphia to Orlando, and one important message implicit in that move was that the old ways were going to be shaken up. Traexler thought an expert system was a wonderful example of exactly that.

As for Osborne, he was excited by the whole project. He

remembers waiting regularly at Traexler's office door at 7:30 A.M. to report on system developments. But Traexler refrained from asking too many questions about this new, rather odd, technology. He especially didn't ask questions he didn't want disagreeable answers to. "Sure things insure small margins," he says now. "Things that aren't so sure have a big risk, but they also have a big payoff. Bob and I had worked together for twenty-five years. I trusted him."

The prototype proved itself in 1979, and the expert system shell whose design was based on the prototype was completed in 1980. Osborne then moved on to the job of building his own organization of knowledge engineers to capture the expertise that would fire the systems he envisioned.

"What we've simply done in the expert system is put the knowledge of the human into the computer," Osborne says. "When we talk to customers, we explain to them that it is basically a tool for giving them what I call 'actionable information.' There's all kinds of information in this world, but what a person needs when he's operating a power plant is information to act on when he needs it."

On-line diagnosis prevents catastrophic failures, and permits planned maintenance. Generators are under surveillance around the clock, and on-line sensors in, say, Texas, feed data to the expert systems in Orlando. The diagnostic output is sent back to the customer site and is also displayed in the Westinghouse Diagnostics Operation Center, a kind of war room, in Orlando, where human experts, also on duty twenty-four hours a day, can spot problems not dealt with by the expert system and contact the plant operators. If a local operator has questions about the expert system's diagnostic output, he can reach the center by telephone to talk to human experts.

In one case, it took fourteen hours to convince a customer that a problem was imminent and it should shut down one of its large generators. Shutdown was completed after another five hours, and a large crack was revealed. But the early diagnostics by the expert system limited the time lost to four days, versus the two to three weeks—or in some cases, months—that are typical.

Utilities that purchase this service for their generators are assured that they are getting the very best diagnostic service available, since the rules for each of the diagnostic systems have been derived from the combined expertise of the best in the field, providing far better quality than any one expert a utility could hire for itself.

Expert systems have not only supplemented the engineers, who were scarce anyway; system accuracy in twenty-four-hour-a-day monitoring translates into important time and money savings.

The payoff for the customer is increased up-time of each steam turbine generator. Each additional day of up-time is worth half a million to a million dollars. Over a two-year period, the average up-time of a machine being "watched" by the diagnostic expert system increased by 0.9 percent, or about three and a half days, representing two or three million dollars per year for each machine. For Texas Utility Electric Company, with seven generators, the savings are enormous. The cost to the customer of the monitoring and diagnostic service is far less than a tenth of these savings.

Chapter 9

A New Business to Be In

A NUMBER OF FIRMS have discovered that not only can artificial intelligence enhance their operations, but selling AI itself is an entirely new business for them. We begin with Texas Instruments, unquestionably the world's leading AI company across its various lines, including its Lisp machine, Explorer; its best-selling expert system shell, Personal Consultant; the systems it builds for customers; its military applications; and its internal applications. TI began as a petroleum exploration company and is now at the forefront of electronics and industrial AI. We continue with Arthur Andersen, the international consulting firm which has developed new business building and selling a great variety of small expert systems. We conclude with Fujitsu, the largest of the Japanese computer manufacturers, which has made a Texas Instruments–like commitment to broad corporate excellence in AI hardware, software, and customer systems.

Texas Instruments: Their Fourth Revolution

George Heilmeier, senior vice president and chief technical officer at Texas Instruments, is not a man people feel neutral about. Those right around him at TI adore him—no other word for it—and speak gratefully of his leadership and vision, which have helped move TI beyond the financial and public relations disaster of its failed personal computer business and into a leading industrial position in artificial intelligence, particularly in expert systems.

"Just after we dumped our home computer business, we spent roughly 25 percent of our time during college recruitment tours assuring potential employees that we hadn't gone out of the computer business altogether," says John Alden, formerly the manager of education marketing. "That's how public our failure was. But then George convinced us all that a big commitment to AI was the next logical step, not only for our company but for American industry in general, and that TI should not only lead technically but take on a sort of missionary project—what we called our 'AI awareness blitz'—to convince the rest of American industry that this is where our competitive edge lies in the future. As a result of that, young people we wanted to hire stopped asking if we'd gone out of the computer business—we hadn't, of course, just the home computer business—and started asking us about AI. They saw it as an exciting thing to be doing at an exciting lab."

If you'd been doing advanced AI research a decade earlier, particularly robotics and speech understanding, you might have a different view of George Heilmeier. As head of the Defense Advanced Research Projects Agency (DARPA) in those days, Heilmeier had virtually killed American robotics, speech understanding, and other AI research, cutting off projects at MIT, Carnegie-Mellon, and Stanford, as well as other research laboratories. His victims saw him as just another know-it-all physicist, displaying a combination of arrogance and ignorance that dismayed scientists in other fields who have different ways of achieving results than physicists do, and can't quite accept that the way physics is done is the only worthwhile way to do science.

When Heilmeier left DARPA and went to work at TI, the company was said to be bragging they'd hired him because he'd been on top of all the best and brightest research funded by DARPA. The AI community laughed: would anybody tell

TI they'd been snookered? Nobody would. Let them find out for themselves.

"I've taken a bad rap on that one," Heilmeier says now. "Yes, I cut AI programs at DARPA, which was already de-emphasizing robotics when I came. But other programs were created. The AI budget was not drastically reduced; it stayed about flat, but it was shifted to some new AI efforts, such as signal interpretation and image understanding. I wasn't against AI per se. How could I be against something I couldn't understand? I might have been the first guy at DARPA to read what these AI people were writing—what they said they were hoping to do. It didn't make any sense to me. Explain it to me, I said. Look, I was told, these are smart people and it's in the national interest to support them, even if they don't always make sense in their reports—even if they don't always *make* reports.

"I didn't think anybody was entitled to the government's money just because they were smart. I wanted to be convinced. And I just couldn't get them to explain, and commit to meaningful milestones."

Veteran AI researchers don't remember it quite that way—in their view, an enormous amount of time was leached from serious, probably strategic, research and spent trying to explain; having explained, more time was wasted in persuading George Heilmeier that even though artificial intelligence research didn't quite fit the model of physics research, it was still pretty important stuff, and results were being achieved. But it all seemed futile; Heilmeier pronounced himself unconvinced.

A decade later, most of the veterans have chosen to let bygones be bygones. Nobody could be a stronger champion of AI now than George Heilmeier. A senior AI scientist says soothingly: "Converts should be welcomed even more warmly than those who've grown up in the faith."

Whatever accounts for Heilmeier's conversion, the fact is that when he arrived at TI as vice president for corporate research, development, and engineering, he was already so enthusiastic that a modest AI effort was begun. By 1979, research began at TI on a project to put a natural language interface to a data base so that you could ask for information in your mother tongue, instead of the arcane commands of computer programmers. Also in 1979 Heilmeier addressed a Morgan Stanley investment seminar, where he said: "I believe that a combination of VLSI (very large scale integrated circuits) and machine intelligence will make possible what I'll call the long-bomb computer—'the instruction-bookless computer'—in the mid-1980s. This will be a machine that will not require one to be a skilled programmer to use it effectively."

Heilmeier then went on to specify some characteristics of such a machine: that you would be able to tell it *what* you wanted done, not how to do it, probably in free-form query and responses (though not necessarily in speech); it would have "audit trails" (you would be able to ask it why it gave a specific answer); it would be fail-soft, meaning it would fail gently instead of catastrophically; and it would be self-teaching, able to communicate with data bases or other processors, rich in graphics, and relatively cheap. Just what some members of the AI community faithful had been saying all along.

By 1980 TI was beginning to build its first expert systems, one for design automation and another for seismic interpretation. Results were so heartening that the "AI awareness blitz" was begun. It started with simple consciousness-raising.

Floyd Hollister, a trim, low-key man with gray eyes behind aviator glasses, who makes a point as eloquently with his hands as his words, remembers that blitz very well. "I joined the AI group in 1981, and George Heilmeier's instructions were, Get the word out. First, inside the company, then outside. We gave five or six major presentations a week inside the company—why we thought AI might be worthwhile, the benefits, could it create new products and what might those new products be, could it improve our manufacturing processes, our design processes, what could you do with it. And we'd answer the questions. What's AI? What makes it different? How do you know it will work? Straightforward questions, but difficult to answer. There was clearly a lot of skepticism at the beginning; there always is when somebody tries to introduce a new technology with a different approach.''

Harry Tennant, a senior member of TI's technical staff, remembers that at the beginning of the blitz, things didn't look very promising. Tennant, a Ph.D. who got his degree for research in AI natural-language techniques, chose Texas Instruments in 1980 because it seemed like the best industrial bet in the country. "My interest was in seeing something come into being instead of just doing research." There weren't a lot of corporations interested in AI then: Xerox's famous Palo Alto Research Center seemed to Tennant "played out"—in any case, Xerox's corporate headquarters was three thousand miles away from its research, whereas AI lived under the same roof with the corporate headquarters of TI. Digital had some things going, but Texas Instruments looked to Tennant like the only company really interested in making a business out of artificial intelligence.

Tennant recalls the early times of the blitz: "We had almost nothing to go on except our faith in the technology. We had stories of Mycin and Macsyma [early expert systems from Stanford and MIT] but when you've heard those stories once, you don't want to hear them again. We'd talk about them, and demonstrate rapid prototyping on Lisp machines, natural-language stuff I was doing. But that, and our general faith, was all we had to work with in the early days.''

Natural language—and faith—turned out to be crucial.

George Heilmeier insisted that the AI group set out its goals in a concrete, realistic fashion. They needed projects that would be perceived as important to customers and could be accomplished within five years.

As the AI group was looking around for something concrete to tackle, the air force published a request for proposals for a system that would let a high-level human decision maker, military or civilian, get information from a very dynamic data base using English instead of a computer language. TI's military systems group hadn't heard of anything quite like that before, so they came around to the artificial intelligence people and asked if this was the kind of thing AI could do.

Harry Tennant had been working on techniques to overcome some of the principal problems that kept natural language from being an easily used technology. His work fit that request nicely. But to build a prototype to show the air force he'd need a data base that the air force was interested in to build his natural-language system upon. Within two days, the air force brought Tennant a "pseudo data base," a mock-up of the real one. Five days later, Tennant was able to show his potential customers a running prototype that permitted the user to get information from the data base by questioning it in English. It meant instant fame around TI for Tennant and the AI lab.

"When I use this example," Tennant says now, "it's always to illustrate the power of rapid prototyping. Building the prototypes was a matter of hours—I worked late one night." More important, the project caught attention around the company because it was a big contract. "It was the greatest single push AI got here, because people were now ready to stand up and say, We're not really sure about this technology, but we understand a $50 million contract," says Hollister.

Under Heilmeier's leadership, AI continued to thrive at Texas Instruments, focused not only on products the company could sell—a Lisp machine called the Explorer, various expert systems, and then a shell called Personal Consultant (an adaptation of a Stanford shell called EMycin) to permit others to build their own expert systems easily—but also on internal systems to be described later too.

The way was not always easy. Heilmeier recalls some monumental clashes with other TI managers. He remembers in the early 1980s getting paged at the San Francisco airport, and being told to call his office immediately. "Things were so bad I figured I was being fired," Heilmeier says.

The home computer business was going through wild times, debates were raging about whether TI was a software or a hardware company, and people in the AI group wanted to leave. Heilmeier persuaded them to stay. He even got a phone call from his daughter, then in business school at Baylor. "Dad, they're using TI as a case study here. Did you really make all those mistakes?"

"Well, not *all by myself!*"

He can laugh about it now.

AI still hadn't proved itself as a product. Don't worry about it, Heilmeier would tell everybody, if all else fails, there'll always be internal benefits, we'll assimilate it across our company. Says Alden: "We had very highly motivated technical people, and a manager with a long history of technology management who understood and believed in this particular technology, who was willing to keep enough money in the bank to let them do the work, and protect them from being diverted to other things. That's not a one-year struggle; that goes on for two, three years."

Heilmeier was also getting full support from the new CEO, Jerry Junkins, who'd been executive vice president when the AI blitz began. Gene Helms, a vice president for corporate staff, recalls that Junkins had what might be termed a crucial appreciation of the technology by the time he had to close down the home computer business. "Junkins had a bewildering challenge: What do we do to have a future anywhere in the computer business? We need something creative, innovative. And here were these guys going around saying AI is the future. So Junkins said, Let's do something a little unconventional."

Talk about unconventional. The next idea was to put artificial intelligence on a personal computer. "That ran right into the existing belief structures in AI," says John Alden. "The AI community always believed if you weren't using a Lisp machine, you weren't doing AI," since Lisp is the favorite computer language of the American AI community, and a computer dedicated to running that language works faster and more efficiently than a general-purpose computer. But Tennant and others had been saying that for expert systems, a personal computer was as good as a mini; for most expert systems, speed was simply not an issue. The point was to work smarter, not faster. Tennant opened their eyes to the real market: customers who didn't want to start with $50,000 to $100,000 machines. They wanted to start with what they knew, the PC on their desks. Strategically, TI realized the opportunity was in selling an entry-level system, which required no great financial investment. Thus its best-selling Personal Consultant, the PC-based expert system shell for small systems.

Texas Instruments also has a division that sells custom-designed expert systems to customers, prototyping rapidly and offering easy, relatively cheap, entrance into the new technology. Among the division's clients have been Campbell Soup, Southern California Edison, Corning Glass, and the Defense Department. For Campbell Soup, TI built an expert system to do early diagnosis of problems with their "cookers," the giant soup-sterilizing machines whose unexpected failure could ruin 500,000-gallon batches of soup. TI helped the Southern California Edison electric utility get started on a system to make judgments about the soundness of earth dams holding their reservoirs. For Corning Glass, TI built an expert system to help control the manufacture of specialty glass products in extremely hot annealing furnaces. In each of these cases, the main goal was to capture the expertise of superb individual performers. In their work for the Defense Department, TI claims a major success in FRESH, for Force Requirements Expert System, an expert system to advise on the deployment of ships in the U.S. Pacific Fleet. According to TI, a typical deployment problem would take an experienced operations officer and his staff as much as a week to solve, but with the help of Fresh, the officer can produce a solution by himself in six to eight hours.

Expert Systems Inside TI

George Heilmeier had predicted that even if AI couldn't be sold outside the company, it would make a difference within. Nothing illustrates this better than an expert system put together by a group in TI's business development division of the defense systems and electronics group for the ordinary engineer who wants to buy a new piece of capital equipment and needs to justify its purchase to a capital investment committee.

Any business needs capital investment to keep or improve profitability; if a business fails to invest in itself, it might not be able to take advantage of new technological advances, and it will probably incur extra costs maintaining old equipment. Engineers might know why they need a new piece of equipment, but they don't know how to justify such a need to a skeptical capital investment committee, or how to compose a convincing business plan.

The system's godfather and primary expert is a capital accounting expert named Bill Illingworth, a feisty, enthusiastic, and to-the-point man whose intensity is a bracing contrast to the laid-back engineers all around him. He explains that when a unit in a corporation wants to make significant capital expenditures at TI (anywhere from a thousand to a million dollars or more), it must go before a board to make its case.

"My group has the capital responsibility for our division—we have to prepare these packages, justify them, even stand up and take the insults when they're done wrong," Illingworth says. "Mostly managers send people they don't care for—here, you present this. And it's true, you have to justify why you want it, you have to have clear-cut goals, they have to match corporate goals—and there's a lot of information you have to gather to support that. This is a committee looking to say no."

In 1985 TI's defense systems and electronics group management authorized over fifteen hundred capital packages, about 60 percent of the packages presented. The packages not only originated from different sources but used a variety of engineering and accounting principles, making the board's evaluation task even more difficult.

"I said, we gotta have a way where we know what we're doing. I think myself that 20 percent of the capital, which in total is like $300 million a year at TI, isn't even required. We wanted to find this out *before* we bought the equipment."

Gathering the information to make up a capital proposal package requires consulting many experts, controllers and investment accountants, engineers, cash-flow experts, labor cost experts, and so on. Each aspect of the proposal requires a document, and typically, the preparation of such a package can take twelve hours, usually spread over five to ten days. "This doesn't count the time spent gathering information—

we can't put a handle on that—only time spent preparing it for presentation. Our numbers are very, very conservative. There's probably much more cost than we indicate."

Jack Gary, one of the knowledge engineers for this system, says that if it had only been a matter of seven or twelve hours to do a package, the system would never have been written. But what really happens is that package preparers must consult experts who aren't always available when they're needed. "It's an incredible task to get that many different people all lined up in a row—you just can't do it; you're here till one in the morning and still you miss deadlines because you can't coordinate all the people you need to talk to. That problem's been solved, because the guy who needs to know has the information right now."

Instead of the burdensome information gathering and writing, a user can now sit down for a thirty-five-minute consultation with the capital expert system on a personal computer. The system asks questions, analyzes requirements, generates uniform packages that are ready to present, and performs at or above the level of human experts. If the user fudges—not an unheard-of problem, which has caused Illingworth's group embarrassments in the past—the system quietly stops. The user can try again, when he's feeling more realistic. Moreover, the system adheres to TI corporate capital guidelines, provides support data, and does an individual package analysis, pointing out weak and strong aspects of a given user's case.

The productivity improvement using the capital package is about 20 to 1 (more if the time saved to gather the information is included), although, as Illingworth says, that was an unanticipated benefit: the primary motive had been to avoid capital overspending. In 1987, the system saved better than a million dollars in preparation costs alone. Over the next five years it is expected to show cumulative savings here of nearly ten million dollars. And this figure doesn't count what TI might be avoiding in unnecessary capital costs—though everybody believes the biggest savings probably lie there.

None of this counts the intangible advantages of standard forms and unbiased data. Illingworth says, "Everybody has a different way of doing payback analysis, and most of those different ways are favorable to their particular proposal. The expert system was an opportunity to standardize payback analysis. You'd be amazed how biased people are, but the expert system isn't. The people on the capital committee now say, Has this been done on the capital expert system? They know we use standard data—it's getting high acceptance." In other words, engineers soon began to notice that requests were more likely to be approved if the system had been used. "With the change in tax laws relating to capital expenditure, we've also had to update the system, which was very easy," Illingworth adds.

The capital expert system was the work of two young industrial engineers, Laurie Dowell and Jack Gary, who were sent off to TI's instructional center to learn knowledge-engineering techniques, and then implemented the system on a personal computer running the TI Personal Consultant shell. The system took two and a half person-years to develop at a cost of $250,000, which was paid back in three to four months. By the end of 1987, the system was scheduled to be in the hands of a hundred capital administrators at seven TI sites.

In the way of corporate cultures, Illingworth's group did not have a charter to do software—the capital expert system was something they did alongside their regular work—and they ruffled some feathers by stepping beyond their usual concerns. Just after the capital expert system was implemented, Laurie Dowell sat down at a table full of Texas Instruments AI people who asked her what she did. She replied she'd just finished demonstrating her expert system, which she'd designed using TI's Personal Consultant software. Oh, they sniffed, that's interesting . . . but not to us.

"The AI people don't like it when I say this is just a hobby with us," Illingworth adds wickedly.

The capital expert system has been so successful that sixteen more expert systems are under way in Illingworth's group alone, which is only one part of the company, a microcosm of how expert systems are becoming a way of life at TI.

Indeed, that usual fortress of corporate resistance to AI,

the main management information systems group, known at Texas Instruments as information systems and services, or IS&S, even has its own artificial intelligence team, which sponsors projects and works as a codeveloper with other segments of the IS&S team at twenty-five places around the world. At TI, IS&S doesn't mean just payroll; it also means running manufacturing as well. Thus anything that can be done to cut the downtime of their computers is vital. The IS&S-AI group has designed a Computer Operator Advising and Training expert system, for "training and advising new operators in the Land of Cobol," says Tom Barrett, a system analyst. "Usually, it takes three to five years to train a new computer operator to where you have confidence he or she can handle anything. So we've got a dual opportunity here, reducing our mainframe costs by reducing the downtime and helping our operators get up to speed quickly." Barrett and his group calculated that every minute saved of certain failures is worth $2,000, taking into consideration overall costs to the corporation of downtime.

But TI is basically a manufacturer, and so are many of its important customers. Early in 1986 TI pulled together a set of techniques, AI central to them, to automate more manufacturing, its own and its customers'. Thus expert systems are beginning to appear where computers hardly ever were before.

Within TI, an expert system diagnoses maintenance problems for an extremely complex piece of manufacturing equipment called an optical coater. TI has fourteen of these machines, custom built from parts supplied by a number of small vendors. The expert system has improved mean time between failures by about 50 percent on each part of the equipment it has been applied to, and has avoided eleven failures per month, which translates into a savings of about $250,000 per year. Its diagnoses have been correct in 75 percent of the cases—an importantly high number, because the human technicians associated with these machines are relatively inexperienced with them.

Says Bob Barnett, the manager for factory integration who instigated this project: "It's much more important to us that a $750,000 machine is up and running than any other savings we make. With our improved maintenance, we've freed up the equivalent of a fifteenth machine. That's a one-time savings of three-quarters of a million dollars right there."

Another troubleshooting expert system has been designed for a complicated piece of equipment called an epitaxial reactor, which grows a molecular layer on a silicon slice. With the expert system, reactor availability has been doubled from 40 percent of the time to 80 percent, thereby saving TI the cost of having to buy a second million-dollar machine. In addition, the two years it used to take to learn to operate the machine has been cut to between four and six months.

The epitaxial reactor expert system, created in about three months, was the work of an engineer with a fresh bachelor's degree from Central Florida State University in Orlando, not exactly a leading center of AI research.

"I hadn't even heard of artificial intelligence, and I certainly hadn't heard of expert systems before I got to TI," Katherine Hunter says, her precise, almost blunt, diction a contrast to her delicate physical frame. "If I were doing it again, I'd learn a lot more about the theory instead of just jumping in with a piece of software, the Personal Consultant, and trying to do what a process engineer said I was supposed to do. I didn't know anything about AI or expert systems. The guy who suggested it to me didn't know much; none of my superiors knew much about it. The two-week course I took, to tell you the truth, really wasn't very helpful: I didn't have the knowledge to utilize that information. I didn't know how to go about it. I just kind of picked it up. It was frustrating the first couple of weeks. I had a false start trying to put this all together—things just went all over the place."

After a few weeks, Hunter formed a panel consisting of several different experts, including the field representative of the company that had built the reactor, the process engineer, a TI equipment engineer, and a service technician. The panel met once a week for three hours for about three months—by that time they had their basic system up and going.

Knowledge engineers often dislike the step of gathering experts for knowledge acquisition because it's so hard to wrestle with experts' egos, but Hunter says: "We were pretty lucky—we didn't have much problem with that."

TI puts enormous effort into AI education. Some of it grows out of the great AI information blitz, which has matured into a continuing series of courses (nearly twenty different ones in computer science and artificial intelligence in the fall of 1986). A TI education group in Austin offers courses to both TI employees and TI customers, and the company will send its employees to outside seminars and pay for further university education in AI. But perhaps the most notable education effort has been the satellite symposiums, broadcast free to anybody with equipment to receive them. By 1987 some 100,000 scientists, engineers, and managers in the United States, Canada, Europe, and parts of Latin America had seen the symposiums. The first one cost $600,000, a hefty sum for mere goodwill, but well worth it, TI believes, for explaining what expert systems are all about and forging a link in corporate minds between TI and the industrial application of artificial intelligence. The video conferences are said to be the largest in history, and have made something of an international star of Harry Tennant, who once picked TI as a place to work because he was eager to see things happen.

At TI's Dallas headquarters, buildings are a gloomy marriage of federal-contractor minimalism and engineering sufficiency: painted cinder block walls; chairs offering the creature comforts of church pews; floors of clean, serviceable, but unexceptional vinyl tile. The contrast between TI's buildings and their mirrored-glass neighbors that dot the suburban Dallas landscape could hardly be more striking. But the mirrored-glass neighbors—architectural clichés of the 1970s, and emblems of equally dated values—are half empty, and decidedly mortuary in spirit.

At TI, on the contrary, the atmosphere is charged. A jokey camaraderie prevails among the researchers, and in a display of implicit self-confidence he couldn't fake, a senior member of the technical staff says dryly: "Oh, we lie to each other to build enthusiasm, and the more we lie, the closer we have to come to reality, and the closer we come to reality, the sooner the sales force can go out and sell this AI stuff." But this is a company that's come through very hard times, survived, learned from its experience, is beginning to prevail. Its ascetic headquarters suddenly seems prudent, mature, the home of people who understand in their bones the idea of lean and mean: less Texan than New England.

Texas Instruments people like to say they've already been involved in three of the great revolutions: the transistor, the integrated circuit, and the hand-held calculator. They think artificial intelligence is the fourth.

Arthur Andersen: A Strategy of a Mile Wide and an Inch Deep

Bruce Johnson first heard about artificial intelligence in after-hours bull sessions with friends when he worked at the Johnson Space Center in Houston during the 1960s. Now he is a partner in the worldwide management consulting firm of Arthur Andersen, its resident specialist on expert systems, and in 1988 the founding head of AA's new Center for Advanced Technology. The Arthur Andersen company, which began as an auditing firm in the 1900s but then branched out to tax advising and consulting, operates as a partnership, which means the seventeen hundred worldwide partners make no salary, but simply share the firm's profits.

"As a result, we don't have much in the way of turf battles," Johnson explains. "We're very loosely organized, and just in there working with each other." He himself works at Chicago headquarters and is accustomed to getting phone calls from any of the 215 offices in 60 countries where the Arthur Andersen group is found.

When the firm decided to move into a new business called expert systems, it faced a number of problems, both with its staff and with its customers. Introducing a new technology is always difficult, particularly in as far-flung a network as Andersen's. "People who do the work at Andersen must sell what they do, so they lean toward what they can already do most easily," says Johnson. "Bringing in new technology of any sort, but especially an abstract technology, is a real problem. You show them something on a Lisp machine, and they can't get beyond the hardware." They can see the example in front of them, but they have difficulty generalizing from that example.

The firm decided it needed a special approach for AI technologies, what Johnson calls the "mile wide and inch deep" approach. The program that Bruce Johnson has designed, responsible for expert systems development and deployment at the firm, makes sure that in every Arthur Andersen office throughout the world, there's at least an "inch-deep" awareness of expert systems. That way, when a possible application arises, the local consultants are aware that such solutions exist, and can call on a task force from regional headquarters for help. The inch-deep awareness comes from courses, the distribution of literature, and occasional meetings.

But how can consultants or their clients recognize when a problem might lend itself to expert systems applications? Johnson's group handles that by producing concrete examples, studying industries to find problems common to them, and conceiving solutions that might help.

"We don't hit anybody's exact problem, but we're close enough so that it can be used to demonstrate the idea to the client, and explain how it might be changed to fit his situation. That's what's important; we're not after a product, we're after an opportunity to solve a particular business problem."

As an example, Johnson cites the truck-routing advisor that the firm did for Southland, the company that owns the 7-Eleven convenience stores. Southland was operating with a relatively crude fifteen-year-old computer program to route its supply trucks to its retail outlets, a system whose results would have to be modified each night by a human designer to take into account many odd rules about loading frozen items, produce, and removing empty cartons. The Arthur Andersen people built an expert system to automate many of those odd rules, considerably inproving the designer's productivity. As Johnson points out, that particular system was useful only to Southland, but the very phrase *truck routing* evokes a rich group of similar problems from consultants and their clients.

This kind of concrete example is as important for the clients as it is for the consultants. "I have found that fewer than 15 percent—maybe only 5 percent—of people in the business world know what to do with new technology. But they can take an idea that's close and do a variation. People simply can't generalize from abstractions, but when they're shown a series of applications, they respond: I need this and this one, but I don't need that one." The AI group will often build a rapid prototype, sketchy and even wrong—it doesn't matter, since it's only to illustrate—instead of writing a proposal to a client. "If a picture's worth a thousand words, a running system is worth at least a thousand and one words."

Above the mile-wide-and-inch-deep local level, there are a much smaller number of Andersen offices with AI task forces. These in turn are supported by research, development, and funding from Chicago headquarters. The headquarters AI organization defines the initiatives, cheerleads, channels the funding, educates staff in formal workshops and classes, and deals with AI vendors and their products. It also acts as an information conduit for AI efforts: "We synthesize the firm's AI experience and periodically redistribute it."

Most Arthur Andersen AI efforts are small, four to five people working on expert systems that take several months to build, but that will have a quick payoff. "As a consultant, I say to my clients that a quick success is more important than a big kill. That's partly because we're always driving for the business problem, and partly because we're aware of many organizational issues that clients must cope with. We're trying to bring them along with the quick success; we'll go for the big kill later." Johnson describes his approach as the mean between two extremes, represented by Digital, which is building its business around central expert systems, and Du Pont, which has many one-man-month single-user systems.

When the firm is trying to show staff or customers what AI can do for them, it begins with the concrete examples. Johnson presents them in ten or so clusters—diagnostics programs, configuration programs, and others, each with a long list of concrete examples, arranged from the most basic to the most advanced.

One he likes is what he calls publishing, or the delivery of active knowledge. "These aren't advisory systems so much as they're the fact finders, but presented in much easier form than if you got them in a book. Another kind of cluster is the advisor—active knowledge with some judgment added." Others include rule-based transaction processing, schedulers, designers, planners, and natural-language processors.

Arthur Andersen's clients for these systems come from among their customers for other services. For example, Pioneer Savings and Loan in Seattle, Washington, for whom Arthur Andersen designed an advisor to help mortgage officers make loan decisions, had used Arthur Andersen for other consulting services first. The Andersen firm has designed other financial advisors both in the United States and abroad, as well as industrial advisors, such as one for a chemical industry client.

"The most successful of our systems have been major steps forward for us and the particular industry where the expert system was applied," Johnson says. He calculates that three quarters of the Arthur Andersen expert systems have been new value, new products, and new services, as opposed to mere cost reduction. If cost savings is the only goal, it's too limiting. Manpower saved through expert systems isn't nearly as important as faster response, improved quality of service, and competitive differentiation.

A group that isn't out in the field making money on direct applications is somewhat countercultural at Arthur Andersen. But Johnson doesn't see any other way of introducing this new technology but investment, which, he believes, will have immense long-term payoffs. "We're more than breaking even on this, but our customers get the big payoffs. However, we think the biggest payoffs of all are still in front of us, because what the technology's really helping us do is cope with complexity. That's the main theme of our presentations."

And so Johnson's group is leading from the technology,

as they put it, which means they are offering a solution to some business problems based on a technology that not everybody in the firm understands. At the beginning, around 1983, that was an uncomfortable position, given the firm's way of doing business. "Nonetheless, it was a necessary position, otherwise the new technology never comes in. But we try not to be zealots; we look at the business problem first." Now that revenues are in the many millions of dollars, Johnson sums up the advantages to Arthur Andersen of having moved into expert systems: first, a separate and unique service line, opening new markets and building new kinds of systems; second, a new product line; and finally, the most important, using and improving a new tool that enhances the firm's regular consulting business.

Fujitsu: The Continuity of Old with New

Fujitsu, the largest of Japan's computer manufacturers, has made a Texas Instruments–like commitment to artificial intelligence across its business in hardware, software, and building customer systems. Much of this commitment has been due to the efforts of Dr. Takeo Uehara, who not only manages the central laboratory's artificial intelligence research but has been key in persuading the company that this is one place where its future lies.

Uehara had been searching for innovative computer research projects for Fujitsu, and in early 1979 went to a Stanford industrial affiliates program where he heard about knowledge engineering. He came away convinced that this could be an area of innovative breakthrough for Fujitsu. In 1981 a young Fujitsu engineer, Fumihiro Maruyama, was sent to Teknowledge for six months to take its intensive knowledge-engineering course; he then spent another six months at Stanford. These were Fujitsu's modest beginnings in expert systems, though Uehara's insight had led them into the world of AI-style Lisp programming a year earlier.

By 1982, a combination of events, including the start of the Japanese government's Fifth Generation project, all helped to solidify Fujitsu's earlier decisions, and the company was able to quadruple its AI research staff. The new young people were eager to do fifth-generation research, which led to the rapid development of both hardware and software products. The AI research group wasn't officially formed until December 1984; until then, all AI work had been done in the Fujitsu central laboratory's software group. By April 1985 AI had its own software division.

The Fifth Generation project had a great impact on work that had already begun. Half of Fujitsu's growth in AI work was funded with government Fifth Generation funds, and the whole Fifth Generation project created a high excitement in young researchers: AI was what they wanted to work on. Subsequently, Fujitsu has sent a number of people to the government's cooperative laboratory, known as ICOT, for the Institute for New Generation Computer Technology, for fifth-generation research in Tokyo.

Fujitsu's AI development laboratory in Kamata, near Tokyo, is an effervescent, upbeat place full of young engineers who sense that their past accomplishments are sound and that those accomplishments are now beginning to permit Fujitsu to differentiate itself from—perhaps even pull ahead of—other Japanese computer manufacturers.

One of Fujitsu's main AI products is a back-end Lisp machine called FACOM-Alpha that runs attached to Fujitsu's conventional mainframes. It was the first Japanese Lisp machine. Its design was begun in 1980, very early as such things go, and by 1983 a prototype was finished and a technical paper published. However, the decision to manufacture and sell this new AI product was difficult. The conventional computer people at Fujitsu were very skeptical.

As a rule, when Fujitsu decides to market a new product, that decision is the result of careful market studies. But a courageous middle manager, Shigeru Sato, bucking the conventional wisdom, decided to go ahead with the production, reasoning that the usual market forecasts are based on two factors: past machines and the competition. In this case, Fujitsu had a unique machine; there was no past, no competitors to measure against. He feared the conservative decision would be made and the project dropped. Rather than get an answer he didn't want to hear, he simply went ahead. As it was, at the insistence of Fujitsu's computer systems people, the product was modified from being a stand-alone workstation to being an attachment to a mainframe, because mainframes are Fujitsu's major business. By 1985 the first customer deliveries were made, and by the end of 1986 thirty of these Lisp machines had been sold.

In software systems, Fujitsu reimplemented and adapted a Stanford expert systems research shell to market a commercial expert system shell called EShell. EShell is used for various kinds of generic applications such as diagnostics, planning, and control. By the end of 1986, the company had distributed over three hundred copies of EShell, mainly to manufacurers whom Fujitsu actively supports as they move into AI applications. Diagnostics programs—which are large, relatively shallow reasoning programs—were the most popular at first, but now a shift has taken place to applications in design and control; for example, the Nippon-Kokan Steel blast furnace application, which captures the catastrophe-prevention expertise of the twenty-year veteran "furnace god." According to a report of the Japanese Information Processing Development Center, Fujitsu's market share in expert system software tools is the largest in Japan, around 25 percent, and going up.

Fujitsu is selling its shells to both end users and data-processing people (50 percent or more). Fujitsu engineers note the well-known reluctance conventional MIS people display toward AI systems, but in Japan, which is presently enjoying something called "AI fever," top management puts great pressure on its programmers to begin implementing AI applications, so MIS people don't have much choice.

People at Fujitsu are candid: so far, AI and expert systems are not making money for the company directly. But they see these as an investment in their future, good public relations for selling their mainframes, and a badge of their cutting edge commitment. AI and knowledge engineering are a companywide effort, involving people from research labs, systems engineers, and field engineers. "Cooperation is a great factor in our work," Uehara says, noting that many parts of the company are moving toward the same goal, which means not much infighting, and a great deal of synergy.

Fujitsu's systems engineers are using AI to enhance conventional applications by adding AI software and the FACOM-Alpha hardware. This fusion of AI technologies with large conventional environments is what Fujitsu believes will lead to large-scale AI applications, which company people don't see coming about any other way or from any other Japanese vendor.

With its large-scale commitment and its pioneering products, Fujitsu sees itself correctly as the leading AI company in Japan, a position that it not only intends to keep, but that it believes will put it at the forefront of all Japanese computing companies.

Chapter 10

The Fifth Generation in Japan and Europe

In Japan we have developed what might be called "expert system fever." In the world of Japanese industry, there are well over a hundred expert systems that are either already being put to practical use or soon to be. Industries engaged most actively in the research and development of expert systems are steel, electric power, manufacturing (particularly the automobile industry), and construction. These are also the industries with the most expert systems in operation. . . . Expert systems now under development are advanced enough for use in strategically important applications like design and planning.

—FROM *JAPAN COMPUTER QUARTERLY* (No. 69, 1987), A PUBLICATION OF THE GOVERNMENT-SPONSORED JAPAN INFORMATION PROCESSING DEVELOPMENT CENTER (JIPDEC)

FIVE YEARS AFTER their dramatic announcement of a national research project in artificial intelligence, the Japanese were experiencing what they call an "AI boom." Japanese top management, energized by media attention to expert systems and trade shows held by both Japan's leading business newspaper and various business associations, were pressing their middle management to move into the new technology. Within the major industrial, banking, and trade groups— Mitsui, Mitsubishi, Sanwa, and others—the cooperative mechanisms already in place for learning a new technology had organized study groups, foreign travel groups, lectures, and courses to train company people to lead expert system development teams.

In Britain, AI pioneer and entrepreneur Donald Michie, founder of a leading British expert system software company, told an old friend sadly but optimistically, "The British market [for expert systems software] has been asleep, but we hope it will wake up in 1987 and 1988." The British government said it was going to end funding for the British national project, Alvey, which supported expert systems work under the title Intelligent Knowledge Based Systems. Efforts were being made to convince the government to extend the project.

In the European Economic Community, funding for the community project, ESPRIT, which supports some work on expert systems, was renewed. Among the companies, isolated examples of small systems could be found at work, but one searched in vain for applications with significant economic gain. Was Europe simply years behind, or was the activity cloaked by proprietary secrecy? It was hard to tell. Inscrutability is something we usually attribute to the East, not the West.

Japan: The Fifth Generation Project and Expert Systems Fever

Artificial intelligence is a science with a thirty-year history. During its first twenty-five years it led a quiet life as the exotic subspecialty of computer science studying intelligence and performing experiments on how to make computers intelligent. For most of this time it was supported generously by the U.S. Defense Department and, in a much smaller and more focused way, by the Japanese government in the PIPS (Pattern Information Processing System) national project of the 1970s. In 1981 the quiet obscurity of AI was transformed into highly visible frenzy by the dramatic announcement by Japan's Ministry of International Trade and Industry (MITI) of the establishment of a program of advanced research and development in AI, a project the ministry named Fifth Generation Computer Systems (FGCS). Coming on the heels of MITI's highly successful efforts to promote Japanese prowess in consumer electronics and computer chips, the announcement set off alarm bells in capitals and companies of the West. The story of the founding of the project was told in the book *The Fifth Generation: Artificial Intelligence and Japan's Computer Challenge to the World*, and in a remarkable retrospective of the key players and their motives, published in Japanese only, *Japanese Dream* by Junichiro Uemae. Six years have passed. The ten-year project has now passed its midpoint, and it is interesting to take a look at Fifth Generation progress and problems.

The Fifth Generation project was set up to develop computer hardware and software for systems the Japanese called generically Knowledge Information Processing Systems (KIPS), the same computer development that we have called knowledge processing. The KIPS work was keyed to a specific methodology called logic programming, originally developed in Europe. The FGCS concept was breathtaking in scope, in the performance promised, and in the vision of a society transformed by KIPS. The FGCS plan promised extremely high-speed problem solving, parallel computers for achieving this, and interaction with KIPS in natural (human) language, speech, and pictures.

The project period was nominally ten years (though realistically the planners admitted that more might be needed), broken into phases of three, four and three years.

A central research institute, the Institute for New Generation Computer Technology (ICOT) was established in Tokyo under the direction of an elite scientific management team from MITI's own laboratory, the Electrotechnical Laboratory. The team was headed by a brilliant, unorthodox, and charismatic scientist, Kazuhiro Fuchi. To the laboratory came forty young engineers and scientists (most in their twenties) from the eight Japanese computer firms cooperating with MITI in the project.

The firms were Fujitsu, Hitachi, NEC, Mitsubishi, Toshiba, Matsushita, Oki, and Sharp. Each established an internal counterpart to ICOT (usually called a Fifth Generation laboratory or something similar) consisting of a "cooperating" part and a proprietary part. The cooperating part contracts with ICOT for MITI funds in support of ICOT-planned or ICOT-directed work and also work thought to be of importance to the community effort. The proprietary part is funded by each company for its own proprietary goals. So a company's participation is threefold. It lends people to ICOT. It connects to its people and the rest of ICOT work through the cooperating part of its lab, which in turn passes knowledge to company colleagues in the proprietary part of the lab.

Under the ICOT staffing plan, the scientists and engineers rotate back to their respective companies at the end of each phase. This accords not only with the demands of the companies to have their prized young people back, working within the corporate family, and with the technology transfer imperative. It also implements what some believe is the most important goal of the FGCS project—the training of a large number of highly qualified people for future work in AI and knowledge processing in Japanese companies. Mr. Konishi, one of the young and bold MITI planners who conceived the Fifth Generation project (now a planner for NTT), in a speech he gave for a conference in Tokyo in December 1986, put this training goal at the top of a list of FGCS goals initally set by MITI planners. We will return to this later.

Phase One began immediately with a judicious pruning of the grand vision. Work on speech and picture understanding was given to the industrial research labs. Language understanding research was maintained but shared with Kyoto University. The focus was on logic programming. An early model of logic-processing hardware was designed by ICOT and manufactured by Mitsubishi, for internal use and later as a commercial product sold internationally. The machine is a minicomputer workstation called PSI (Personal Sequential Inference machine). A more recent version, three to five times faster, is called PSI-2. A high-speed version of PSI, called CHI, was built by NEC for ICOT. ICOT also reworked and extended the original logic-programming language Prolog into a powerful programming tool, in which they were able to write the operating software of their machines. This effort, done under contract by Mitsubishi, resulted in the largest Prolog program by far ever written and established the Japanese as heavyweight champions of the Prolog world. ICOT designed, and Hitachi built, a machine for knowledge bases (technically speaking, a relational data base machine), but the machine was not efficient and practical, so the idea was dropped in Phase Two.

The public relations bridge between Phases One and Two was a large conference held in Tokyo in November 1984 to exhibit the results of the first two and a half years and build enthusiasm and consensus for Phase Two. Conference attendance was oversubscribed. ICOT people were surprised by how many people from a broad spectrum of Japanese industry were in attendance. A disappointment was the small number of university people who attended. The biggest disappointment was felt by some American and European attendees, who came expecting to see the fruits of a revolution and saw instead the considerable achievements of a fast catch-up exercise.

Phase One came to an end in March 1985. Almost everyone except Fuchi and his cadre of group managers rotated back to the member companies, and Fuchi selected a new batch of scientists and engineers from the companies. To a Western research manager, what they did was incomprehensible. On a single day, a highly trained team of (by then) forty-eight technical people whose collective skill was ICOT's own knowledge base, and whose esprit de corps was built to a high level, evaporated and was replaced by new initiates. If they could survive this at all, it would mean slow going for the first year of Phase Two.

Phase Two, according to plan, was scheduled to be the period of most innovation and creativity (for these too were FGCS goals), the period for intense focus on parallel computers. Parallelism for high-speed economical computation is a worldwide goal of the computer industry, but for ICOT it meant parallel logic processing, or PIM (for Parallel Inference Machine). ICOT says it regards logic programming as "the bridge between knowledge processing and parallel machines." The initial PIM is a cluster of PSI machines whose cluster architecture is not much different from that of DEC, Encore, Alliant, Sequent, and other Western companies. Later PIM machines will consist of clusters of the original clusters (a design also under development in the United States). Still later models will substitute PSI-2 machines for PSI. If the software can be made to control and distribute the work efficiently among the many processors (always the big "if" in parallel computing), then ICOT says it can deliver on its promise of many millions of logical inferences per second.

Software is where the action is, and ICOT has had some difficulties with its software. ICOT was successful in extending Prolog. But neither Prolog nor its competitor Lisp are good languages for practical knowledge-processing use. The developer needs higher level languages that we have been calling shells. This difficult work did not build well on a Prolog base, and in any event did not receive the attention it deserved. In 1986, ICOT announced that it was rectifying this, beginning with a survey and study of the "problems involving the capabilities and performance of commercially available tools (e.g., KEE, ART, KC, etc.)." These tools are the large expert system tools developed by three U.S. firms.

In June 1985 ICOT started a new effort (the Fifth Laboratory) for building expert systems and expert system tools. Fuchi understood that the focus on logic programming without coupling to practical knowledge processing carried a risk. He said recently, referring back to the FGCS kickoff conference in 1981, "It was the most controversial issue at the conference, criticized as a reckless proposal without scientific justification." Nonetheless, in Phase Two the Fifth Laboratory was established, in the words of the ICOT journal, to work on "the verification and enhancement of the fifth-generation computer technologies from the viewpoint of applications in order to ensure the capability of the new-generation computer now under development. For this purpose, R&D on expert systems has been selected as our main theme."

The expert system task domains are these:

- diagnosis system for an electronic switching system
- intelligent office secretary system (scheduling business trips and meetings)
- design of a computer room layout
- design of large-scale computer chips
- design of analog electronic circuit chips
- intelligent support system for project planning and management

Computer understanding of human language has always been an important goal of ICOT. As we discuss in Chapter 13, it is essential for a natural interface to a knowledge system. For the Japanese, it is critical for machine translation of language, a goal that the Japanese pursue assiduously, partly because they need a high volume of translation to support their export businesses and partly because they feel keenly the linguistic isolation that the Japanese language imposes upon them.

In language understanding research, the important problem is neither words nor grammar but concepts and meaning. Concepts and meaning are embodied in knowledge. At the moment, there is no way for a computer to get the necessary knowledge except for people to codify concepts manually and "engineer" the knowledge structures for the machine. (The need for large knowledge bases is discussed in Chapters 13 and 14.) ICOT is proud of the research it did in Phase One, relating grammar processing to logic programming. But the message about knowledge was finally understood.

ICOT laid out a plan in which computer-readable dictionaries with a total of 800,000 words would be prepared. In addition, a "concept classification dictionary" was to be prepared containing 400,000 concepts, including a general thesaurus. Finally, they would engineer a "concept description dictionary" which would contain semantic descriptions of the 400,000 concepts, an extremely large knowledge base by today's standards. To carry out this plan requires an enormous and disciplined human group effort. The problem was how to mount such an effort within the constraints of ICOT's structure and its limited government budgets.

The answer was a masterstroke of improvisation. In 1986 the Japanese government was planning the privatization of NTT, the Japanese telephone company. NTT, a quasi-governmental corporation, is the largest company in Japan, the AT&T of Japan. The sale of a portion of government-owned stock in NTT was expected to yield $2 to $4 billion. Rather than take this windfall back into the treasury to offset government debt (exactly what the British government did when it privatized British Telecom), the Japanese decided to put the money into a fund managed by a new agency called the Japan Key Technology Center for "the promotion of private-sector research and development of fundamental technologies."

Suddenly, billions were to be available, some of which might be tapped for the large knowledge base project. But how? ICOT was in the government sector, not the private sector. The answer came with the formation by the member companies of ICOT, in association with the Key Technology Center, of a new company called Japan Electronic Dictionary Research Institute, Ltd. (EDR). The Key Technology Center invested more than $100 million for a seven-year program of research. After seven years, EDR is supposed to be self-sustaining from royalties received for the use of its dictionaries and knowledge base, as they find their way into commercial application, and royalties from licensing specific programs. The Key Technology Center is the biggest shareholder, and the remaining shareholding is split among ICOT's member companies. EDR's management is separate from ICOT's, but the offices of EDR are located in the annex of ICOT's building in central Tokyo.

The conception goes well beyond language understanding. In a diagram illustrating "the tree of knowledge-information processing," the "advanced large-scale electronic dictionary" is shown at the root. The trunks are natural-language processing and knowledge-based inference. The application areas that are the leaves of the tree are:

- intelligent word processing
- intelligent office automation
- machine translation
- speech understanding
- expert systems
- computer-aided design
- computer-aided manufacturing
- decision support systems
- intelligent robots
- computer-assisted instruction

Even those Westerners who were skeptical that the original Fifth Generation goals were achievable agreed that the national project would serve to train a large number of Japan's young computer engineers in the new knowledge technology and make the field glamorous enough to attract the attention of university students. Because Japan was behind and needed a fast start, this training could only be done "on the job," by doing, by championing, by lectures, seminars, and information centers (the recently established AI Center run jointly by ICOT and JIPDEC—Japan Information Processing Development Corporation—being an example). As the MITI planners had envisioned, training was the Fifth Generation project's number-one goal, and today it is the number-one achievement. ICOT managers count about one thousand trained engineers by the end of Phase One (1985), including ICOT researchers, engineers in the "cooperating" sections of member company laboratories, and engineers in the "proprietary" sections. They expect that number to increase tenfold by the end of the Fifth Generation project (1992). It would not have been possible to bring about this kind of "training effect" in any other way. Under the best conditions, universities cannot move this quickly, and in Japanese universities the best conditions do not obtain, since they tend to stand aloof from industry and its needs. MITI and the Ministry of Education are not historical allies. No matter what happens in Phases Two and Three of FGCS, the legacy of ten thousand trained engineers will be of immense value to Japan in the 1990s as knowledge technology reaches full adulthood.

We studied the Fifth Generation scene and had conversations with many Japanese industry managers and government officials. From these, we draw some summarizing views. The Fifth Generation project is widely admired, not necessarily for its technical achievements but for its boldness, its pursuit of innovation, its enthusiasm, and its drive—as we heard it put, "the spirit of ICOT." There is gratitude that FGCS got the ball rolling in applied artificial intelligence. The enthusiasm is infectious, but ICOT technology is not—yet. Those companies, even ICOT member companies, which are having successes with knowledge technology are making little or no direct use of the ICOT research results. For example, Fujitsu, the commercial AI leader in Japan, sells a Lisp machine of their own design (derivative from U.S. Lisp machines), not a Prolog machine; their expert systems shell, EShell, the best selling expert systems software in Japan, is Lisp-based and derives from Stanford University software. The Nippon Life Insurance expert system sketched in this book was developed using U.S. software on a U.S.-made Lisp machine. The Fifth Generation project has opened a new era of cooperation between university researchers and government-sponsored industrial research projects. While at the top the chill undoubtedly still exists, the "spirit of ICOT" at the working level has fostered scientific friendships and collaborations similar to those found in the government-industry-university cooperative efforts in the United States. Finally, Dr. Fuchi told us that "a turning point has been reached. Our computer manufacturers want more practicality. Our researchers want more advanced research." It is a classic dilemma. For now, at least, with its new Fifth Laboratory for Expert Systems, and its spinoff of EDR, ICOT seems to be moving in the direction of more practicality. ·

Expert Systems in Japanese Companies

"Japan is an engineer's paradise," observed Gordon Bell, noted computer architect and entrepreneur, and former vice president for engineering at DEC. In a paradox in which the new coexists with traditional Japanese forms and "style," the Japanese are technology addicts. The dawn of knowledge technology in Japan represents for many Japanese not just the latest in intriguing technology but the ultimate in technological prowess and promise. For fans of expert systems, it is fun to be in Japan these days to see Japanese firms excitedly experimenting with knowledge technology.

"Expert systems fever" has spread widely to hundreds of Japanese firms across the entire Japanese economy. Unsurprising are the applications in engineering-intensive industries, heavy machinery and materials industries, construction, chemicals, insurance, and financial services. More surprising are applications such as:

- the shopper's cosmetics advisor of Kao
- design of prefabricated homes by Sekisui
- advisor for newly opened liquor stores and restaurants by Suntory
- gift assortment advisor by Dai Nippon Printing (one has to understand the Japanese gift-giving tradition to appreciate the need for this)
- design of paper boxes by Toppan Printing
- work schedule planning for soybean growers by the Ministry of Agriculture, Forestry, and Fisheries
- production control system for potted flowers by the same ministry

Some of the leading expert systems vendors and developers have been discussed in this book. We could not include them all, but some deserve mention.

The earliest expert systems in Japan were done by Hitachi. In some cases, their work moved quickly from development to commercial use and sale. They produced early systems to assist steel making, to diagnose problems with municipal water systems, and to control train braking for passenger comfort. The train-braking system, which has been sold to several railways, including the train systems of the cities of Sendai and Sapporo, is a small but fascinating system. It was noticed that braking systems based on mathematical control theory were effective but not comfortable for riders. They were unpleasantly jerky. Interviews with the railway people revealed many rules of thumb, or heuristics in the jargon of expert systems, that people who brake trains manually use to smooth the rider's experience. Those were then incorporated into the Hitachi expert braking system by the knowledge engineers. Hitachi's nuclear division developed a complex and advanced expert system for nuclear power plant monitoring, but it has not been put into use. Hitachi also developed an expert system for Tokyo Electric Power that designs layouts for an electric power substation. Layout problems that previously took twenty-four hours to solve are now solved in two to three hours using the system.

Mitsubishi Electric rivals Fujitsu in the depth of its commitment to knowledge technology. In hardware and software offerings, it has adopted the role of technology transfer vehicle from ICOT to users. It developed the commercial version of the PSI machine and its software, SIMPOS. Mitsubishi's motivation to develop a wide variety of commercial expert systems arose from a simple observation. As they began to define for their internal use a variety of expert systems, they realized that most were not Mitsubishi-specific, that Mitsubishi was simply a microcosm of the economy, and that if the systems were valuable internally, they could form the basis of a new line of business.

NEC, a talented computer manufacturer, is marking time. Early on, its engineers produced a high-speed Prolog machine and several demonstration expert system applications. But the corporation, unlike Fujitsu, has not yet decided to commit to the new knowledge technology, so an unsettling confusion of goals and purposes exists at the working level.

IBM Japan got a slow start in expert systems but is now in high gear. The work is done at the IBM Research Laboratory in Tokyo. For internal manufacturing, it produced an expert system for the computer printer production line in Fujisawa. The system solves problems of allocating workers to positions on the assembly line based on various production factors that change from time to time, such as the number of subparts that have arrived, the number of printers to be produced, and the organization of the assembly cell. The expert system solves the problem in minutes, and overall reduces the number of workers needed by 10 percent. For a customer, NKK Steel, IBM built a system that schedules the movement of materials and products and does the assignment of workers to tasks. The expert system was put into operation in September 1987. It produces in half an hour a schedule that previously took ten hours to prepare, and saves the company 100 million yen per year (about $700,000).

Among Japan's construction industry giants we chose to feature Kajima's applications, but the other firms in the industry have been very active. Takenaka Komuten, for example, built a system to advise on the most appropriate utilization of land from knowledge of the land's environment, applicable laws, and profitability targets. Fujita is developing an expert system for management support in airport construction.

Similarly, in steel making we described the Nippon-Kokan blast furnace diagnosis system, but other steel companies have been building expert systems as well. The largest effort is at Nippon Steel, with four systems, including a system for diagnosing problems in a continuous smelting process.

In the transportation group, scheduling of personnel, for operations and for training, is a hot topic. Systems are under development at Japan Air Lines, All Nippon Airways, and Japan National Railways.

Both the Kyowa Bank and the Japan Federation of Bar Associations are at work on expert systems for advising about Japan's inheritance tax laws. The Central Research Institutes of the Electric Power Industry have developed an expert system that advises utilities operating dams on the repair-versus-replace decision for dam gates. This difficult problem is solved with knowledge of the dam gate's structure and the nature of corrosion present. The system obviates the need for expensive, time-consuming visits by specialists from the Research Institutes. Finally, nuclear power plant operations support and diagnostic systems are being built by an electric utility (Kansai Electric Power) and a systems company (Mitsubishi Atomic Power); a government agency (Power Reactor and Nuclear Fuel Development Corporation) has a system in support of operations for plutonium conversion facilities.

Expert Systems in Europe

The announcement of the Japanese Fifth Generation project generated deep anxiety in Europe. The Europeans were accustomed to hearing of bold, expensive technology initiatives from the Americans and had long since comforted themselves with a number two role. But the Japanese-European trade in key areas had eroded in favor of the Japanese (for example, in automobiles and cameras), and now the Europeans imagined a critical strategic erosion in the information-processing industry. In Britain, there was a special sense of irony. Britain had been a world leader in artificial intelligence in the 1960s, but a loss of confidence by the Science and Engineering Research Council had terminated most funding support for AI. The flow of students through university AI programs effectively ceased, creating quite literally a generation gap. In 1981 the British AI scientists could say (and did), "I told you so." On the Continent, AI research was scattered in a few isolated university centers and a handful of pioneering companies. So the anxiety felt by countries of the Continent was more the anxiety of the unknown than alarm.

Large-scale projects to counter the Japanese move were quickly set up. The European concern was broader than just AI, so the project goals were stated broadly to cover a range of information technologies. The British government repented of past sins by funding the Alvey project and its AI component, Intelligent Knowledge Based Systems. The primary purposes of the Alvey project were to provide funds to subsidize companies to educate themselves in the new technologies by doing—by attempting substantial projects, in teams and with university cooperation; and to repopulate the base of trained scientists and engineers by filling the university pipelines. Similar goals motivated the parliament of the European Economic Community to establish the ESPRIT project (European Strategic Program for Research in Information Technology), with considerably more funding than Alvey. As usual with things European, the terms were complex. Teams were required to be multinational, and connections with university groups were deemed to be of high priority. The ESPRIT proposal to the parliament was cast in terms of the fading presence of European companies, not only in the world market but even in supplying Europe's own needs. Minister D'Avignon of the EEC, addressing a conference in the Netherlands, used this familiar metaphor in closing his speech: "In information technology, the last boat is leaving. Europe has got to be on it."

Despite problems, Alvey worked. Industrial and commercial Britain came alive to the promise of knowledge technology, and university AI research and teaching were brought back to a reasonable state of well-being. Big projects, called "demonstrators," were launched and served to focus the efforts of disparate groups. The Alvey participants, with funding support, invented a cooperative mechanism similar to what the Japanese trading and banking groups provide in Japan. These were the Alvey "clubs," ad hoc associations in commercial sectors (for example, insurance) that organized common projects so that the members could teach each other how to build expert systems effectively.

The effects of the ESPRIT project are more difficult to sense, perhaps because the Continent, with its many countries, is more diffuse. ESPRIT supported many projects, some quite large (thereby absorbing most of the funds), but there were few in expert systems. EEC administrators prodded companies to adopt a greater spirit of multinational cooperation in the service of common purposes, instead of using ESPRIT money to push forward the companies' private research agendas.

Expert Systems in Britain—1987

Searching for expert systems in real use in Britain is like searching for clams at low tide. You've been told there are plenty hiding in the sand, most small but some of meal size. But it takes much digging to find just a few.

Britain is the land of the microcomputer-based (PC) expert

system. These are the rabbits that Ed Mahler of Du Pont champions. But nowhere is the dominance of the PC expert system so complete as in Britain. Why? Expert system shell vendors believe that British company managers are simply risk-aversive, and the smaller the outlay for hardware and software, the smaller the risk. They're willing to experiment with a technology, but not if it costs too much. But the focus on the small systems of limited functionality also limits one's vision of what can be accomplished with knowledge technology. Lists of British expert systems prepared by consultant firms overstate the number of expert systems actually in use. There are very few.

British Petroleum (BP), the computer manufacturer ICL, and the chemicals company ICI have systems that are among these few. Among BP's expert systems, the most widely publicized is an advisor for the design of gas/oil separators. Its use has returned cost savings of several million pounds per year. ICL has developed two systems for use. One of those solves the same configuration problem for ICL's Series 39 computers that DEC's XCON/XSEL solves for Vax computers. (DEC's systems are described in Chapter 11.) The time to configure a Series 39 machine has been reduced from several days to about one hour. No incorrect configurations have been noted, and the system is reported by ICL to save five million pounds per year. The other ICL system is an advisor to assist customers in doing their own capacity management in a data-processing installation. It is sold as a software product. ICI has developed many systems, but they are rabbits like Du Pont's. They deal with chemical judgments (for example, assessing corrosion behavior of certain alloys) and the manufacture of chemicals; but one widely publicized system deals directly with the public, advising farmers on crop diseases and their appropriate treatment with the chemicals that ICI sells.

Expert Systems in Western Europe

Brian Oakley, former head of Britain's Alvey project, said recently about the countries of the Continent that they have a strong academic tradition in artificial intelligence, but results have remained largely in the universities.

France has the most lively software industry in Europe, which would lead one to look for a lively French interest in expert systems. The approach to rationality taken by the knowledge engineers should also feel comfortable to the Cartesian minds of the French. Logic programming was invented in France in the early 1970s; the French have university centers of excellence for AI research in Paris, Marseilles, Grenoble, and Toulouse, among other places; and two very important companies with French roots did pioneering work in expert systems. The first, of course, is Schlumberger, whose story is told in Chapter 8. The other is the French national oil company, Elf. A third French company, Framatome, the atomic power plant manufacturer, actually forged an alliance with an American firm, Teknowledge, and started the first expert systems specialty company in Europe, Framantec, still one of the leaders.

The disappointing news is that few systems in France have emerged into regular commercial or industrial use. This is true even among the pioneers. Both Elf and Framatome have been very tentative about the exploitation of their early developments. Renault, however, has a system reportedly in regular use to assist mechanics in Renault repair shops in diagnosing and repairing a complex and usually unfamiliar part of the car: the automatic transmission (most French cars are manual shift). The system is distributed on microcomputers to the local Renault repair garage. The companies Aerospatiale Dassault and Airbus reportedly make use of expert systems for maintenance and design.

Germany is a puzzle. Until fairly recently, German work in artificial intelligence research was almost nonexistent. Now they are playing catch-up, with major experimental investments by the large German firms. But almost none of these systems has yet emerged into use. BMW and Mercedes have used an expert system for engine diagnosis experimentally. Consultants report that Siemens is the largest user of expert systems in Europe, with 40 projects and 150 to 200 people employed in knowledge processing. But none are visible. Nonetheless, the Germans are serious and moving fast.

Finally, Scandinavia. The Swedes have academic centers of excellence in artificial intelligence and a vigorous orientation toward industrial application. The success of a small company named Novacast, working originally in metallurgy and foundry technology, tells the Swedish story. In the early 1980s the company created three expert systems in their own area of expertise: foundry processes. Sales of these systems were good, and a fourth system, a casting defect analyzer, is their latest product. Since the technology seemed to them so powerful, Novacast established a new line of business in expert systems. They built an expert system to analyze postal rules, seeking the cheapest way (in the maze of regulations) to mail a particular parcel or type of shipment. It also tells what documents are needed. Costs savings to user companies range from 10 to 30 percent. Novacast builds systems for clients and distributes British expert system shells. Its customers are in metallurgy, steel, margarine manufacturing, banking, auto manufacturing, aircraft manufacturing, shipyards, and a long list of other industrial areas. Finland has begun its own small but bold "Fifth Generation" project, whose goal is to raise the level of national capability in what is regarded as a strategic technology well suited to Finnish talents and Finnish economic circumstances.

The United States, Japan, Europe: A Summing Up

The United States has great breadth and depth in the exploitation of knowledge processing. It has a deep reservoir of trained people, a university system that has geared itself up to produce many more, a managerial frame of mind that has allowed the technology to move swiftly into companies, a large government project, and an expert systems/knowledge-processing industry of innovative venture start-up firms supplementing (and often pushing) the large companies.

The Japanese have the Fifth Generation project and a highly receptive management outlook. The Japanese managers, like the Americans, are not reluctant to spend money to develop major projects. The Japanese are rapidly building their pool of talent. From an industrial viewpoint, they are rapidly closing the gap with the Americans.

The Europeans constitute too diverse a collection of managers, projects, and attitudes to allow simple generalizations. But two observations stand out. The first is the inclination of Europeans in the private sector to pursue small, low-cost, risk-free projects, usually developed and delivered on microcomputers. The second is the paucity of reported systems in actual use in 1988, an observation that of course could be an artifact of company confidentiality. Brian Oakley had this to say in 1987: "The European view is more pragmatic and geared toward short-term benefits. In the long term, the U.S. approach could lead to a widening of the competitive gap, as U.S. users will be better placed to develop large, high-payoff applications."

Chapter **11**

Restructuring a Business to Enlarge Customer Choice

THESE ARE NEW TIMES. Customers demand products that suit their individual needs, and businesses have to figure out some way of delivering those customized products cost-effectively. Trying to produce truly customized products inevitably leads to the combinatorial explosion, an attempt to connect so many pieces in so many different ways to meet differing demands that the human brain quails—and fails. Along with stress, costs rise stratospherically.

For Digital Equipment Corporation, this problem was at the heart of its minicomputer business. DEC decided to solve it—not by ignoring it, or by telling customers they couldn't have what they wanted, but by using expert systems to offer à la carte products.

Here is another example of a newly evolving corporate intelligence. Rudimentary now compared to what it someday will be, it is a community intelligence—it contains an amount of knowledge that no single human or group of humans can possibly know, and makes decisions about corporate processes based on that knowledge. In short, it solves problems that are too hard for people to solve. To be sure, the expert systems at DEC avoid costs—a configuration and sales expert system saves, as a conservative estimate, some $40 million a year. But to focus on that is to miss a more important point. DEC is the business of the future, an expert company that serves each customer individually—a thoughtful corporation in every sense of that phrase.

And lest anybody think this can only be done by a computer company, we also offer the story (for now, a story in progress) of that all-American icon, the highway truck, product of Navistar, a company that's also stepping smartly into the new age of thoughtful, flexible manufacturing.

Digital Equipment Corporation: The Complexity Problem

Try, for the moment, to think of Digital Equipment not as a computer company but rather as the manufacturer, seller, and servicer of a highly complex product, a product whose complexity is increased all the more with the company's policy that the customer can order it in a shape to suit himself.

It's a policy opposite from Henry Ford's—the customer, Henry Ford told us, could have any color Model T he wanted, so long as it was black. Ford was selling to the masses his mass-produced autos, every matching component interchangeable with every other, each ensemble indistinguishable from the next. He'd applied Adam Smith's notions about the division of labor and brought to auto manufacturing the assembly line, making cars and (as it happened) social revolution simultaneously.

But DEC's product is a set of boxes for processing information, in all its wondrous plasticity and variety. DEC's customers are individuals with very different aspirations, needs, circumstances, budgets, levels of competence, and expertise (so were Ford's customers, perhaps, but too bad for them). With such a product and such customers, the economic and time advantages of large-scale production must be married to bespoke tailoring; standard parts must be put together a new way every time. Furthermore, playing no small role in the drama, DEC is a highly decentralized company, even, some say, anarchical; it encourages a variety of approaches, risk-taking, innovation. It draws people who like to do it their own way and are impatient with direct orders. The corporate culture encourages small, temporary, low-overhead alliances, where workers explore a task together but then are just as likely to part and go off to do other things. In DEC's experience, people carrying ideas in their heads across organizational boundaries is the fastest, most efficient way to transfer technology.

Here, then, is the multi-billion-dollar New Age manufacturer: decentralized authority that shapes and is shaped by a network of diverse expert systems far greater than the sum of its considerable parts, all in the service of giving each customer exactly what he wants.

In 1981, with business doing well, the Vax family of midrange computers starting to sell briskly to a market that had been neglected by other manufacturers, a group engineering manager for worldwide systems manufacturing by the name of Dennis O'Connor (now the senior group engineering manager of the intelligent systems technologies group) began to think about where DEC's commitment to à la carte computing would place the corporation in the coming decade. He was stimulated to this in part by a series of discussions he and his colleagues had been having about the corporation's future.

O'Connor examined the major cycles of the business. Was there a way to improve, for instance, the order process cycle, where an order is taken, checked, scheduled, built, shipped, and then serviced? Could DEC live with the burgeoning number of final-assembly-and-test plants, or the number of technical editors (those specialists who check and modify computer configurations) that business growth required? No, the firm would have to have clean—that is, workable—orders from the outset, or it was dead.

An order might come in for six Vaxes of a certain configuration, and in the course of things, four of them would be built at one plant and two of them at another, with the individual plant deciding how the final system should look. All the products would work—in that sense the order was clean—but they'd be different, which would mean a big headache for the engineers who had to service them in the field. Not that they didn't have headaches enough already. In fact, where was the company going to find, or train, sufficient numbers of field engineers for its anticipated growth?

Without change, the firm might not survive.

The general solution O'Connor began to conceive grew out of a modest attempt, implemented the year before, to fix one important corporate bottleneck, the technical editing process. If the solution—an expert system called R1, to help edit computer configurations—could be expanded, that might be the solution to the whole order process cycle. If it couldn't, the future he saw would be very troubling indeed.

The new product line, the Vax family of minicomputers, promised success, yes; but in its very success lay corporate strangulation. So complex was the product, so further complicating was the process of customization, that every single order going out DEC's door had to be put together and tested on the factory floor before it was then disassembled, packed, and shipped to the customer. Of any hundred shipments, ninety of them would be different from each other. O'Connor foresaw five, perhaps six, new final-assembly-and-test plants to accommodate healthy corporate growth in the 1980s, and he thought there ought to be a better way than that. How, he wondered, could the manufacturing cycle time be shortened when the product was growing ever more complex?

The bottleneck O'Connor had already begun to fix a year earlier had been at the stage DEC calls "technical editing." This is where a sales rep's order (which might run from five lines to several thousand, depending on the system being sold) was checked by experts to see whether, in fact, the components actually all worked together, whether the sales rep had remembered to put in extra housing for extra components; whether, in fact, parts could be made, assembled at some point on the schedule, and shipped as promised. Automatic configuring programs were being used, but they couldn't keep abreast of the continuous changes being made. Over half the orders had to be changed in the technical editing stage, and a large number of those were so seriously flawed they required the sales rep to return to the customer and renegotiate, bad business in every way.

Yet this technical editing was exacting and challenging work for trained experts, editing not words but computer configurations, checking the grammar, so to speak, of orders as they came in to make sure they really worked, met all the rules that existed somewhere in the company about what could be configured and what couldn't.

And what happened to orders with problems? They sank into the reconfiguration cycle, delayed for one to two months. Later, the company might have to give equipment away if a customer had already been assured he could have a given configuration, and then extra backplanes or cabinets had to be added. You could even err in the other direction by overconfiguring: the customer would return the excess parts for a refund, and the company would have to try to sell them somewhere else. It was bad customer relations, and, historically, faulty configuration had been a significant drain on the company's profits.

As a possible solution to the technical editing bottleneck, an expert system hadn't immediately suggested itself. O'Connor's background was manufacturing; he didn't know that much about AI, and what he did know didn't thrill him. Still, his problem was real, and when Samuel Fuller, DEC's corporate vice president for research, suggested that research at Carnegie-Mellon University might be interesting and applicable, O'Connor remembers now that he thought he'd make a small investment. Using some discretionary funds earmarked for another project, he spent $60,000 to buy a few months of the time of John McDermott, a young professor of computer science at CMU, to see if an expert system was feasible to help with the technical editing problem.

"I chose that problem because tech editing would impact the whole food chain," O'Connor says. "Clean orders up front would have a large impact on every phase of the business from inventories to shipping." And although the major revenues of the firm were then coming from the PDP-11, the Vax family of computers was expected to provide DEC's major revenues during the 1980s, which is why the focus was on Vaxes.

But some of O'Connor's colleagues, particularly Gordon Bell, vice president for engineering and the chief architect of the PDP-11 and the Vax, and later the assistant director for computing at the National Science Foundation, remember that O'Connor ran an amazing risk. It took nerve, Bell says; O'Connor's reputation was on the line. "A few of us were involved, but ultimately it was Dennis going around with the tin cup. He got the sales organization involved, for instance." And that involvement of other segments of the corporation was going to prove to be important.

Carnegie-Mellon's John McDermott had been looking around for ways of applying artificial intelligence to real-world problems, away from the chess and the puzzle-solving and the arcane scientific applications university researchers had favored for AI testbeds up to then. He welcomed the chance to give it a try.

DEC's technical editing problem certainly had the right criteria: lots of messy detail that must be dealt with by rules of thumb and that, once automated, would have a big impact on the company's profits. He began to put together a prototype at CMU in December 1978. Since configuring a computer is an idea many industrialists can grasp, whereas the value of a chess-playing program, or even a program that can do spectrographic analysis, is more elusive, the configuration expert system (at its prototype stage called R1: "I always wanted to be a knowledge engineer, and now I are one," McDermott loved to say) began to get a fair amount of publicity early in its career. That had unforeseen effects of its own.

For McDermott, R1 was a memorable lesson in the difference between academic prototypes and real-world production systems. When, in April 1979, he and his team believed they had a system that worked with 95 percent accuracy on any problem they could think of giving it, they took it to the field. The system instantly swooned to only 80 percent accuracy. Chastened, they redesigned. By January 1980 the system had improved enough so it could begin to be used for all Vax orders. These days, just before order execution time in the manufacturing plants, the expert system assists the technical editors by revalidating an order and providing detailed configuration information about it, including spatial relationships among the order's components, additional components required to build the order, components that cannot be configured (and reasons why), switch settings for component addressing and vectoring, system cabling information, and unused system capacity.

As R1 moved from prototype to production, O'Connor thought it was appropriate for DEC to take it from its university researchers and assume responsibility for further system development. By now it was renamed XCON, for eXpert CONfigurator, and Ginny Barker, an econometrician out of M.I.T. who'd come to DEC a few years earlier as a senior-level analyst in management information systems, was put in charge of that move. "For a long time the Xcon group had been in a very loosey-goosey R&D mode, and it was time to get into a serious production mode, which is a different way of operating if the company is dependent on you. That's the change we've made over the past four years," she says.

In the next few years Xcon became so deeply embedded in corporate operations that DEC executives say if Xcon were turned off the company would feel the impact within three days: it wouldn't be able to sell its product. A number of products are so complicated and their volume so high that DEC factories simply refuse to build them unless they've been processed by Xcon, a message that has had its impact.

"In our business, we're always dealing with exceptions. And expert systems handle exceptions superbly well," O'Connor says.

In 1987 Xcon processed some eighty thousand orders (up from fifty thousand the year before, and up from four thousand the year Xcon was introduced), although this represents only the product lines Xcon knows about: DEC's total annual orders, including sales of other lines, are confidential. Xcon knows about some twenty-four families of central processing units, and it knows about more than twenty thousand hardware and software entities. It's used worldwide, which introduces another level of complexity, because different configuration issues appear overseas—different power, which makes the configuration different; different metrics;

and different traditions in the ways of doing business. By mid-1987 Xcon was being used by DEC's Galway, Ireland, and Ayr, Scotland, plants and would soon be used by other plants abroad.

As DEC's products change, Xcon undergoes related changes. For example, these days DEC sells clusters of computers instead of single computers: Xcon now reflects that difference. Keeping a big, dynamic system up to date with current knowledge—the task of knowledge base maintenance—is a major issue in expert system projects. DEC spends $2.5 million per year on the maintenance of the Xcon/Xsel suite of programs and employs fifteen people to do the work.

Beyond Configuration

But before all this happened, before expert systems had proved themselves in a corporate structure, O'Connor and his colleagues had spent a fair amount of time in 1981 avidly discussing the ten-year future of the company. Where should DEC really be five years, ten years, from now? Was there a better way to go from a new concept to a new product than the way it was being done?

Even as McDermott had begun solving the configuration problem, both he and O'Connor realized that this was only part of a larger problem. Moving in either direction from configuration, you ran up against difficulties, dealing with the sales force in one direction, or in the other, with what manufacturers call sourcing, exploding the order down to the most basic components that must be manufactured and assembled to fill an order.

The larger problem, in a word, was knowledge. Never mind the factory of the future, O'Connor said to his colleagues as they met in 1981 for a day to consolidate their year-long discussions and set a course for DEC in the coming decade: Imagine the business of the future; imagine the knowledge network. It was elegantly simple in concept: a smooth-flowing loop of information that connected the customer to marketing and sales, which then connected to order administration, to manufacturing, to distribution, and back to the customer. In the center of this loop were two functions, engineering and customer/field service, which connected in spoke fashion to each of the outer points of the loop.

But if the concept was simple, the implementation was something else again. O'Connor's year or so of success with Xcon as a production system, a system actually working in the real world every day, rather than a prototype, had been very visible across the corporate structure. The risks had been taken and were past, it seemed; at least one expert system was a proven thing, and the small group of expert system developers at DEC were backlogged with requests. O'Connor suggested that the integration of expert systems across the corporation was one answer to getting the knowledge network under way. The question was which, of the many functions that were clamoring for attention, should get the next expert systems treatment.

It was plain that Xcon didn't address the problem of how to get a clean order in the first place. And the reason so many bad configurations came in was because the sales reps just didn't know enough about putting orders together. Partly that was because the sales force was changing; instead of engineers, it was now predominantly business types. But with twenty thousand saleable parts, it was really asking the impossible for anybody to stay on top of them all, especially when DEC went through one of its periodic major product changes. Corporate sales knew this was a problem. Indeed, as Dennis O'Connor had been going around with his tin cup to get support for what was then a very unproven concept, corporate sales had been the second largest contributor to invest in Xcon.

And so, in January 1981, just as DEC was taking over responsibility for development of Xcon, research for Xsel was begun at CMU. It wasn't enough to send an order back to a sales rep saying it had to be fixed, which is what Xcon did. Instead, sales reps needed help putting together clean orders in the first place. Xcon might keep you from doing dumb things, like building things that didn't work, or that had to be rebuilt, but it didn't fix the order-processing cycle.

Xsel could. It was closely coupled with Xcon, invisibly checking orders for validity and then presenting a graphical document of a working system. At least it was supposed to do all that once in place. But it had to be a system that would work for thousands of salespeople, each with an individual style, a different way of working with customers; it had to be a system that would work for novice sales reps as well as for veterans. In July 1981 a research prototype was tested, and in October that year a user group was organized to advise the designers. These were the people who'd actually be using the system, sales managers and sales reps who faced the problems day in and day out; they got to set the priorities, choose the trade-offs. The first thing they asked for was accuracy; don't embarrass us, they said, by giving our customers bad configurations. Whenever the design group talked about smooth interfaces, fancy graphics, the users said, No, never mind if it means compromising the accuracy in any way. Stick to the basics.

By July of 1982 DEC had taken over development from McDermott and his team, and in October that year field testing for Xsel began.

Getting Xsel in place was something else again. Bruce Macdonald, then the Xsel program manager, remembers sitting at a meeting the very month field testing was beginning for Xsel, October 1982, with several vice presidents and other senior executives. He was already feeling a bit intimidated by the surroundings and the generally towering seniority when the vice president for sales eyed him and said: "You've been working on this thing for three years now. Isn't it ready?"

Xcon and Xsel had been receiving splendid publicity, so it might seem as if three years' work had gone into them, but by most measures, the systems were barely out of the prototype stage. The development group had taken over Xcon from the academics less than two years earlier, and had taken over Xsel only three months before.

Macdonald started to protest that the publicity far outweighed the accomplishments, but the vice president for sales wasn't about to stop. He asked a hardware man about sales terminals: "How soon can we have one on every sales rep's desk? Three months?"

The hardware man turned to Macdonald: could he have the software up and running in three months? Macdonald, white-haired, with striking blue eyes, obviously the product of millennia of ancestors who marched through the gorse, bagpipes skirling, tugged at his big white mustache and said, uh, he thought they'd better talk it over in their group. He suspected if he said no outright, the funding would be cut off, but he saw eight, not three, months of work ahead.

The vice president for sales was gleeful: "Good, we'll have this out by Christmas, a Christmas present for the sales force." Macdonald was thinking, This is my Christmas goose, cooked.

Nothing went according to plan. The hardware wasn't ready by that Christmas after all; it needed another year, given the cost of computing in 1982 and 1983. And there were really no alternatives to the sales terminal: communication costs prohibited the program from being run centrally with lines reaching out to the individual sales offices, and anyway, the system didn't respond very well in such a time-shared environment. They tried a portable terminal, but it didn't work well and wasn't a great success. What was really needed, but wouldn't be available until four or five years later, was a powerful micro-Vax in the district offices or wherever the sales reps worked.

Xsel began as a program with over two thousand rules, some of them shared with Xcon. By mid-1987, its rules now doubled, it was being used by between 25 and 30 percent of the sales force worldwide, with that use projected to climb over the next five years to 100 percent, yielding, by the most conservative estimates, a $40 million return over those five years from the U.S. sales force alone, although worldwide returns will actually be much more. Xsel reduces the time a salesperson takes to do a configuration from between one and three hours to about fifteen minutes. Orders come in accurately through Xsel 99 percent of the time, as compared to 70 percent of the time without it. Frank Lynch, the group engineering manager of Advanced Systems and Tools at DEC's AI Technology Center in Hudson, says, "That 29 percent difference is what lets us stay in business." Xsel is particularly helpful in the huge, complex orders that stretch human minds to the breaking point; thus in 1987, though only between 25 and 30 percent of the entire Vax order flow went through Xsel, that represented 80 percent of the income flow.

Despite Xsel's obvious advantages, it wasn't adopted immediately and universally for a number of reasons, and they deserve some examination. Perhaps the most important is that, given the DEC corporate culture, nobody was compelled to use the new system. "We're a carrot company, not a stick company," Macdonald says. Thus if the job could be done the old way, it generally was, habit being the most difficult of human behaviors to change.

"People don't like to change their procedures, they really don't," Ginny Barker says. "Though you identify the usefulness of the tool for them, and they agree the tool is very useful, they'll still demand that the procedure they've always had continue to be followed until you can convince them they're doing something they don't have to do."

In addition, everybody remembered some of the early hard times with Xcon/Xsel. At one point, when it was on the verge of gaining widespread acceptance, some implementation problems came up: the system would break down at a critical moment, or the performance would suddenly degrade, and even the most enthusiastic users felt betrayed. The skeptics nodded knowingly and continued with pencil and paper.

What gave Xsel its biggest boost was not a spectacular improvement in the system (though it was and continues to be steadily improved) nor a perception that in the long run it would help improve sales productivity ("Our sales offices are probably the least automated part of our business," one DEC engineer says, "and I bet that's true in most companies"). Instead, Xsel's salvation was external. A series of changes in the product base almost totally transformed it within nine months, and salespeople were forced to use the system, which was continually updated, just to find out what was happening. Suddenly they loved Xsel; almost every piece of equipment being ordered was new, but they didn't have to memorize all that, the machine had it.

Now they saw that even if Xsel didn't save them great amounts of time, it improved the quality of time spent generating an order. The AI gurus at DEC's Hudson facility might be able to show that the usual one-to-three hours had dropped to fifteen minutes for doing a configuration, but the sales reps saw it differently: in the same amount of time they'd once spent doing a configuration manually to satisfy a customer's requirements, they could suddenly generate two or three different configurations, give the customer a real choice. They could think of optimal configurations instead of merely workable ones. A nifty new addition to Xsel also pleased them and their customers: another little expert system appended to the main system did floor layouts of the equipment so that the customer could visualize how it would all look at his site. Customers, the sales reps felt, responded very positively to this much more professional way of doing business.

And the success stories were assiduously circulated. There was the midwestern guy who'd sold a huge order to a university, only to hear that big changes were needed in the configuration, and needed the next day, to present to a monthly trustees' meeting. Thanks to Xsel, he was able to get the documents in front of the trustees in time. Huge, complex orders were being won because DEC could guarantee the systems would be delivered on time and would work. People were beginning to ask how they'd got along without this tool. The Xcon/Xsel systems, with over ten thousand total rules, now generate sound orders. But all orders don't come in that way. Sometimes a sales rep doesn't have access to a machine (sometimes it's not available personally, or not available when the order is called in); some reps are just "too macho to use the system," in the words of one DEC developer. But in the next five years that will change, and the least automated part of the company will automate even as everybody else has. However, in the district where DEC's biggest customer is found, Xsel has been mandated by the regional sales manager; for one thing, that customer insists on the Xsel/Xcon output for its own peace of mind. When customers don't ask for it, the documentation often finds its way into the files of the field engineers for guiding future maintenance.

DEC's own most conservative estimates are that, including maintenance and systems quality-control costs, the collection of Xcon/Xsel programs saves the company about $40 million per year. This figure includes the savings realized by not building the five or six new final-test-and-assembly plants that O'Connor had foreseen the company would need to keep up with growing sales, and includes the costs of hiring and training new technical editors. O'Connor estimates it would take hundreds of new technical editors to handle the volume of orders DEC does today. Instead, the numbers have remained about the same as they were prior to Xcon, but each technical editor processes at least ten times as much business as he or she did before.

DEC executives anticipate new business opportunities with Xcon/Xsel; already very large customers have expressed interest in accessing the systems for reconfiguring and adding to their own computer layouts, and experiments are under way permitting OEM's, the firms that repackage DEC products under their own names, to try out Xcon/Xsel.

The Bigger Picture

On the utility of artificial intelligence, specifically expert systems, there's been a gradual dawning at DEC rather than a sudden conversion. At the highest levels of the company, a commitment has been made to expert systems and artificial intelligence in general as a new and very important way of doing business; it's now a corporate strategic goal for this $9-billion-a-year company, named among the United States' most competitive "lean and mean" corporations in a recent *Business Week* cover story.

Expert system implementation is under way everywhere; in sales, for example, AI programs are used in training courses and in management analysis; in manufacturing, the order process cycle has been described, but AI systems also control shop and factory schedules and other operations; an expert system exists for strategic planning, including planning the growth of the work force. New products are being planned.

But DEC's history with expert systems isn't a tale of non-stop success. Some areas, such as planning and scheduling, haven't noticeably yielded to expert system treatment, though prototypes were designed and built.

Still, from the ten major expert systems in place, Dennis O'Connor estimates that DEC realizes $70 million a year in materials and time savings and cost avoidance. "A nice return on my original $60,000 investment," he says.

However, DEC has deliberately adopted a strategy that aims not so much to change existing systems as to make them gradually "smarter," the better to serve customers. Everyone knew that direct labor down on the shop floor had largely been driven out of the equation. Across American manufacturing, the general rule of thumb is that direct labor, "touch" work, only accounts for about one third of corporate costs. Even if "touch" costs are driven to zero, nontouch, or indirect, labor and support still represent the other two thirds. The manufacturing population won't grow, but the support—the nontouch workers'—population is growing, and the support structure has to change faster; that's where opportunities are seen to lie for working smarter. DEC now makes commitments in monthly increments: it can promise a customer a system in April, or May, or June; but it hopes to get down to weekly, and then daily commitments, aiming, its people say confidently, to be the best firm to do business with.

An "AI Board of Directors" has been set up, composed of all the vice presidents (of manufacturing, field services, marketing, engineering) plus Sam Fuller, the vice president for corporate research. The board decides what makes sense strategically for the company. For example, all internal applications are aligned with major business goals, such as shortening the order process cycle or transforming a concept into a new product. DEC's planners are asking how AI can help manage the business, both at an operations level in a two-year period and at a strategic level in a three-to-five-year period.

At the Hudson facility, a 1970s concrete office building on a hilltop, its hallways bright with paintings, sculpture, and primary-color supergraphics, its denizens tweedy and rumpled as any on a university campus, an AI center has been formed where some three hundred people are at work on AI projects. They report to the AI center manager, Scott Flaig, as well as to their functional vice presidents, and working together at Hudson makes sure they all talk to each other. An equal number outside the center are working on AI, too, including some sites abroad: France, England, Japan, and Australia. The center's mission is research *and* technology transfer: "We want to get this technology into the hands of everybody around DEC who's had problems, because we've been starting to see that this stuff really works," says Frank Lynch.

Nevertheless, DEC imposes some constraints on AI development. For example, engineers who want to learn AI techniques can't just sign up for the company training; they must have a specific application in mind to undertake, which also requires their manager's sponsorship. "We just can't afford to go off solving problems that aren't important," Lynch points out. Moreover, every system that's built must have a corporate sponsor, someone who signs the paycheck, whose word has weight, somebody who can legitimize change. In addition, there must also be an advisory group made up of users to tell the designers what real needs are. This also ensures what DEC calls buy-in, meaning that users will not only advise realistically but will also have high personal commitment to the system, a working knowledge of exactly how it's going to help the company's business. That also helps eliminate not-invented-here resistance.

But at lower levels, people suspect—and to a certain extent, correctly— that Xcon/Xsel and other expert systems will impose a kind of uniformity that DEC has never had before, and the prospect makes more than a few people nervous.

Cynthia Lund, the user support manager for Xcon, whose job is to find out from users what they want, was running into this nervousness continually in 1987. DEC people wanted to do things their own way, the way they'd always done them, but as Xcon was spreading out through the company, well beyond the technical editing stage and into manufacturing and other places, it was getting clearer that doing things your own way might eventually be less easy.

And something else was happening with the wider use of these tools. As Lund moved out among Xcon users to find out what they wanted, she discovered that much of the unhappiness with Xcon that appeared to be caused by flaws in the tool was really caused by flaws in the larger business process that Xcon exposed.

For example, the technical editors would sometimes look at an Xcon configuration and say it wasn't right, based on other documents and sources of information they used regularly. But analysis would show that Xcon *was* right; its information was current, whereas the technical editors had relied on a variety of sources for information, not all of them current or correct.

If the Xcon/Xsel group had it to do all over again, one thing they'd change would be the initial relations between themselves and the plants. Certain of DEC's plants resisted Xcon in the beginning because it seemed to impose what they perceived as unnecessary and pesky regularities. Ginny Barker remembers doing missionary work on behalf of Xcon, telling plant managers how useful it was, and hearing about one plant where the tool wasn't useful. "When we looked into it, it turned out they were using Xcon. But their manufacturing process was very different from that used in the other plants. This had a clear impact on their view that the tool was cumbersome for them to use effectively. The point is, if you didn't have a good solid relationship going with the user base, then you wouldn't know they had a different process out there, and they wouldn't be getting any advice on how to work the tool into the process they had; they'd just be hearing how other people used it; they'd try to use it that way, and it wouldn't work out. So we'd have done that differently—and we did for Xsel."

Then she stops to reflect: "Oh, perhaps we'd have done

many things differently, but Xcon was the first thing, so how could we have done it differently? We learned a lot of the lessons that make what we do now so good."

Navistar: The Phoenix of the Rust Belt

A truck is just a truck to most people. It hauls everything from steel to produce along the highways, and is central to the mythology that endures around the trucker and his life on the open road. But the uneducated eye would be astonished to see that well beyond the gross differences between flatbed or refrigerated, semitrailer or tanker, trucks come in an almost infinite variety, depending on the cargo they're intended to haul, the conditions they'll be working under, and the desires of the individual owner.

What makes truck design and manufacturing so complicated isn't just that cabs can come on top of the engines or behind them; or that engines can be of varying horsepower; or that the number of axles and wheels depends on the truck length and loading. What makes it so complicated is that a change in one component cascades through other related components—a certain kind of chassis must have a special hole in just the right place for mounting a certain kind of air conditioner, and if it isn't there, the chassis has to be pulled out of production and sidelined until the hole can be drilled, a delay that causes ripples up and down the assembly line, affecting the suppliers, ruining schedules.

Navistar has been manufacturing trucks for years, originally under its old name of International Harvester. In the early 1980s the company was bashed from all sides—not only by the general circumstances of corporate contractions prevailing just then in the United States but also by multiple shocks that hit its particular products, trucks and farm machinery, with special impact: energy shortages, agricultural gluts, domestic trucking deregulation, economic instability in the foreign markets where the firm had traditionally done well (the Middle East, South and Central America), and foreign competition at home.

Yet even as memorials were being read in the press for International Harvester, R.I.P., an energetic manager of North American truck operations named Neil Springer (who would subsequently be named CEO of Navistar International Transportation Corporation, the new name for the operations portion of the corporation's new life) was urging everybody to use all the imagination they had to save the company.

One who took him at his word is John Bowyer, staff vice president for information systems services at Navistar. Bowyer has worked at the company for nearly thirty years, is approaching retirement and frankly looking forward to it; for years he's been commuting daily from his suburbs-of-Chicago executive job to his farm in Indiana to look after his prize herd of cattle, and he happily anticipates full-time cattle raising. The salubrious life shows on him—he's a trim, ruddy-faced, Clark Gable lookalike.

But in the early 1980s, what should have been a pleasant glide toward retirement suddenly threatened to be a head-on crash with unemployment.

Bowyer watched his company undergo a painful set of changes. In 1980, the company needed one manufacturing employee for every 6.1 trucks it made in a year; by 1986 each manufacturing employee was producing 13.1 trucks a year. In 1981 inventory had amounted to 108 days' supply; by 1987 that had dropped to 28 days' supply. Navistar began buying from fewer suppliers, but controlled them more carefully for quality; and kept an open mind for arrangements with others.

But John Bowyer worried that all this wouldn't be quite enough. It was doing the same thing much better, but it was, after all, the same thing. Was that really enough for a whole new world of trade? How could his company gain a competitive advantage? How could it offer a buyer exactly what he wanted in the way of an incredibly complex product like a truck? How could a salesman price that custom product, how could the company know ahead of time what it was going to cost to manufacture, when some twenty thousand parts had to be taken into consideration, and every choice made cascaded throughout the machine's structure, meaning that hundreds of details had to be just right?

How could the company offer, not necessarily à la carte trucks, but a much wider choice of trucks than it was offering (Navistar is already the largest manufacturer of custom trucks), buildable trucks, taking into consideration what it had material for, what the assembly line was engineered for? In short, how could it offer its customers cost-effective custom trucks with consistently high quality?

There was the central problem.

The expert system to help master the problem is one that Bowyer calls a "truck specification system" (or, in a wider view, a product specification system). He gives four main reasons why the system is being built:

- the need for a strong (indeed, novel and unique) orientation to customer needs
- the need to capture and standardize the core knowledge of Navistar's truck engineers
- the need to reduce errors "upstream" of the manufacturing floor
- the need to reduce the complexity that attends the introduction of a new part

As the head of Navistar's data processing, Bowyer breaks the stereotype of the fusty, cautious character we've seen so often in data-procesing departments. For one thing, he keeps himself informed, and when a visitor came by from SRI International, a consulting firm, and described something called artificial intelligence, Bowyer was intrigued. However, he needed to understand it all better, how it contrasted with classical management information systems. Because he's a man who pays attention to detail, he took himself and a colleague to a day-long seminar on the AI language Prolog, and then to a week's course in AI techniques.

Bowyer said later, "I just got converted. I had an in-body experience there, and it really turned me on—at least to the point that I thought that the methodologies of AI held promise." Pause. "Even some of the things that were being oversold had some truth to them if you just didn't sign up on the first day of conscription."

He came back and persuaded his management to make a million-dollar investment. He mentions it almost offhandedly, yet it gives an outsider pause: Dennis O'Connor had to filch his first $60,000 for DEC's expert system from another project; Ken Lindsay and Bob Joy of Northrop Aircraft grew pale at the idea of $100,000.

But John Bowyer has the persuasive powers to walk away from Neil Springer, Navistar's chairman, with a million dollars, and anybody in the same room with him understands it instantly. This is a master rhetorician, a voice of endless nuance, one part Old Vic, one part tent evangelist, one part spellbinder.

Still, a million dollars. And for once, the project Bowyer was proposing wasn't prepared by the book, with a business plan, financial analysis, projected cost savings and detailed quality improvement, and so on.

He's intense: "People involved know the problem's got to be fixed. The chairman of the company *knows* the problem's got to be fixed. We"—he gestures around the room—"have made no commitment. We have sized the job—and we're probably wrong. Looking at the technology, I was convinced that if ever this problem is solvable, it's now. I told my boss, Neil Springer: *This can be done.*"

Bowyer began Navistar's expert systems efforts by trying to put together a small demonstration system with a couple of knowledge engineers and a domain expert to determine the manufacturing process for a part in a truck's electrical system. Solving that problem would prove to the company, he believed, that AI had applications in their world, "isn't clairvoyancy." The first system was exciting, and behaved more consistently than the human experts who'd supplied the knowledge. "It's going to do more than we promised." Then he laughs. "That's not 'cause we underpromised. It's just that we didn't know what lies to tell! We know a little more what lies to tell now, and that—that may be our undoing."

Meanwhile, he began trying to hire people with experience in expert systems. He found Jay Yusko, who'd worked on expert systems at AT&T, and Scott McIntyre, a young engineer who'd worked with Bob Joy and Ken Lindsay at Northrop. He told them to start hiring until he said stop.

So that all work wouldn't be done in-house, another part of the million dollars was put on a second horse in case the jockey fell off the first one, as Yusko puts it. The second horse is an outside vendor, IntelliCorp, which helped build the underlying AI software for the big expert system. It will be nothing less than a DEC-style configurator, but for trucks instead of computers, that will issue precise orders to the factory and to suppliers for just-in-time manufacturing. Bowyer has midwifed that system's birth.

In late 1987 it wasn't at all clear that the effort would succeed. "I'm not certain we're bright enough," Bowyer would say thoughtfully. He meant bright enough to solve the problem, bright enough to keep his newfound AI people challenged. All that. But he was certain the job could be done by somebody. He wanted it to be his people, his company. He hoped for success with the full knowledge that he might fail. ("Let's say we have a very heavy correlation between my retirement date and the proficiency of that system.")

The system Bowyer envisaged will do more than just organize the building of a truck. It will permit the customer and the sales rep to sit down at a terminal and design exactly the truck the customer wants, if Navistar has the parts to make it. It's a configuration and sales system that's a first cousin to DEC's Xcon/Xsel, informing the customer of the precise cost and delivery date. Later, it will be able to sell a customized insurance policy for exactly that truck and propose customized financing. Unlike the other expert systems we've described, Navistar's is a system-of-promise—not yet, in 1988, a system-in-fact. The full-scale prototype will be running on a Lisp machine in the fall of 1988. The introduction into factory use will take place in April of 1989 at a small Navistar factory in Ontario, Canada, that manufactures their top-of-the-line 9370 truck, a kind of pilot run for the later and broader use across all their truck lines. When complete, the expert system will contain about six thousand rules. It is built using a version of KEE specially customized for Navistar.

What's the capability of the first system? Like DEC, Navistar has sales reps who take customer orders and "order coders" who make sure that each order reflects a buildable truck. The order coders fill in missing parts, correct errors, and if an order is too confused send it back to the sales rep. The order coders face the same basic problem DEC's technical editors faced: complexity. There could be as many as twenty thousand different parts involved. If for some reason a different engine transmission is needed, all of a sudden the frame has to be different, brackets have to be different, bolts have to be different, and they in turn cause other changes.

With the expert system the order coder enters the two to three dozen order entries to the system, and it determines whether the truck is buildable nor not. If some order entries are not compatible—for example, the power requirement to drive a transmission cannot be met by the engine ordered—it will list other engines that would do the job. From the list, the order coder can select his favorite. Once the truck is deemed buildable, the system will do material explosion and list all the parts needed for the truck, down to the number of nuts, bolts, and washers. Each part is identified with a name, the manufacturer, the part number, the quantity required, and so on. In addition to making the complex order process simple and accurate, it allows the customer to try what-if games of truck design, optimizing his order.

Bowyer likes the word *courage*, and uses it often. Asked what it means, he defines it in terms of the situation: It takes courage for the chairman to put so much money into expert systems when other problems also need attention and that million dollars. It's a word he learned the meaning of in the difficult times the company went through in the early 1980s.

"It takes courage to do the unusual, to *not* take the comfortable route. Many of the people running our company today exemplified, in the most trying moments, a great deal of courage, and came out of those experiences with a willingness to take risk and pursue an advantage. . . . And then this opportunity came along."

He's hired a scientist to work on voice recognition; he's examining neural net computers. "Once you develop this cadre of AI experts, you've got to keep them challenged. We just can't stop at present stuff." He muses: "I want this company to be there. I want these people to be there, *the day before it breaks* and prepared to use it, knowledgeable, involved in it. We can't wait till you can go down to Computerland and buy it. There's no competitive edge in that!"

Jay Yusko says, "John not only goes to courses, he reads a lot of books, watches tons of videos, so he keeps up. Sometimes I hate for him to see something new because then, all of a sudden we have heavy assignments, new projects."

Later, Bowyer would reflect on his role. An AI champion, he'd tell the National Computer Conference in 1987, needs courage—*in abundance*—because to introduce AI is often to tread where there are no footprints. An AI champion must clearly seperate the hype from the reality, must be able to distinguish vendor product from vendor prototype, to distinguish demo from real demonstration of capability. An AI champion must be charismatic to the technical people in his firm, and must be credible high enough in the organization to command peer respect. Finally, the AI champion must be a risk taker, willing to go into uncharted areas. If every venture in your corporation must early on be 100 percent successful, then you're in big trouble.

Yet Bowyer now walks a very fine line between cutting-edge research and the demands of staying in business. "I never want to lose understanding of what it takes to stay in business; that's been brought home very clearly the last few years. Those who passed the course understand what it takes to stay in business. That, I hope, is the vision that we've gained. But maybe going forward I can play more the role of being an academician in business—without credentials— to help encourage and incite and direct people and projects toward new ends. That's the new role that perhaps I didn't pursue vigorously in the past." He speaks gratefully of Neil Springer, who let him do that, unafraid to shed the old ways.

"Having survived the traumas of this company, you want so much for it to realize what it expects of itself now."

Chapter 12

Stimulating Innovation Through "Working Smarter"

WE'VE POINTED OUT the earliest stages of the evolution of the expert company. We've summed the money saved, the expertise preserved, the new business developed, and a host of other advantages accruing from expert systems. We conclude our case studies with two companies (both Japanese, perhaps significantly) that have begun to implement expert systems for reasons that include but transcend all the reasons other companies use them. To be sure, both companies are capturing precious expertise and realizing significant short-term savings. But these seem trifling savings over the long perspectives these companies maintain. Much more important, both companies are looking ahead, infused with the belief that the most profound effect of expert systems for them will be the fast innovation of design that the technology permits—in one case for camera lenses, in the other for large-scale construction methods.

Interestingly, both companies began their experiments with expert systems thanks to the vision of one or two mid-level employees who worked independently to explore this technology, evaluate it, and bring it into the company.

Canon

The Canon Research Laboratories, in a lovely suburban valley ringed by mountains in Atsugi, Japan, conducts the research for one of the largest and most successful of the Japanese optical products companies: Canon, Inc. As everyone knows, following World War II the Japanese gradually invaded and then won a market that Europeans (especially Germans) once called their own: the market for high-performance cameras. Japan continues to dominate this market, and Canon is credited with some of the earliest and most significant innovations in the Japanese camera industry.

For the past fifteen years, Canon's corps of eighty lens designers has used a conventional computer-aided design system to help produce both still and television camera lens designs. The CAD system runs on a Hitachi mainframe and is accessed by some fifty terminals. (As it happens, the first Japanese domestic computer, the FUJIC, was motivated by lens design problems.) The CAD system has evolved over the years and is now extremely elaborate: 300,000 lines of Fortran code. During the process of lens design the designers use the system for complicated calculations of ray tracing, calculating the path light will take through a combination of glass and air from the object to the film or the retina.

A zoom lens, for example, consists of many pieces of glass in precise configuration so that the rays bend correctly. In such a lens design, there are between fifty and seventy different variables to control; designers must find different configurations to satisfy the different optical goals of the various instruments, using the CAD system to assess how well a given combination of optical glass and air performs.

But in the early 1980s Toshiaki Asano, himself a lens designer, began to wonder whether the CAD system was enough. There was certainly no pressing need to worry. Unlike Northrop, Canon wasn't having trouble finding expert designers, and unlike Navistar, Canon hadn't at all suffered from hard times. Indeed, everything seemed to be going well for the company—it was preparing to move into its award-winning research center, a luxurious building by

Japanese standards, especially with its "quiet room"—soundproof carrels with windows that look out to the mountains, where people can come to sit, think, and write, away from the normal pandemonium of Japanese engineering rooms.

But insofar as lens design went, it struck Asano that very little had changed in the basic methods designers used. "I saw technological revolution everywhere. But lens designers had been using essentially the same technology for over ten years. We do it better now, but that's due to progress made in computer hardware—bigger memories, faster cycles—but the basic way we do things hasn't changed. I worried that the lens designer would be left behind, his lot never improved!"

This dissatisfaction, this worry, led him to start looking for a new technology for his lens designers. Asano himself wasn't a technologist—he'd been a scientist and was now a manager—but he was eager to find some new ideas to help his designers do their jobs better. His search eventually brought him to a book by Professor Fumio Mizoguchi, of Tokyo Science University, called *Introduction to Knowledge Engineering*.

He read the book with growing excitement, and then went to call on Professor Mizoguchi. The whole idea of expert systems, he explained, seemed very interesting, but would such a system be applicable to lens design? He hoped Mizoguchi would be enthusiastic, for to Asano, expert systems looked like the breakthrough technology he'd been looking for. If it was, he was eager to get going. Mizoguchi listened and nodded, encouraged Asano to pursue it, and eventually became a kind of consultant to the project. In 1983 work was begun at Canon Research on an expert system for lens designers, and in 1985 prototype testing began.

And so for the past few years an expert system called Optex has been developing at Canon for the TV camera development division. At present, Optex assists a human lens designer with the detailed internal design of a zoom lens—the configuration of glass pieces that will achieve an optical goal and be manufacturable. The designer states a goal to the system, and Optex gives shape to the concept—

works out the details and presents a design to the designer. It knows about manufacturability and how to run the complicated ray-tracing CAD system, and it can evaluate its own design.

For example, the designer might begin by specifying a certain type of zoom lens. He then says to the system, Modify the lens configuration such that the focal length of the second bloc is changed from -15 to -20. Optex uses its knowledge base to provide actual details about the nature and the arrangement of different pieces of glass that must go into the lens to achieve that goal. The knowledge base knows about handling some forty to fifty different conventional lens types. In the course of trying to meet the designer's goal, it will run into different kinds of optical problems. Some have to do with glass thickness (too thin, and it can't be manufactured, too thick and it won't fit the casing) or with glass shape (certain shapes bounce rays back instead of transmitting them forward), or light being transmitted forward will be transmitted at an incorrect angle, or marginal contact between two pieces of glass won't work properly to bend the light. Optex can correct those errors and come up with a workable lens system design. It then generates the information needed to test and evaluate its design using the Fortran CAD ray-tracing program.

In its first year of use, Canon was able to document a twelvefold gain in productivity for the lens designers who use the system.

Canon calculates its gains in five ways. First, time is saved. Optex permits the designer to discover limitations in a design concept and switch to a new concept much earlier than with the old CAD system alone. The second way Canon gains is from optimizing: A design might be good but not optimal in terms of cost/performance; with the expert system, many more design points can be explored more systematically in a shorter period of time, permitting an optimum combination of glass materials. Third is a savings in automated generation of patent data, and fourth is a savings in programming cost by reuse of old designs or their subsets. Finally, Optex creates the opportunities for design trials that were simply too costly before.

For example, using an existing zoom lens design as a prototype to be modified, a lens was to be reduced in size but was to preserve the same optical performance. This job would normally take a designer three hours to do; with Optex running on a Lisp machine, it was done in fifteen minutes. Moreover, the exercise uncovered some flaws in the original design—without those, the designer assisted by Optex would have taken even less time to do the job.

In another instance, this time a carefully controlled experiment, a particular design job was done in the old way by four people in a month and a half, or six people-months. Using Optex, the same work was done by one person in two weeks, or half a person-month. That speedup permits many more trials, several runs per day, leading to an optimal cost/performance design after a couple of weeks. Nobody can reliably calculate the savings realized by reaching optimal cost/performance designs quickly, but taking measurable cost savings into consideration, the present version of Optex saves Canon 100 million yen, or $700,000, a year.

But Canon's main interest is not in returning cost savings to the company. Instead, the time and money saved are invested in new designs—working smarter to get more of them.

Toshiaki Asano's English isn't as good as his physics or his business acumen; softly and somewhat stiffly he reads a canned presentation on the Optex system to visitors before showing them about. But then, as he begins describing his problem and the system he built to solve it, his pride transforms him dramatically: in Japanese he grows passionate; Optex works even better than he dared hope.

But neither he nor his company is complacent. Always looking to the future, the company has established an Intelligence Engineering Division, thirty researchers divided among four advanced projects: a knowledge engineering group, a natural-language processing group, a voice-recognition processing group, and an image-recognition group. Asano heads the knowledge engineering group, which has developed Optex.

Optex is one of the few expert systems intended for design work, an unconventional, innovative step forward. It was developed early on by Canon's own knowledge engineers, who've paid a price for being first: had they waited a few years, they might have been able to use an expert system shell to build their first expert sytem, but in 1983 when they began, no such thing existed. As a result, the 1987 version of Optex had some problems: it ran on a Lisp machine and the CAD program ran on the Hitachi mainframe, which posed two-systems difficulties sometimes found when expert systems are set up to be used with an existing program. And the CAD system itself was designed for human users, not for another computer program, which posed some special interfacing problems.

But all these were temporary obstacles that gradually dissolved. What matters to Canon are the long-run advantages offered by the system (and others planned like it) for keeping the company at the very leading edge of product design.

Further into the future, Asano wants Optex to act as an intelligent interface between the designer and the CAD system by automatically analyzing exactly what the designer is doing, automatically capturing his creative design knowledge, his cognitive processes. As quantitative changes in lenses and cameras transform themselves by their numbers into qualitative changes, Canon is confident of reaping the rewards of innovation from its pioneering initiative.

Kajima:
Expert Systems in Heavy Construction

When Japan decided to end its self-imposed isolation from the West, around 1860, it was Kajima that built the first European-style commercial building in Japan, as it happened, for the Hong Kong–based Jardine Matheson & Company. Kajima then moved on to help build the Japanese railway system, and these days, Tokyo's skyline is being reshaped by Kajima high rises, thanks to the company's pioneering efforts in earthquake-resistant construction. From Asia to Africa, from North America to Europe, Kajima can also be found constructing power stations, dams, highways, refineries, dry docks, steel mills, manufacturing plants, airports, and harbors.

The company has a long tradition of innovative construction methods—it even has a large research-and-development division devoted to improving construction techniques and diminishing hazards—and so perhaps it's not surprising that Kajima has also taken up expert systems, not in research and development, but enthusiastically introduced by its electronic data-processing people.

When, in 1982, the Japanese Ministry of International Trade and Industry formed ICOT, the cooperative laboratory in Tokyo that would do research in fifth-generation computing, a young engineer at Kajima's information-processing center, Motoo Matsuda, got into conversations with a friend assigned to the new laboratory. Convinced that what was happening at ICOT was deeply important, he persuaded several of his colleagues at Kajima to begin learning about expert systems. "It was a kind of personal innovation that hadn't been officially sanctioned by the company," Matsuda says.

However, as ICOT's visibility in Japan grew, and as the artificial intelligence activities of Japan's computer manufacturers increased, an official proposal to management was made and accepted in 1983. The proposal involved studying the basics of AI, acquiring the expert system shell KEE, and building a prototype for hands-on experience in expert systems. The prototype was a Stairways Planner for configuring stairways in buildings, based on building codes and architectural design. That exploratory application was finished in November 1985, and, satisfied they had mastered KEE, in December 1985 the newly constituted team—numbering ten knowledge engineers and thirty domain engineers—began the real work of designing expert systems for everyday construction use under the direction of Atsuo Nishino.

The company has moved rapidly into applications, combining not only what they call "engineering common sense" and "industry standards" but also proprietary knowledge the company has accumulated over its nearly a century and a half in business. Across the company, some 140 areas are under study for expert system treatment. Kajima's expert systems are available to construction sites by means of networks and communication lines.

One interesting system helps deal with soil liquefaction problems. This important problem involves a judgment not only about the proper structural design for a site but also about digging to avoid water problems with construction equipment. As a rule, data produced by on-site earth borings suggest where water will be found. Civil engineers then employ several different methods to compute the chances that certain amounts of water will be found at certain layers in the soil, and sometimes those computational methods yield different results. A major element of judgment involves putting those several models together for a particular case to form a cumulative judgment that will lead to the correct design for the structure at that site, and that will also protect equipment during construction. This expert system assesses the probability of liquefaction at different depths in different layers under the ground, based on boring data and various standard interpretations.

Another expert sytem advises on the best type of pilings for a structure and the best ways of driving them. The system's goal is to select a pile that not only does the job but does it at minimum cost. The system knows the characteristics of two different kinds of piles—prestressed concrete and steel pipe—and various methods of driving them: diesel hammer, oil pressure hammer, or driven-bore. Certain conditions shape the decision, such as environmental noise, vibration, the scale of the structure, and the load-bearing characteristics of the soil. The expert system also knows about a third kind of pile that's cast in place instead of being driven, in which case the earth must be drilled and bored to pour the concrete in place.

Engineers assess the conditions of the site and the ground composition, make a rough selection of the type of pile and method, and then with the help of the system proceed to refine that selection. Once the feasible candidates for pile materials and driving methods are presented, the expert system then calculates the various costs, permitting the selection of the best combination of feasibility and cost, whether one nine-inch pile, two four-inch piles plus a third, and so on.

The Kajima knowledge engineering group has an interesting rule of thumb for choosing the best problems for expert system treatment. They seek a problem that usually takes a professional about a day to solve, and using an expert system, transform it into ten minutes of work. The immediate saving, of course, is a professional day eliminated from a design or estimating job.

Kajima makes varying estimates of the cost of a day's professional work: anywhere from $250 to $400 per day. Thus, to take the example of piles, between two hundred and one thousand pile design-and-estimation jobs come up a year. Using the minimum figures, two hundred jobs a year at $250 per job, the expert system saves $50,000 per year; at the maximum, one thousand jobs at $400 per day, the savings are $400,000 per year. In addition, Kajima saves time, of course, and increases the quality of job performance since the expert system has pooled the knowledge of several construction experts.

The cost of putting together a system that reduces one day's professional work to ten minutes is a knowledge engineer plus a domain expert working with a tool like KEE for a month. Thus two professional man-months invested in system building pay back a minimum of $50,000 a year. The Kajima knowledge engineers intend to design specialized tools that will permit the end users to build their own expert systems without help from a knowledge engineer.

But as American Express also reported, Kajima believes current savings are only lagniappe on the real yields from expert systems. As Motoo Matsuda explains: "In this construction company, experienced engineers are our most valuable asset. Therefore it's important for us to capture their expertise." Kajima has done demographic profiles of its engineering staff between 1985 and 2010, which show an aging population, the younger engineers representing an ever-smaller percentage. In 1985 the bulk of Kajima engineers were aged thirty to forty-nine, but by 2010 the largest group will be aged fifty and above, including a big group over sixty.

Kajima engineers tell several different stories about those population figures and how they figure in Kajima's motivation for getting into expert systems.

The younger people say the company was motivated to do expert systems partly because there will be so few young people to manage on-site construction that they'll need the multiplication factor, so to speak, offered by expert systems to help them. They add that construction technology is changing so quickly that young engineers will be needed to get the new knowledge into expert systems for on-site use, implying that the older people are less flexible and can't pick up the new technology; expert systems will compensate for the paucity of young people.

Privately, older engineers say the real reason for getting knowledge into expert systems is because the older engineers have wisdom and experience that must be captured in expert systems to preserve it for the future.

Presumably all these are viable reasons.

But Kajima is looking even further ahead. It expects to open new business ventures by selling its knowledge to customers, and it sees its electronically dispersed knowledge bases and expert systems as a prototype for the intelligent office of the future, knowledge located everywhere in the "intelligent building."

Perhaps most important, company managers argue that high-quality work no longer guarantees high sales and high profits in what they call the postmodern society. As an example they cite how, in the past, the quality of Nikon and Canon cameras allowed those companies to capture large market shares. But as mass production of high-quality goods has taken effect, even the highest quality items are sold at low prices in the electronic bazaars of Shinjuku. To increase sales in the camera business requires innovative design, innovative products, marketing skills, and planning. The same is surely true, they say, in their own business of construction project design, engineering, and building.

"We must now automate not only for high-quality production, but also introduce automation for high-quality planning and design," says Mr. Shoji, who manages Kajima's electronic data processing. Expert systems are Kajima's companywide key to automating that high-quality construction planning and structure design.

Chapter **13**

The Second Era of Knowledge Processing

THE HISTORY OF TECHNOLOGY shows us that we overestimate what a technology can do for us in a few years and underestimate what it can do in a decade or two. As we have seen, expert systems technology, even in its first era of application, has given rise to remarkable corporate gains. Let's look at the technology in the years before the century turns, and call this the second era of knowledge processing.

Knowledge engineering itself will change greatly. The direction of that change is already with us. Experts, and the companies they work for, will be able to build their expert system software without hiring knowledge engineers as technological intermediaries. As we have seen earlier, some companies are doing that today. How is that possible? The trick is to codify for computer use the very knowledge that is helpful in building expert systems.

The business of developing and selling software tools for expert system development is intensely competitive. The competition drives the software firms to perfect the product, incorporating each year, in the new versions of the tools, the latest practical developments in the underlying science of artificial intelligence. At the same time, they are improving the builder's interface to these tools. There's an easy way to describe what the knowledge-engineering tool designers are doing: they are trying to put as much of the knowledge engineer as they can "in the box." In a decade or so, there may be no knowledge engineering expertise that is outside the box.

In the second era of knowledge processing, a widening reconceptualization of what is meant by an intelligent system will take place. In the wider concept, the intelligent system will be conceived as the colleagues' relationship between an intelligent computer agent and an intelligent person. The computer and the person will each perform tasks that it/he does best, and the intelligence of the system will emerge from the collaboration. If the interaction is seamless and natural, then it will hardly matter whether the relevant knowledge or the reasoning skills needed are in the head of the person or in the knowledge structures of the computer.

Natural, smooth interaction with one's expert system is important. Expert systems of the first era were largely "back office" assistants, in places like trading rooms and laboratories where awkward interactions are tolerated (and, perversely, sometimes admired). In the second era, the systems will be moving out into front offices and into places of public exposure and use, in, for example, sales situations or in consumer-advising roles. "Naturalness" will be essential.

Progress in artificial intelligence is more difficult in some areas than others. One of the most difficult parts of the technology deals with the processing of natural (human) language. A consequence is that expert systems of the past have been constrained by a rigidity of grammar and stylistic expression, of vocabulary, and of concepts. For example, the interactions rarely allow synonyms and never handle metaphors. In the second era of knowledge processing, major research-and-development efforts will force the emergence of natural interfacing.

The task of understanding and using language is as much a thinking task as any other we have described. Some would say it is the quintessentially human task, the very definition of what it means to be intelligent. Language use, like all other cognitive tasks, is a knowledge-based activity. Language has meaning only because the language user has general knowledge about the world and specific knowledge about the area under discussion and the context of words and sentences. Expert systems usually contain enough knowledge to support some language understanding about their problem areas. In the coming decade, language-handling programs will make greater use of the knowledge already in expert systems about areas of specialization.

Harbingers of "naturalness" already exist. Some systems are based to a large extent on pictures rather than words. In the Oncocin project at Stanford, a system intended to help physicians in the very complicated treatment of certain cancer patients, the research team invested great effort to provide the doctor with a seamless transition between paper forms for entering patient data and electronic versions of those forms. What emerged was an electronic flow sheet, guiding the doctor step by step, and often substituting signs and symbols for words. Some commercially available expert system software tools contain powerful packages for creating pictures that show both the reasoning of the expert system and the results.

But pictures are not enough. Understanding the natural flow of language (words) is essential. Fortunately, one of the largest research efforts in artificial intelligence is focused on natural language understanding. A few limited language-understanding systems have already made it into commercial use, an example being the Intellect system of Artificial Intelligence Corporation. Though the problem is difficult, excellent research progess is being made, particularly on the problem of bringing the program's knowledge to bear on its task of understanding words, sentences, and concepts. In the second era of knowledge processing, it will become commonplace for systems to interact with users in human language, at least within the scope of the system's own knowledge.

Typing is not "natural." Speaking is. Today we all type to our computers, but natural fluid speech understanding is coming in the second era. The barriers that exist are engineering, linguistics, and knowledge. The engineering barrier will be broken by the rapidly falling cost of computer chips and by parallel operation for higher speed. Knowledge and linguistic barriers will fall as much larger bodies of knowledge are given to computer programs, and as research in language understanding by computers' progresses.

A limitation of expert systems to date has been their brittleness. Since they must be knowledgeable to perform well, their performance drops from excellent to zero when one poses a problem outside the scope of their knowledge. For human experts the fall is also steep but more gradual, because people, who today have vastly more knowledge than computer systems, can use the more general knowledge that underlies highly specific and specialized knowledge. For example, if an engineer is diagnosing the failure of an electronic circuit for which he has no specific knowledge, he can fall back on his knowledge of electronics, on circuit analysis methods, and on handbook data for the components. It may be difficult for him, but he is not helpless. In other words, overcoming brittleness will require more general knowledge and more general reasoning processes. The research is being done in AI laboratories. The solution will require the construction of large knowledge bases of generally useful knowledge, rather than just knowledge of highly specific task situations.

As the second era of knowledge processing moves toward more versatile intelligent systems, it will be useful and important to give these systems some common sense. But what we call "common sense" is itself knowledge, an enormous body of knowledge distinguished by its ubiquity and by the fact that it is rarely codified and passed on to others, as more "formal" knowledge is. For many AI scientists, the weak but general forms of thinking that we call "commonsense reasoning" constitute the ultimate goal in the quest for an artificial intelligence. For others, the computer with common sense is not a Holy Grail but yet another technique for enhancing the naturalness of the interaction between people and their electronic assistants.

For example, imagine an expert system that is an advisor on personnel policies and legal requirements, advising middle managers on how to apply correctly the complex web of policies and requirements in particular cases. If a case at hand involves a female employee, then the system will automatically bring into play knowledge relevant to maternal leaves and pregnancy expenses. It knows some "common sense," that women have pregnancies and men do not. But if the data file on the employee shows an older woman, then more common sense knowledge will remove the relevance of rules about maternal leaves and pregnancies.

Reasoning methods will change, too, in the second era. Today most reasoning methods used by expert systems are based on logic and probability. In the future, reasoning by analogy will be added to the power tool. Analogizing is a method for bringing more knowledge to bear on a particular problem than would ordinarily be done by strict application of logic. It can be used to construct interesting and novel interpretations of situations and data. It can be used to retrieve knowledge that would be overlooked by the usual methods of search, because no one had anticipated its use in some particularly novel way.

Using an analogy process to interpret new experience in terms of old will also be an important part of computer self-learning (or learning, for short). It comes as an exciting surprise to most people that computers can learn. While it is difficult scientific work, right now, to make them do this in interesting and practical ways, the concept itself is simple to understand. Learning means acquiring new knowledge that enhances subsequent performance. Knowledge is represented as symbols and collections of symbols. During learning, these are stored in the knowledge base, where they become available to affect later performance. Today's practical systems do almost no self-learning, though a few commercial systems are advertised as having a (minimal) inductive learning ability. Their knowledge is constructed without computer help by knowledge engineers (and occasionally by the experts themselves). In other words, today's expert systems learn only by being told. But experiments aimed at second-era learning abilities have been under way for several years. Analogizing has been shown to be a powerful method for using the computer itself to assist in the building of knowledge bases. The learning program suggests an appropriate analogy between a present situation and some stored experience, and the knowledge engineer modifies, enhances, and corrects the analogy.

In other experiments, the scientists have built "learning apprentices" that carefully observe their human users performing complex tasks. They have been given knowledge that allows them to be of some assistance to the users. But by watching, these programs learn new knowledge to improve their performance. For example, suppose design experts have given a design apprentice program knowledge to assist in engineering design, and the program offers assistance during a design process. By observing which of its design recommendations the users accept, and what alternate design steps the users decide to take (in lieu of the program's advice), the program can enhance its own competence at offering designing advice.

Not all knowledge is learned by being told, or by watching. People acquire much of their knowledge by reading. On the horizon are learning programs that read text in areas of expert specialization (for example, journals and textbooks) to augment their knowledge bases.

Learning is the "magic bullet" that is needed to help with the building of the large knowledge bases that we earlier said were essential for the more versatile intelligent systems of the second era. These knowledge bases will contain hundreds of thousands, perhaps millions, of facts, heuristics, concepts, relationships, and symbolic models. Interestingly, learning will become easier as the knowledge bases grow larger. The task of learning is just another reasoning task, and the knowledge principle applies to learning. Learning programs will be more competent at learning as more knowledge supports their performance. In other words, the more a computer (or a person, for that matter) knows, the easier it is to know more.

The Library of the Future

The physicist Niels Bohr once remarked, "It's hard to predict, especially the future." But let us shift our horizon beyond the year 2030 and envision what knowledge processing of that time might be like. To call to mind very large knowledge bases, we've chosen the metaphor of the library, but we could as well be suggesting a company or government knowledge center. Those familiar with the AI science might find our attempts at envisioning mundane because they will recognize extrapolations of current work and trends. If we knew what the big surprises were going to be, they wouldn't be surprises.

Marvin Minsky, MIT professor and one of the founding fathers of AI, envisioned himself in the library of the future, reflecting back on the early stage of knowledge processing that we are in today: "Can you imagine that they used to have libraries where the books didn't talk to each other?"

The libraries of today are warehouses for passive objects. The books and journals sit on shelves, waiting for us to use our intelligence to find them, read them, interpret them, and finally make them divulge their stored knowledge. "Electronic" libraries of today are no better. Their pages are pages of data files, but the electronic page images are equally passive.

Now imagine the library as an active, intelligent "knowledge server." It stores knowledge in complex knowledge structures (perhaps in a formalism yet to be invented) so that crossovers and connections between categories are routine. It can use its knowledge to assist its users in problem solving and other complex thinking tasks. The needs of users are expressed naturally, with fluid discourse. The system can, of course, retrieve and exhibit (the electronic textbook). It can collect relevant information; it can summarize; it can pursue relationships.

It acts as a consultant on specific problems, offering advice on particular solutions, justifying those solutions with citations or with a fabric of general reasoning. If the user can suggest a solution or an hypothesis, it can check this, even suggest extensions. Or it can critique the user's viewpoint, with a detailed rationale.

It pursues paths of associations to suggest to the user previously unseen connections. Collaborating with the user, it associates and draws analogies to "brainstorm" for remote or novel concepts. More autonomously, but with some guidance from the user, it uses criteria of "interestingness" to discover new concepts, new methods, new theories, new measurements.

For example, envision a "brainstorming" assistant for new product ideas. Let's say it first proposes and searches the possibilities for extensions and revisions of current products and comes up with a list of a few dozen plausible candidates. It then shifts its attention to possible new markets for the company's products, proposing and searching product ideas targeted for those markets. As it does so, it might propose a product with a plausible market that is already on the list to be considered because it was put there by the previous search for product extensions and revisions. The same idea came up twice, by different lines of reasoning. That's interesting! The assistant immediately focuses attention on this idea from among the many that have been generated. Of course, there are a very large number of ways of specifying what is "interesting," and the one we just gave is among the simplest.

The user of the library of the future need not be a person. It may be another knowledge system—that is, any intelligent agent with a need for knowledge. Such a library will be a network of knowledge systems, in which people and machines collaborate.

Publishing is an activity transformed. Authors may bypass text, adding their contribution to human knowledge directly to the knowledge structures. Since the thread of responsibility (authority) must be maintained, and since there may be disagreement as knowledge grows, the contributions are "signed," incidentally allowing for the computation of royalties for access and use. Knowledge base maintenance (updating) itself becomes a vigorous part of the new publishing industry.

Will there be such a knowledge system? As we see it, the only open question is when.

Chapter 14

Looking Around and Looking Ahead

THE INFORMATION-PROCESSING INDUSTRY may not yet be the world's number-one industry, but it is certainly the knife edge for all the sectors and industries of an advanced national economy. New and innovative use of computers leads the economy and pulls progress and productivity.

As we have seen in this book of portraits, a major new computer technology, knowledge processing, has grown to early adulthood in the 1980s. Much has been expected from this technology since it derives from a science, artificial intelligence, that studies one of man's great questions: What is the nature of thought and intelligence? The arrival of knowledge processing and its expert systems is not the answer to this deep question, any more than the arrival of the steam engine was the answer to the deep questions of physics. The expert system "engines" are early spin-offs from the science.

The Technology and Its Insertion

Much has been expected, and much has been delivered. By mid-1987 fifteen hundred expert systems were in use worldwide. They assist human intellectual work over a wide range of tasks that are called "knowledge-intensive" and "information-oriented." Examples are found in every area of corporate life, from the CEO's office to the personnel function, from the sales office to the factory floor.

The pace of the technology insertion has been rapid by historical measures. According to Professor Nathan Rosenberg, a well-known economic historian, new technologies diffusing into industrial practice often take decades to achieve widespread use. He thinks the diffusion of the new knowledge technology is probably happening faster than the historical curves.

The expert systems turned out, in most cases, to be much simpler to build than even the technological optimists had believed. The software tools used to write the programs have allowed the knowledge of expertise to be readily expressed for the computer so that, unexpectedly, many experts, after short training courses, have become their own expert system builders. The tools provide the reasoning processes. What is critical is the flow of specialized knowledge from the expert to the computer's memory.

Expert system activity in companies is now merging with the mainstream of information processing dominated by conventional data-processing work and machines. That is a sign of success and of maturation. The early adopters did their development work on high-performance workstations. The mainstream developers of the late 1980s are demanding expert system software that runs on their conventional mainframe machines. IBM dominates the mainframe market and mentality, and has announced software products and product plans to speed the transition of expert systems to IBM mainframes. Fujitsu, the largest Japanese computer manufacturer, from the very beginning of its activity in expert systems conceived of the expert systems business as seamlessly interwoven with the conventional data-processing business. Fujitsu's special-purpose hardware (the FACOM-Alpha Lisp machine) was offered as an optional attachment to a Fujitsu mainframe. Even more significantly, the Fujitsu specialists in the expert systems area retained the conventional job title of the analyst's function, system engineer, intentionally making a statement of their view that expert systems work was simply part of the mainstream of computing.

The Dimensions of Gain in Review

The expert systems now in use are showing extraordinary economic gain to the companies that developed them. Here, in review, are some of the aspects and dimensions of that gain:

- Costs saved on internal processes. For some systems, millions of dollars per year, and even tens of millions. For smaller systems, returns on investment in the thousands of percent. Recall American Express's Authorizer's Assistant; IBM Burlington's work-in-process planner; DEC's Xcon/Xsel computer configuration and sales assistant; or the many Du Pont "pebbles," small expert systems on microcomputers.
- Speedup of problem solving. Almost always greater than ten times, usually twenty to forty times, a big boost to personal productivity for expensive employees.
- Preservation of the company's know-how, its expertise. Capturing the knowledge of the best and distributing it widely to boost average performance. Protecting against volatility caused by resignations, retirements, and other departures of critical experts from the company. Training the novices in company skills and preserving in an explicit form what those skills are composed of. Recall Lend Lease's construction time estimator, Schlumberger's engineering design aid, Northrop's manufacturing process planner, and Nippon-Kokan's "god" for steel making.
- Improvement of quality and consistency. Insuring that company knowledge is used systematically and the problem solving done carefully (computers are good at "detail work"). Efforts of companies to improve the quality of work are now of first priority.
- Changing the way the basic business works. The flexi-

bility of action that high-speed reasoning can bring to business processes—for example, manufacturing and sales—allows these processes to be reconceptualized for new markets or to better meet the needs of customers. Recall the Navistar truck manufacturing and sales system.

- New revenues from new products and new lines of business. Knowledge is power, and customers will pay for the assistance of expert systems that yield big gains. Recall Westinghouse's diagnostic service for turbine generators and the major new line of business that Texas Instruments has opened.

- Stimulating innovation. High-speed problem solving serves as a power tool to allow creative professionals to explore, understand, discard, and rework many more pathways to a solution than they would otherwise have had the time and patience to do. Recall Canon's lens design assistant.

Quality and Productivity

In today's business environment of intense international competition, it is worthwhile to revisit concerns with quality and productivity of work.

How to improve the quality of work is a hot topic of business soul-searching. Jerry R. Junkins, CEO of Texas Instruments, a company that has trademarked the term *knowledge technologies* and is the world's leading firm in selling and using knowledge processing, has written, "Not too long ago, the ability to manufacture defect-free products consistently and at low cost was viewed as the pinnacle of quality achievement. Today it is a minimum requirement for staying in business." James Houghton, the chairman of Corning Glass Works, an early user of expert systems, has said, "Last year [1986], IBM estimated that it would take $2.66 billion of additional revenue to generate the same amount of profit that could be realized if each employee removed work product defects that would save just $1000 per year." Quality as a key concern is summed up in the slogan "Do it right the first time."

Expert systems do not always "do it right" (because their knowledge is heuristic, experiential), but for most expert systems the error rate is astonishingly small compared with human performance. Because of the large number of configuration designs done, DEC has good statistics on Xcon's performance: configuration errors occur less frequently than one time in ten thousand! In some cases, investment in expert system building stops at the 80 percent or 90 percent level because the remaining "difficult" problems can best be handled by the human user. Dr. Robert Fallat, who worked with a Stanford team in developing a lung disease diagnostic assistant (PUFF), said in a television interview, "If the computer can handle the routine 80 to 90 percent of the cases, that's OK. It frees me to work on the other 10 to 20 percent, which are the really interesting medical cases."

Another important issue that concerns business and trade analysts is productivity. Increases in productivity provide the push for rising standards of living. During the years 1950 to 1985 the average annual productivity gain in the manufacturing sector was a "poor" 2.5 percent for the United States and an "excellent" 8.5 percent for Japan. In activities related to offices and knowledge work, productivity gains are poor, near zero, in all countries. The productivity gains from the use of expert systems that we have reported are often hundreds of times greater than even the "excellent" 8.5 percent. Since knowledge work is coming to dominate manufacturing work and other service work in advanced economies, the importance of the productivity effect of expert systems as a "turbocharger" cannot be overestimated.

If the average performer were given a "turbo" to allow him to perform at the level of the best performer, would that make a difference? Norman R. Augustine, the CEO of Martin-Marietta, in his book *Augustine's Laws*, discusses "concentration of productivity," saying, "In virtually any undertaking it is found that a very small fraction of the participants produces a very large fraction of the accomplishments . . . Amazingly, the top 1 percent produce nearly fifty times the per capita output of the bottom half." Undoubtedly, then, capturing and distributing the expertise of the top performers to assist the average and below-average performers would produce a very large gain in overall productivity.

Dimensions of Pain

The introduction of a new technology into people's work, into organizational processes, and into society's patterns and laws is never easy. We see some problems: in the development of knowledge technology, in the evolution of human expertise, and with the inevitable societal effects.

Orderly development and deployment of knowledge processing in companies will require the smooth integration of the new technology with the traditional data-processing activities and machines that represent massive company investments and commitments. In most corporations, the traditional data processing was centralized decades ago and is located in the company dukedom called management information systems (MIS). MIS is the nervous system of the modern company, and MIS managers are justifiably reluctant to perform intrusive experiments. They've been burned too often in the past, and prefer to be the last to move, not the first. For the harassed MIS manager, every day brings demands and crises, leaving little time to explore the new, little motivation for vision. MIS managers are rarely heroes. In the line activities of companies—for example, in manufacturing or engineering—this is a time of feverish search for new information-processing technologies. It is also a time of frustration and bitterness as the champions of the new make war with the powerful MIS establishments that control access to corporate data bases, control purchase of equipment, and control most of the "computing" dollars in the organization. MIS is strong. These days it is even trendy for companies to appoint a "chief information officer" (CIO), usually the Duke of MIS. The challenge is to convince the majority of MIS managers to follow the examples of vision and alertness that we saw at Du Pont, Navistar, and Nippon Life. The tragedy of the MIS inertia is this: Turtles beat hares only in fairy tales, not in competitive businesses.

Another issue of development is the setting of standards. The industry surrounding electricity would have had difficulty growing were it not for standards of voltage, cycles, and even plugs (the interface). The emerging knowledge-engineering business is vigorous but chaotic. It contains several large companies and hundreds of small companies, selling various kinds of software, hardware, builder interfaces, and user interfaces. IBM has not yet achieved the dominance in knowledge processing that would allow it to set de facto standards. The vendors pursue unnecessary idiosyncrasies as they carve out their niches in the highly competitive business, and in the process are confusing their markets and their customers.

One of the things that MIS managers worry about most is the security of their company's data—against unauthorized access and outright theft. Consider how much more valuable than data is the company's knowledge. In some cases it's unique expertise. Will the standard methods for protection suffice? Or has the nature of the threat changed? If company expertise is distributed around to micros and minis in the work areas, is the company knowledge secure?

Who owns the knowledge anyway? The new technology casts the knowledge in physical, tangible form—symbols stored in complex ways on, say, a floppy disk. In the past, this knowledge was hidden away as part of the mental apparatus of a company expert. The expert's salary is essentially a series of rent payments for the use of his knowledge. Now what? Does the now-tangible knowledge base belong to the company? Logically it would seem so, but how will that sit with the expert who is nervous about his continuing flow of "rent payments" and who, understandably, feels a sense of ownership? Similar vexing questions arise concerning copyrights and copyright protection. It's difficult enough for the law to deal with the copyright of conventional software. Who gets to hold the copyright on an expert's lifetime of experience in performing his niche task? Pirating is also an issue. Think of an expert system as a kind of active "book of knowledge" about a specialty. If pirating means going to a photocopier with a big book, then it's awkward and time-consuming (and yet some people do just that). If pirating means copying a floppy disk, it can be accomplished easily and swiftly.

Large Knowledge Bases: A Problem of Infrastructure

The more knowledge an expert system has been given about its domain of work, the more competent will be its performance. Today's expert systems deal with domains of narrow specialization, and they are given much knowledge about that narrow specialization to allow them to perform at expert level. For expert systems to perform competently over a broad range of tasks they will have to be given very much more knowledge. The problem of the large knowledge base was discussed in the previous chapter.

The next generation of expert systems, beyond those whose portraits we have sketched in this book, will require large knowledge bases. These do not exist today. How will we get them? One possibility is to give expert systems the processes that will allow them to learn from experience, in that way allowing them to build their own large knowledge bases. Self-learning is one of the deep issues in the science of artificial intelligence, and is being worked on by AI laboratories around the world. But transfer of the technology to workaday systems is still at an early stage. Another possibility is to buckle down to the task of creating, without much computer assistance, a giant "encyclopedia of knowledge" for use in the next generation of knowledge-based systems. It would be a huge task, and could be done either in the private sector or the public sector. The MCC computer research consortium owned by seventeen private companies already has such a project under way. The Japanese Fifth Generation project has spun off a company, Japan Electronic Dictionary Research Institute, that will use public funds and private company personnel to create a large knowledge base primarily for use in tasks of language understanding and translation (the knowledge base is called Concept Dictionary). One could think of the large knowledge base as a necessary piece of national infrastructure (like the Library of Congress or the National Library of Medicine) and request the government to fund its construction. This indeed has been the subject of preliminary planning among AI scientists in the United States. Or one could view the construction task as too vast for a centralized effort, requiring many people in many places to build small pieces of the large knowledge base, and requiring an incentive structure to motivate their work. The concept is called "the knowledge market." The incentives are royalty payments for use of someone's small piece of the knowledge base. The knowledge flows from place to place over an electronic data network, but other than this, the knowledge market resembles the publishing business. The appropriate analog for the small segment of the knowledge base that an individual would construct is the textbook. However it is built, the large knowledge base will be extraordinarily valuable and necessary for the future of knowledge technology. The policy issue of how to get it built (nationally? internationally? private sector consortia? university consortia? IBM?) needs to be addressed in the next few years.

The Impact on Knowledge Workers

There are fears that professional work will suffer from the introduction of expert systems. For every manager who feels that consistency in decision making is a worthwhile company goal, there may be a professional who feels that the uniformity that results is stifling. In our portrait of DEC, we told about just these feelings. If an expert system assistant can solve the problem at hand for its user 99 percent of the time (levels easy to achieve today by careful knowledge engineering), is there enough substance in the difficult 1 percent remaining to nourish the need for novelty and creativity felt by the human user, his need to extend the boundary of what he knows and enrich his store of expertise? If the answer is an optimistic yes, would the answer be the same at performance levels of 99.99 percent? The issue is real, because such levels are realistic. There probably will always be a need for human expertise at the highest levels of competence and creativity. But many who are regarded as experts do not perform at these levels, and will find their jobs threatened. Knowledge workers have been largely insulated from the effects of computerized automation because until now there has been little that computers could do that impacted their area of work. But since expert systems can speed up a professional's job by a factor of ten or more while maintaining quality, it is likely that some companies at least will extract this productivity gain in the form of fewer workers of that type. There is nothing novel about the labor displacement and retraining problems that follow from this, except that a new class of worker, one that previously thought itself exempt from these problems, will begin to feel the heat.

Widening the Gap

Will knowledge processing open wider the gap between haves and have-nots? Knowledge is power: economic power, cultural power, technological power, the power to change one's circumstances. The haves are largely in control of the knowledge engine. Now, with their knowledge technology, they have created a turbocharger for that engine. In the developed nations there is a sense of urgency about building the so-called knowledge-intensive businesses to earn back the wealth that has been lost as manufacturing work has moved to less developed countries. In the truly globalized world economy that is developing, the rising economic tide from the more effective utilization of knowledge should float all the boats. But we are not optimistic. In today's world it seems as though the knowledge-haves are not about to give away knowledge to the knowledge-have-nots. The haves want to sell knowledge and the high-value-added products and services that attend knowledge, but the have-nots do not have the money to buy. We seem to be taking one more trip through an old story, the gap widening each time.

National Wealth and Change

Nations are investing heavily in knowledge processing and other advanced information technologies. Examples are the U.S. Strategic Computing Project, the Japanese Fifth Generation project, the European ESPRIT project, and the U.K. Alvey project. Projects with similar goals, but on a smaller scale, also exist in Finland, Canada, and Singapore. Why are the nations concerned?

The noisy anger from the capitals of Western nations, and the quiet anger in response from Japan and the rapidly developing countries of Southeast Asia, have at the root one overriding concern: the wealth of nations and hence the standard of living of their citizens and the prosperity of their businesses. Wealth floods and ebbs, measured by trade surpluses and deficits. Adjusting an ebb by lowering the value of a nation's money is negative and unsatisfactory since it leads to lowering the standard of living of the people. Witness the vivid contrast between the British decline of the 1960s and 1970s and the stunning rise to affluence of the Japanese people during the same period.

National wealth arises from many different factors, and the importance of each factor in the wealth equation changes as the world economy adapts to changing circumstances and technologies. One hundred years ago the rich nations, and the soon-to-be-rich, were those with a plentiful supply of natural resources, particularly iron ore and coal for making steel. Now these resources (with the exception of oil) are becoming virtually irrelevant to the new wealth of nations. The recent international furor about the semiconductor industry—the trade in microelectronic chips for computers—is about . . . what? A fraction of a gram of sand, exquisitely refined and manufactured to the finest tolerances ever achieved, using for its design and manufacture a huge body of scientific knowledge.

"For the first time in the history of mankind," said Carlo DeBenedetti, the chief executive officer of Olivetti, "innovation is the fundamental raw material. Real strategic resources are no longer represented by coal, steel, or oil but by the cleverness and cognitive capability of man."

In 1985, to celebrate its one hundredth birthday, the magazine *Iron Age*, the trade journal of U.S. manufacturing management, took a look back and a look ahead. It surveyed the great technologies of yesterday and then ranked them according to their importance to manufacturing. Then it projected the great technologies of tomorrow and ranked these by the same criterion. The most important of yesterday turned out to be the Bessemer steel furnace. Number one for tomorrow was artificial intelligence. Here is what the editors said: "Of all the technologies expected to shape tomorrow's factory environment, none will have a greater impact than artificial intelligence. . . . AI will be the software that ties existing technology tools together. In the form of an expert system, AI will be able to capture age-old skills that are rapidly disappearing from the shop floor."

Artificial intelligence is the science behind the new knowledge technology. Knowledge is at the focus of national efforts to manipulate the wealth equation. In the late years of the twentieth century, knowledge is economic power. Knowledge drives the economic engines of economies that prosper from selling high-value-added goods and services. A nation that invests in its knowledge technology makes a strategic investment in its economic future. In a widely quoted section from the plan for the Japanese Fifth Generation project, the planners of the Ministry of International Trade and Industry said: "Japan, which has a shortage of land and a population density about forty times that of the United States, cannot attain self-sufficiency in food, and her rate of self-sufficiency in energy is about 15 percent and that of oil about 0.3 percent. On the other hand, we have one precious asset, that is our human resources. Japan's plentiful labor force is characterized by a high degree of education, diligence, and high quality. It is desirable to utilize this advantage to cultivate information itself as a new resource comparable to food and energy, and to emphasize the development of information-related knowledge-intensive industries which make possible the processing and managing of information at will."

In the United States the big investments in information technology R&D, including the investment in artificial intelligence, have been made for the nation by the Defense Department's elite research agency, the Advanced Research Projects Agency (ARPA). ARPA's scientific managers are skilled at managing military systems research, but their interest in artificial intelligence is of broad national scope and of long duration. In 1972 Dr. Lukasik, the director of DARPA, at a meeting of all the principal scientific investigators doing research under contract to his agency, sketched the patterns of DARPA funding for new technologies. He sketched how they ramp up, then decline, over a five-year period. Then he drew a horizontal line straight across the blackboard. "This is the funding for artificial intelligence. Artificial intelligence is my long-term investment." With the Strategic Computing Project of the 1980s, the amount invested multiplied manyfold.

A long-term vision of the power and significance of the science and the knowledge technology that spins off it was articulated in 1987 by the eminent mathematician and member of the national Academy of Sciences, Dr. Jacob Schwartz, who presently serves DARPA as director of information science and technology. In an article for the *Encyclopedia of Artificial Intelligence* (1987) on the limits of artificial intelligence, he wrote: "If artificial intelligences can be created at all, there is little reason to believe that initial successes could not lead swiftly to the construction of artificial superintelligences able to explore significant mathematical, scientific, or engineering alternatives at a rate far exceeding human ability, or to generate plans and take action on them with equally overwhelming speed. Since man's near monopoly of all higher forms of intelligence has been one of the most basic facts of human existence throughout the past history of this planet, such developments would clearly create a new economics, a new sociology, and a new history."

The expert systems whose stories we have told are windows on the new economics, the early economic results from the first technology spin-off of artificial intelligence. Even in the light of early dawn, the returns on investment, the productivity increases, the consequences of preserving and distributing company expertise, the enhancement of quality, and the other gains are remarkable. In the international competitive environment, the early adopters will not easily be displaced by latecomers. The competitive opportunity presents itself now. When will another, as widely useful and powerful as this, come along?

Appendix

EXPERT SYSTEMS IN USE by Paul Harmon

Agriculture Applications

Grain Marketing Advisor. For sale by Purdue University.

Based on its analysis of the futures market, the Grain Marketing Advisor helps farmers choose marketing or storage strategies for their grain crops. Developed with Personal Consultant Plus, the system runs on TI or IBM PCs. For more information, contact Dr. Larry Huggins at (317) 494-1162.

Aquaref. Distributed by United States Department of Agriculture (USDA).

Aquaref provides references to sources of information on aquaculture, similar to the work of reference librarians. The system was developed at the Aquaculture Information Center at the National Agricultural Library using 1st-CLASS. It runs on IBM PCs or compatible equipment. For more information, contact Samuel Waters at (301) 344-3780.

Communications Applications

Automated Yellow Pages Production. For sale by Expert Technologies.

Automated Yellow Pages Production is a composition system designed specifically for formatting yellow pages. It positions ads and lays out pages. To create this system, Expert Technologies used their own development tool based on Cartesian geometry. The system runs on Sun Microsystems or TI Explorer. For more information, contact Jim Gay at (412) 621-0818.

ACE. For sale by AT&T Bell Laboratories.

ACE is an equipment diagnosis and preventive maintenance planning system. Its purpose is to help telephone operating companies reduce the incidence of phone cable failures. The system analyzes operating and repair data and identifies areas for preventive maintenance and further repair. ACE examines two data bases: the Cable Repair Administrative System (CRAS) and the Trouble Repair Evaluation and Administration Tool (TREAT). ACE helps free up the time of a limited number of expert cable analyzers who before had faced a discouraging volume of data. The system was developed with a combination of OPS4 and standard Unix-based development languages. It runs on AT&T 3B2 workstations. For more information, contact Fran Henig at (201) 580-5310.

GEMS-TTA (Generalized Expert Maintenance System–Trunk Trouble Analyzer). Developed by Bell Laboratories in AT&T network.

GEMS-TTA diagnoses faults on telephone trunk lines. It was developed using OPS83 to run on a Unix machine. For more information, contact Paul H. Callahan at (201) 615-5199.

Newspaper Expert Systems. For sale by Crossfield CSI.

Newspaper Expert Systems assists newspaper editors in making decisions about layouts, and in the planning and scheduling of printing runs. Advertising, editorial, and production decisions have implications for the other departments. Use of the system leads to better integration of the functions of the editorial, advertising, and production departments. Newspaper Expert Systems was created using ART to run on a Vax network. For more information, contact Anne Hamlin at (213) 417-7997.

COMPASS. Developed for internal use by GTE.

COMPASS (Central Office Maintenance Printout Analysis and Suggestion System) assists telephone switch maintenance personnel by analyzing operating data and recommending appropriate maintenance actions. Field tests have shown COMPASS to equal or exceed human experts in analyzing operating data printouts. COMPASS upgrades analysis to the level of the top expert in the country. The time saved is a secondary advantage since it is run off line. Compass was developed using KEE and runs on a Xerox Lisp machine. For more information, contact Dr. David Prerau at (617) 466-2611.

Press Line-Up Advisor. For sale by Rockwell International Corp.

Press Line-Up Advisor analyzes newspaper format and suggests a configuration for placement of printing plates for the press. The system was developed in Interlisp on a Teknowledge S.1 EShell and runs on a Xerox Lisp machine. For more information, contact Morton Balban at (312) 656-8600.

IDEA (IS4000 Diagnostic Expert Advisor). For sale by Pacific Bell.

IDEA helps technicians diagnose trouble situations in the Infotron IS4000 Local Area Network, a complex telephone switching device. IDEA is capable of solving a significant percentage of problems, with a typical consultation lasting five minutes or less. IDEA was developed using an experimental product called Metashell, with Exsys. For more information, contact Kevin McElroy at (415) 823-8983.

Computer Applications

COCOMO1. For sale by Level Five Research.

Cocomo1 helps engineers and managers schedule and staff software development projects. The system predicts the labor, cost, and time involved and forecasts the productivity of projects. Managers not trained in Cocomo1's particular cost modeling are able to use the system to develop estimates and schedules. Cocomo1 was developed with Insight 2 and TurboPascal and runs on PCs. For more information, contact Don Ahrens at (305) 729-9046.

CSF Advisor. Developed for internal use by IBM.

CSF Advisor guides the development of cost estimates for the relocation of major data-processing equipment. It was developed with ES Environment/VM to run on IBM mainframes. For more information, contact Gordon Ratica at (919) 848-5647.

Diag 8100. Developed for internal use by the Travelers Corp.

Diag 8100 diagnoses problems and failures of the company's IBM 8100 computers. Use of the system has reduced the time needed to solve a typical problem from forty-five minutes to five minutes, reducing computer downtime. Diag 8100 was developed with M.1 and runs on a PC. For more information, contact Teknowledge at (415) 424-0500.

Information Engineering Workbench. For sale by Knowledgeware.

Information Engineering Workbench assists systems analysts in the planning, analysis, design, and construction of management information systems. Use of the system eliminates the bottleneck caused by slower production of manually drawn diagrams. Also, the ease of changing components of a design seems to allow for more experimentation with alternative designs. The system was written with C and Prolog. For more information, contact Steve Kahan at (404) 231-8575.

Intelligent Peripheral Troubleshooter. Developed for internal use by Hewlett-Packard (HP).

The Intelligent Peripheral Troubleshooter provides a level of expertise comparable to a technician with years of experience in troubleshooting HP's disk drives. IPT was developed on an HP-RL shell and runs on an HP3000 workstation. For more information, call George Gottchalk at (415) 691-5662.

DASD Advisor (Direct Access Storage Device). For sale by Boole & Babbage Inc.

DASD Advisor uses information gathered by the DASD/RM program to identify DASD performance problems, analyze their causes, and recommend corrective actions and thereby improve overall system performance. Use of the system improves productivity of computer tuning personnel, and it improves computer performance at sites without a DASD specialist. The system also helps in training DASD tuners. DASD Advisor was developed with the Aion Development System and runs on an IBM and compatible mainframes. For more information, contact Dennis White at (415) 961-3138.

Cabling Configurator. Developed for internal use by Ferranti Computer Systems, Ltd.

The Cabling Configurator determines efficient arrangements of wires connecting circuit boards. Cabling Configurator does in one day what used to take a skilled engineer two months or more to accomplish. The system was developed with ART and runs on a Symbolics Lisp machine. For more information, contact Anne Hamlin at (213) 417-7997.

TIMM-Tuner. For sale by General Research Corporation.

TIMM-Tuner assists managers in tuning the Vax/VMS operating system. In testing, TIMM-Tuner improved the performance of Vax more than 10 percent. TIMM-Tuner was written with TIMM. For more information, contact General Research Corp. at (703) 893-5915.

Permaid. Developed for internal use by Honeywell.

Permaid helps diagnose problems and suggests preventive maintenance of large disk drives. Permaid paid off its development cost in three months. Permaid is written in Loops and runs on a Xerox Lisp machine. For more information, contact Tom Howell at (602) 862-4486.

CA/ISS Three. For sale by Computer Associates Inc.

CA/ISS Three manages computer capacity for better use of resources. It also helps ensure that cost-effective recommendations are made for future equipment upgrades. The system was written in C for use on IBM PCs. It has a mainframe component MVS analyzer written in SAS, reducing RMS and SMF (measurement and accounting data) which they generate about themselves, then is downloaded to microcomponent-capacity planner. For more information, contact David E. Y. Sarna at (212) 972-4400.

ESPm. Support contract which includes ESPm for sale by NCR.

ESPm analyzes computer maintenance logs to identify possible future problems. Use of ESPm increases system availability and improves efficiency of service operations. ESPm was written with S.1 and runs on the NCR Tower 32 machine. For more information, contact Tom Hansen at (619) 485-3179.

The DBA Assistant. For sale by Knowledge-Based Engineering, Inc.

The DBA Assistant helps design and evaluate problems with data base structures within an IDMS/R environment. The DBA Assistant was developed with the KES II tool to run on IBM PCs. For more information, contact Ricki Kleist at (703) 276-7910.

BDS. Developed for internal use by Lockheed.

BDS troubleshoots a large signal-switching network called a Baseband Distribution Subsystem. The system is reported to have cut troubleshooting time by a factor of five. It calculates test points quickly and easily with fewer miscalculations than the previous method. BDS was developed with the Lockheed Expert System development tool to run on Vax. For more information, contact Walt Perkins at Lockheed's Palo Alto Research Center at (415) 354-5239.

Intelligent Software Configurator. Developed for internal use by Honeywell-Bull.

Intelligent Software Configurator helps configure software for Honeywell-Bull's data-processing customers. The system has cut configuration time down from three days to a matter of minutes, greatly speeding customer service. The system was written in Loops to run on Xerox Lisp machines. For more information, contact Barbara Braden at (617) 552-6351.

SYCSON. Developed for internal use by Honeywell.

Syscon was designed to configure the details of DPS 90 mainframes for Honeywell's customers. It was developed with OPS5 on Honeywell's Multics system. For more information, call (602) 862-5412.

Dragon. Developed for internal use by Systems Designers Software.

Dragon is an expert system to aid salespeople in configuring ICL's Series 39 computers. It was developed with Envisage on a Lisp machine. For more information, contact Anne Stevenson of Systems Designers Software at (302) 323-1900.

CONAD (Configuration Advisor). Developed for internal use by Nixdorf.

Conad is used by Nixdorf sales personnel for the configuration of Nixdorf's 8864 systems, products, and service ranges (computers, process plants, machines, networks, financial counseling, insurance packages, etc.). Conad was developed with Twaice and runs on a Nixdorf 8890 and Nixdorf Targon 35. For more information, contact Gordon Graham at Logicware, Inc. (416) 672-0300.

Ocean. Developed with Teknowledge, Inc., for internal use by NCR.

Ocean is part of a customer order-processing system that aids in the configuration of NCR computer installations. It validates computer system orders to make sure they are correct from an engineering standpoint. The system greatly reduces order-processing time while also reducing errors. Ocean was written with a proprietary tool to run on an NCR Tower 32 (Unix machine). For more information, contact James A. King at (513) 445-1090.

SNAP (Simplified Needs Assessment Profile). Developed for internal use by Infomart.

SNAP helps shoppers at Infomart, a Dallas computers-only shopping center, to assess their personal computer needs. In one five-month period SNAP received overall favorable response from the more than 3,300 visitors who used the system. SNAP was written with TI's Personal Consultant to run on a PC. For more information, contact Texas Instruments. (800) 527-3500.

Titan. Developed for internal use by Radian Corp.

Titan helps train and assist technicians servicing the TI 990 minicomputer. Written in RuleMaster and Unix, Titan runs on a PC. For more information, contact Steve Pardue at (512) 454-4797.

Mask. Developed for internal use by Norcom.

Mask assists helpline personnel diagnose customers' problems with a screen management software product sold by Norcom. With Mask, entry-level staff can be used on the helpline instead of senior technicians. Mask has been able to solve in three minutes customer problems which used to take a week. Mask was developed with 1st-CLASS and runs on a PC. For more information, contact John Andersen at (907) 780-6464.

Hotline Helper. Developed for internal use by Texas Instruments.

Hotline Helper assists customer service operators in diagnosing problems with Omni printers. The system allows nonexperts to handle most calls, thus freeing experts for more productive tasks. Hotline Helper also speeds the training of new operators. The system was developed with Personal Consultant and runs on a PC. For more information, contact Texas Instruments, Inc. (800) 527-3500.

BEACON (Browser/Editor and Automated Configurator). Developed for internal use by Unisys.

Beacon is a sales aid which ensures correct and complete configuration of Unisys computer systems. It also allows for direct updates of inventory entries. Beacon was created with KNET, an internal tool. For more information, contact Bart Dunning, Unisys Knowledge Systems, at (612) 851-3350.

Disk Diagnostician (RBEST). Developed for internal use by Hewlett-Packard.

Disk Diagnostician analyzes the results of computer-run disk-memory tests to diagnose disk failures. Technicians used to spend hours analyzing these reports, a task which Disk Diagnostician does in one to two minutes. The system was written in Lisp and runs on the HP9000. For more information, contact Terry Cline, Hewlett-Packard, at (415) 857-7559.

Expert-Tek. Developed for internal use by Motorola.

Expert-Tek aids in the diagnosis and repair of computer systems and helps plan for customer service needs. Use of Expert-Tek has led to quicker resolution of customer problems over the phone. Expert-Tek was created with S.1 and runs on a Unix machine. For more information, contact Teknowledge at (415) 424-9955.

DEFT (Diagnostic Expert for Final Test). Developed for internal use by IBM San Jose.

DEFT diagnoses defects in IBM 3380 Direct Access Storage Devices (DASD) during Final Test, a stage at which the devices are installed, configured, and operated in a manner that simulates the actual conditions at customer locations. The Final Test ensures that the DASD hardware meets performance and reliability standards before it is shipped to the customer. DEFT was developed with ESE/VM. For more information, contact Don Palese at (408) 282–3223.

Seguide/Perform. Developed for internal use by Fujitsu, Ltd.

The objective of Seguide/Perform is to adjust the operational load of on-line systems whose performance is difficult to predict and evaluate. It is used as an intelligent front end for an existing performance prediction support tool which the systems engineers have been using for the M series operating system. Seguide/Perform determines the cause of degraded performance and recommends a solution in the form of job control language code that remedies the situation. It is designed so that software engineers with only two years of experience can perform at the same level as a software engineer with five years of experience. Seguide/Perform was developed in EShell. For more information, contact Fujitsu, Ltd. (in Japan) at (03) 735-1111.

CDES/S (Configuration Design Support for S Series). Developed for internal use by Fujitsu, Ltd.

CDES/S aids inexperienced systems engineers in the configuration of S series minicomputers. The S series is difficult to configure because of the large number of control devices and interface combinations. CDES/S contains knowledge of nineteen categories of configurations. One systems engineer who used to take ten hours to do the configuration now takes only one hour, and another who used to take twenty-five hours now finishes in fifteen hours. CDES/S was written in EShell. For more information, contact Fujitsu, Ltd. (in Japan) at (03) 735-1111.

CASS/X. Developed for internal use by Fujitsu, Ltd.

CASS/X is a batch scheduling system for 140 kinds of computer resources at the Fujitsu Numazu factory. With the exception of rush orders, it is used to schedule all computer usage requests. CASS/X was developed in EShell. For more information, contact Fujitsu, Ltd. (in Japan) at (03) 735-1111.

Machine Room Layout. Developed for internal use by Hitachi, Ltd.

The Machine Room Layout system generates a room layout for computer equipment. The system considers various constraints, including: room for maintenance, visiblity of the front panels to the operator, close proximity of the I/O devices to the entryway, and other proximity constraints such as cable lengths. The system is to adjust to any room shape and to changes and interdevice relations. It previously took five to eight hours to produce a layout plan that is now produced in about thirty minutes. Machine Room Layout was developed in UTILISP. For more information, contact Hitachi, Ltd. (in Japan) at (03) 258-1111.

XCON. Developed for internal use by Digital Equipment Corp.

Xcon was designed to accept orders for large computer installations and to determine exact specifications and layouts of hardware to meet customer needs. By using Xcon, DEC has been able to reduce its technical editor staff and to free up the remaining editors for other tasks. The accuracy is above 99 percent. Xcon was developed with Vax-OPS5 to run on a Vax computer. For more information, contact Julie Kayward at (617) 568-5431.

XSEL. Developed for internal use by Digital Equipment Corp.

XSEL was designed to help salespeople with component selection to configure Vaxes for DEC's customers. During 1986 XSEL was used to process more than 18,000 orders. Xsel was developed with Vax-OPS5 to run on a Vax. For more information, contact Julie Kayward at (617) 568-5431.

CDS (Configuration Dependent Sourcing expert). Developed for internal use by Digital Equipment Corp.

CDS deals with the assignment of fulfillment sites (factories) to line items in computer systems orders. Based on XCON's configuration, CDS determines the factory manufacturing assignment for each item on a configuration order. The old system often required manual intervention, which took from ten to fifteen minutes. CDS has reduced manual intervention to near zero in 70 percent of the cases. CDS is scoring 98 percent correct in its sourcing decisions. CDS was developed in Vax-OPS5 to run on a Vax. For more information, contact Julie Kayward at (617) 568-5431.

Matcher. Developed for internal use by Digital Equipment Corp.

Matcher matches new configuration requests with old orders that were canceled, in order to locate modules or components that were already assembled. If any existing modules can be cost-effectively modified to fulfill a new order, DEC can avoid the cost of tearing down or stocking the canceled equipment. Developed in Vax-OPS5. For more information, contact Julie Kayward at (617) 568-5431.

Dispatcher. Developed for internal use by Digital Equipment Corp.

Dispatcher determines the order in which work-in-progress items are dispatched and determines the workstations to which they should be sent. Dispatcher's knowledge base contains information about components that enables it to make decisions: workstations, route lists, unit loads, and work-in-progress. These elements, along with a validation table that verifies valid workstations, operations, parts, and classes, allow the system to model the state of the manufacturing floor and decide the most effective place to dispatch the work-in-progress item. Dispatcher is in daily use; it makes some 250 dispatching decisions per hour. For more information, contact Julie Kayward at (617) 568-5431.

Mover. Developed for internal use by Digital Equipment Corp.

Mover coordinates and drives the two robots that actually deliver the work-in-progress items. Since their implementation at DEC's Marlborough, Massachusetts, manufacturing facility, the two robots and the pair of expert systems have been in operation six days a week, three shifts per day. During the first month, inventory was reduced by 50 percent and increased inventory accuracy to 99 percent. For more information, contact Julie Kayward at (617) 568-5431.

AI-SPEAR (AI-Standard Package for Error Analysis and Reporting). Developed for internal use by Digital Equipment Corp. to support its field staff.

AI-SPEAR is an expert system that analyzes tape drive failures in conjunction with the SPEAR program. The program helps isolate the cause of tape drive failures by analyzing error messages logged in the system event file. This system is used by DEC service representatives in customer support centers worldwide. For more information, contact Julie Kayward at (617) 568-5431.

VPA (Vax Performance Advisor). Developed to support Vax products by Digital Equipment Corp.

VPA analyzes the computer log of a customer's Vax and recommends various ways to improve its performance. The recommendation ranges from changing system parameters to distributing loads differently and adding equipment. The VPA system is shipped with each Vax that DEC sells. For more information, contact Julie Kayward at (617) 568-5431.

Mindover MVS. For sale by Applied Data Research, Inc.

Mindover MVS allows the user to conduct performance management and capacity planning for the MVS environment. It collects batch data on resource utilization and system performance from Look, an ADR data-gathering package. The data is acquired at intervals that the user establishes. Mindover MVS analyzes the data, reports its findings and conclusions, and offers recommendations. The system adheres to the IBM methodology and cross-references recommendations to appropriate sections of IBM manuals. Mindover MVS was developed in an ADR proprietary tool and runs on a PC. For more information, contact ADR at (201) 874-9000.

Construction and Utilities Applications

Pile Selection. Developed for internal use by Kajima Construction Company.

This system helps in the selection of piling material to be used in the foundations of buildings. Some piling materials are prestressed concrete, steel pipes, and cast-in-place concrete. The selection of piling material is determined by various noise-and-vibration regulations pertaining to local ordinances, load conditions, condition of bearing stratum, condition of ground water, cost, and other variables. The system was developed in KEE. For more information, contact Kajima Construction (in Japan) at (03) 404-3311.

BEST. Developed for internal use by Sekisui Kagaku Kogyo/ ISSAC.

Sekisui Kagaku Kogyo designs and builds prefabricated houses. Given a design of a house, Best aids in the decomposition and selection of parts needed for building houses. The component parts are such items as steel frames, floors, ceilings, and roofs. Best is currently being used at six factory sites for a new series of houses; it is a part of a larger production management system called Happs, which is still under development. Best was developed using K-Prolog. For more information, contact Sekisui Kagaku Kogyo, Japan.

PREDICTE. Developed for internal use by Lend Lease (Australia) by Digital Equipment Corp.

Given a general description of a high-rise building to be constructed, Predicte estimates the length of time it will take to construct the building. The system asks the customer questions about the various materials and characteristics of the building to generate the time estimate.

Layout of Electric Power Substations. Developed for internal use by Tokyo Electric Power Co. with Hitachi, Ltd.

This system provides support in the task of designing the layout of large-capacity electric power substations, particularly during the early stages of the design process. The design must satisfy cost, safety, maintenance, and construction requirements. When a design is modified by a user, the system modifies other sections of the design as needed to maintain consistency. The expected work efficiency gain is tenfold. For more information, contact Hitachi, Ltd. (in Japan) at (03) 258-1111.

Diagnostic Aids for a Steam Turbine Generator (GenAID, ChemAID, and TurbinAID). For sale by Westinghouse.

Westinghouse's Power Generation Commercial Division manufactures and sells multimegawatt steam turbine generators and parts to utility companies. They also sell three diagnostic expert systems that provide continuous on-line diagnostic service: GenAID for the generator, ChemAID for chemical upsets in the boiler and steam system, and TurbinAID for the steam turbine. For more information, contact Westinghouse at (305) 281-3230.

Operational Control of Turbine Generator. Developed for internal use by Tohoku Oil and Fuji Electric Company, Ltd.

A large amount of electricity and steam is needed at oil refineries. At Tohoku Oil, the electricity is provided by an electric power company and by a private power plant. The demand for electricity and steam varies with the operational plan, the weather, the temperature, and the season. This expert system determines the optimal operation of a turbine generator as the load changes. This includes determining whether to use the oil company's own electricity or buy from the power company. The system collects various data every minute; the operational cycle of the system is 0.2 seconds. The system was developed using a tool developed by Fuji Electric. For more information, contact Fuji Electric (in Japan) at (03) 211-7111.

GIO (Diagnosis of Oil Transformer). Developed for internal use by Fuji Electric Co. with Fuji FACOM Corp.

GIO diagnoses the presence of any abnormality inside an oil transformer. The data is continuously collected by an automatic gas ratio analysis device and passed to GIO. The primary data that is collected include quantity and composition of hydrocarbon gas dissolved in the insulating oil of the oil transformer. GIO was developed using COMDEX, an expert system shell developed by Fuji FACOM, Japan.

TOGA (Transformer Oil Gas Analyst). Developed by Hartford Steamboiler Inspection and Insurance Company.

TOGA analyzes insulation oil in order to diagnose faults in large utility transformers. The system was created with RuleMaster and runs on a Vax under a VMS operating system. For more information, contact Don Smith at (203) 722-5472.

Financial Applications

TIARA (The Internal Audit Risk Assessor). Developed for internal use by The Equitable.

TIARA identifies units within the company to be audited in the next audit cycle. TIARA was written with ART. For more information, contact Inference Corp. at (213) 417-7997.

Can Am Treaty. For sale by Buyers Casgrain.

Can Am Treaty gives advice on the legal aspects of trade transactions between the United States and Canada. The program was written with Guru and runs on an IBM PC. For more information, contact Pierre Lessard at (514) 878-3177.

California Sales Tax Advisor. For sale by AD/PR Software Information Services.

California Sales Tax Advisor gives advice on the California sales tax status of financial transactions involving advertising agencies, commercial artists, and designers. It was written with 1st-CLASS and runs on an IBM PC/XT, or compatible equipment. For more information, contact Don Wayne at (415) 671-0990.

Underwriter. For sale by General Data Systems.

Underwriter performs risk analysis and problem solving formerly done by senior underwriters. This system is used for both commercial and personal lines of insurance. The system was developed on the GDX proprietary shell and runs on the IBM 3000 and 4300 series and compatibles. For more information, contact Tom Tarrant at (215) 985-1780.

BEST MIX Portfolio Management System. Developed for internal use by Sanwa Bank and Toyo Information Systems.

Best Mix advises on conservative portfolio management for private accounts with large deposits. It selects investments from tax-free products, a variety of time deposits, government bonds, gold accounts, and mortgage securities. Best Mix was developed in Brains. For more information, contact Sanwa Bank (in Japan) at (03) 216-3111.

Underwriter's Aid. Developed for internal use by Nippon Life and CSK Research Institute.

This system helps an underwriter and a physician team up to determine whether to issue a policy and how much to charge for "difficult" cases. Of the 2.7 million applications processed annually, 1.2 million require a physical exam by a physician, and of those, 600,000 are considered "difficult" cases. In addition to speeding up the underwriting process, the system helps the company produce more consistent policy recommendations. Underwriter's Aid was developed in KEE. For more information, contact CSK Research Institute (in Japan) at (03) 342-0281.

Credit Authorizer's Assistant. Used internally by American Express.

Credit Authorizer's Assistant helps American Express credit authorizers make quick decisions about authorizing purchases for cardholders who are at, or beyond, their normal limit. The system was developed to reduce losses resulting from bad judgments. It is currently used on a twenty-four-hour basis by some three hundred credit authorizers. Without expanding its staff, American Express can now handle an increased number of transactions while simultaneously reducing losses due to bad judgments. In addition, Amex expects to shorten the time needed for each authorization by 20 to 30 percent and thus provide better service to its customers. The Authorizer's Assistant was developed by Inference Corp. using ART. It runs on a Symbolics Lisp machine that can access twelve data bases on an IBM mainframe. For more information, contact American Express at (212) 640-4718.

Capital Expert System. Developed for internal use by Texas Instruments Defense Systems and Electronics Group.

Capital Expert System enables engineers with no special expertise in finance or capital administration to prepare standardized, comprehensive capital packages for the company's decision makers. Before the creation of Capital Expert System, the process required from four to fifteen hours; the use of Capital Expert System has now reduced preparation time to forty-five minutes. The system was developed in Personal Consultant Plus and is delivered on a TI Business Pro. For further information, contact Bill Illingworth at (214) 995-3333.

ExperTAX. Used internally by Coopers and Lybrand.

The Decision Support Group at Coopers and Lybrand, under the direction of Dr. David Shpilberg, developed ExperTAX to help evaluate the application of new U.S. tax laws to clients of the firm. There is a knowledge base organization whose job it is to keep abreast of tax law changes. The system incorporates the knowledge of forty top partners of the firm. ExperTAX replaces a written questionnaire that could run up to two hundred pages and had to be analyzed by one of the firm's senior tax experts. ExperTAX helps audit and tax staff draw conclusions in the tax planning and tax accrual process for the client. ExperTAX was developed in Q Shell (Coopers and Lybrand proprietary product) in Golden Common Lisp and runs on an IBM PC/AT. For more information, contact Harry Schatz, Decision Support Group, Coopers and Lybrand, at (202) 822-4014.

Financial Advisor. Sold by Palladian Software (now marketed under the name **Management Advisor**).

Management Advisor is designed to assist senior managers who are faced with the evaluation of complex business proposals. Using this system, a manager can consider alternative approaches to new product development proposals, evaluate major strategic investments, and consider the consequences of cost-reduction plans and buying and leasing equipment.

The system contains a core of financial knowledge common to all businesses and must be tailored to give specific advice for a particular company or industry. The system allows decision makers to evaluate plans more thoroughly and to consider a variety of alternatives before making a decision. Management Advisor is written in Lisp and runs on either a Symbolics or Explorer Lisp machine. The cost of customization varies from client to client. For more information, contact Tom Murphy at Palladian Software at (617) 661-7171.

Financial Statement Analyzer (FSA). Piloted in a hundred companies by the United States Securities and Exchange Commission (SEC). The successful pilot is now complete and private companies are bidding for ownership.

The Financial Statement Analyzer is an expert system that captures information embedded in the financial statements (specifically 10Ks and 10Qs) that companies file with the SEC, which are stored electronically in the SEC's Edgar system. Because individual companies use a variety of formats and wording, the SEC always reviewed these statements manually. Now FSA can electronically extract the wealth of information in the Edgar files and then perform automated numerical analyses of standard financial ratios such as the Quick Ratio. Once the ratios are calculated the system can highlight companies that stand out because of higher or lower averages, unusual balances, or missing information. FSA was developed by Arthur Andersen & Co., using KEE. It runs on a Symbolics Lisp machine. For more information, contact Joe Carter at Arthur Andersen & Co. at (312) 507-6401.

Letter of Credit Advisor. Used internally and intended for sale by Bank of America (U.K.).

Letters of credit are issued by a bank on behalf of an importer to the bank of the exporter in another country. When documents verifying the terms of the delivery have been issued, the exporter can collect payment. Different banks and companies have different requirements and formats for letters of credit, but they all share basic underlying rules governed by uniform customs and practice. This advisor facilitates the detection of discrepancies between the letter of credit and accompanying documents, and recommends possible courses of action. Letter of Credit Advisor was created using Expert Edge and runs on an IBM PC with 640K RAM. For more information, contact Fiona Bell at Bank of America (U.K.) at (01) 583-9391.

Manager's Broker Monitoring System. Developed for Bear, Stearns & Co.

Coopers and Lybrand worked with Bear, Stearns & Company, a brokerage firm, to develop this expert system to expedite the monitoring of brokers' discretionary accounts. Discretionary accounts allow brokers to invest clients' funds without prior investor approval. In the industry, all firms expect their branch managers to be responsible for monitoring broker activity. A typical branch may register 20,000 discretionary transactions per month. The new system maintains a profile of each broker's activity throughout the year and can identify items a compliance manager would be looking for. The system was developed in GoldWorks, fielded in Lisp and C with a Gold Hill 386 HummingBoard. For more information, contact Barbara Melcher or Fred Katz at Coopers and Lybrand, (212) 536-2045.

Mortgage Loan Analyzer. Developed by Arthur Andersen & Co. for sale by other companies.

Mortgage Loan Analyzer (MLA) helps underwriters assess and make decisions about residential mortgage loan applications. The MLA system reduces the time and risk involved and offers the benefits of consistency and adherence to policy in loan evaluations. As a side benefit, it documents the reasons for an underwriter's decision. MLA runs in Aion's PC-version of ADS and requires a fully IBM-compatible PC, DOS 3.0 or higher. For more information, contact Butch Leonardson at (206) 623-8023.

Client Profiling. For sale from Applied Expert Systems (APEX).

Client Profiling is designed to assist field sales representatives of insurance companies, banks, and other financial institutions to tailor packages of financial products for middle-income clients. It also helps the salesperson plan an appropriate sales strategy for each client. The average agent would take about twenty hours to produce a detailed plan similar to one that the Client Profiling system can supply in fifteen minutes. The system was written in Lisp and runs on a Vax. The sales personnel access it via a PC located in the agent's field office. For further information, contact APEX at (617) 225-2820.

PlanPower. For sale from Applied Expert Systems (APEX).

PlanPower assists specialists in financial organizations and independent financial consultants in the preparation of financial plans for high-income clients. The system helps the planner develop a personal financial plan that can incorporate strategies for handling taxes and inheritance. It has some 6,000 rules and can provide advice on 125 different types of investment products. PlanPower runs on a dedicated Xerox 1186 Lisp machine. For more information, contact Bob Atwell, Vice President–Sales, at APEX at (617) 225-2820.

Foreign Exchange Options Advisory System. For sale by the Athena Group.

The Foreign Exchange Options Advisory System assists in the development of strategies for trading foreign-currency options. It provides recommendations based on market outlook, expected price movements, price volatility, and the investors' risk profile. Primarily aimed at traders with financial organizations, treasurers of multinational corporations, and international portfolio managers, the system is offered with a three-month management consulting plan. The system was developed in ART; the user must acquire an ART run-time or development system in order to use the system.

For more information, contact Randy Reiter at the Athena Group at (212) 605-0224.

Portfolio Management Advisor. For sale by the Athena Group.

Portfolio Management Advisor helps with investment portfolio management. The system contains extensive macro- and microeconomic models of the economy and stock markets. It can search for optimal investment solutions and evaluate a broad range of alternative strategies within the constraints relevant to each individual client's institutional policy, legal limitations, cost and tax concerns, investment goals, and so on. The system was created in ART by Inference Corp. The Athena Group offers the program with a three-man-month management consulting package. For more information, contact Randy Reiter at the Athena Group at (212) 605-0224.

Lending Advisor. For sale by Syntelligence, Inc.

Lending Advisor is designed to help loan officers evaluate credit risks of mid-sized commercial borrowers. The system assists in the analysis of a borrower's historical performance, management, cash flows, and various ratios. It also helps the lending officer evaluate the overall market and the risk of making loans to companies in a particular industry. The primary user of Lending Advisor is a lending officer and the primary function of the system is to ensure that the officer considers all relevant variables, and to minimize the need for the officer to seek advice from senior credit managers and specialists. The system also enables effective and consistent loan decisions. It was developed on a Syntel ES shell and runs on IBM mainframes with PC terminals. Consulting and customization necessary for each installation are generally included with the system. For more information, contact Jim Rossner at Syntelligence at (408) 745-6666.

Underwriting Advisor. For sale by Syntelligence, Inc.

The Underwriting Advisor assists underwriters in underwriting commercial insurance lines of property (fire and allied lines), general liability, workers' compensation, inland marine, and commercial auto. The use of the system enables consistent, higher-quality policies. The Underwriting Advisor was developed on a Syntel ES shell and runs on IBM mainframes and is accessed via IBM terminals. The knowledge in the system must be tailored to the individual client and the system must be connected to the clients' existing data bases. Consulting and customization are included in the price of the system. For more information, contact Jim Rossner at Syntelligence at (408) 745-6666.

General Applications

CASES (Capital ASset Expert System). Developed for internal use by IBM Endicott.

CASES is an interactive system to help in the paperwork involved in the transfer or disposition of pieces of equipment or machinery. It asks enough questions to determine what forms are needed, what must be filled in, whose approvals are required, and where the completed form should be sent. CASES was developed in ES Environment. For more information, contact Joe Caldwell at (201) 329-7000.

Employment Law: Clarifying Dismissal. For sale by Expertech, Ltd.

Employment Law: Clarifying Dismissal contains knowledge about British employment law. The system helps determine if employees are covered under rules of the Wages Act of 1986 and the Sex Discrimination Act of 1986. The system was written with XI Plus to run on an IBM PC or compatible. For further information, contact Keith Clark, Expertech, Ltd., at (702) 831-5655.

Prohibited Transaction Exemption (PTE) Analyst. For sale by Computer Law Systems.

PTE Analyst assists attorneys in analyzing employee benefit transactions governed by the Employment Retirement Income Security Act of 1974. Benefits of the system include increased speed and accuracy for experienced lawyers. The system also serves as a quality control and training tool for inexperienced lawyers. PTE Analyst was written with Personal Consultant Plus and runs on a PC. For more information call (312) 941-3801.

Inner Budget. Developed for internal use at the Georgia Institute of Technology.

Inner Budget interactively analyzes budgets generated with the Lotus 1-2-3 spreadsheet program. This expert system incorporates the expertise of senior accounting and financial staff. It helps department administrators apply policy rules to project funding. Inner Budget is written in Interlisp and runs on the Xerox Lisp machine. For more information, contact E. D. Anderson at (404) 894-2423.

Data Protection Act Advisor. For sale by Helix Expert Systems Ltd.

Data Protection Act Advisor helps managers of British companies comply with a law which requires the registering and monitoring of computerized information held about individuals. Data Protection Act Advisor was created with Expert Edge and runs on a PC. For more information, contact Helix Expert Systems Ltd. (U.K.) at (01) 583-9391.

More. For sale by Persoft, Inc.

More is an expert system that identifies the most profitable prospects on large-scale mailing lists. It is faster and cheaper than less automated methods and provides richer and more integrated reporting. More was written in Cobol and runs on an IBM Mainframe 4300. For more information, contact Persoft, Inc. at (617) 935-0095.

SOPHINA. Developed for use by Ka-oh.

Ka-oh is a large cosmetics company. This expert system is designed to be used by cosmetics customers while shopping in large department stores. The system explains the nature of skin problems, including rough skin, sunburn, or pimples, and gives advice on skin care and recommends appropriate Ka-oh cosmetic products. The knowledge base contains data on the skin conditions of about 160,000 different women, and it uses a theory of skin physiology developed at the Ka-oh laboratory when it analyzes and explains skin conditions.

Pension Advisor. Developed for the Department of Health and Social Security (England) by Arthur Andersen & Co.

The Department of Health and Social Security offers a retirement pension forecasting service. The service enables individuals to determine whether they can expect a state pension when they reach retirement age, and the pension entitlement, if any. Because of the complexity of the pension system, the manual system suffers from lack of timeliness and accuracy. Pension Advisor helps the staff provide more accurate, consistent, and faster service. For more information, contact Arthur Andersen, Chicago, (312) 507-6469.

Manufacturing Applications

SIMLAB (Flight Simulator Scheduler). Developed for internal use by Boeing.

SIMLAB schedules Boeing's flight simulator sixteen hours a day, seven days a week. It was developed in OPS5 and runs on a Vax. For information, contact Barbara Murphy at (206) 773-2816.

Electrical Connector Assembly Expert System. Developed for internal use by Boeing.

The Electrical Connector Assembly Expert System selects the correct tools and materials for assembling electrical connectors. In actual use it has reduced specification research time from an average of 42 minutes to 10 minutes, with more uniform selections. The system was written in Quintus Prolog to run on a Microvax II. For more information, contact Jim Treyens at (415) 965-7700.

Technical Specifications Advisor. For sale by Stone & Webster Engineering.

Technical Specifications Advisor provides information regarding the safety and regulatory related consequences of proposed equipment maintenance and operator actions in manufacturing plants, power plants, and chemical plants. Each type of plant requires its own knowledge base. Technical Specifications Advisor was developed with Exsys and runs on PCs and Vaxes. For more information, contact Gavin Finn at (617) 589-1567.

Thermal Information Program. For sale by General Physics.

Thermal Information Program monitors high exit gas temperatures in electric-power generating plants and recommends steps to reduce waste heat, which would increase the efficiency and profitability of the power plant. Thermal Information Program was created with M.1. For more information, contact Teknowledge at (415) 424-9955.

Component Impact Analysis System. Developed for internal use by Argonne National Laboratory.

Component Impact Analysis System advises nuclear reactor operators on the proper setting of valves and switches. The system was written in Quintus Prolog to run on a Sun workstation. For more information, contact Jim Treyens of Quintus Computer Systems, Inc., at (415) 965-7700.

Crystal Advisor System. Developed for internal use by GHS Corp.

Crystal Advisor System has computerized the expertise needed for growing gallium arsenide crystals, thereby reducing the operator skill and attention requirements for the process while at the same time reducing processing pitfalls. Crystal Advisor System was created with KES for use on PCs. For more information, contact Doc Ardrey at (201) 549-1300.

ASEA Maintenance Assistant. Developed for internal use by Ford.

ASEA Maintenance Assistant helps diagnose problems with ASEA robots in Ford factories. It is used mainly for training mechanics. ASEA Maintenance Assistant was developed with Personal Consultant and runs on a PC. For more information, contact Sheldon Greenberg at (313) 594-1441.

WeldSelector. For sale by the American Welding Institute.

WeldSelector helps welding engineers choose proper weld electrodes. With its use, the time required in this process is reduced from hours to minutes, while weld safety is increased. WeldSelector was created with Personal Consultant Plus to operate on a PC. For more information, contact Dr. Jerald D. Jones at (615) 970-2150.

Brush Designer. Developed for internal use by Delco Products, a division of General Motors.

Brush Designer helps in the design of motor brushes and springs for electrical motors in cars. A nonexpert using Brush Designer can produce in under an hour a design that formerly took days. Brush Designer was created with S.1 to run on a Vax. For more information, contact Teknowledge at (415) 424-0500.

Photolithography Advisor. Developed for internal use by Hewlett-Packard.

Photolithography Advisor diagnoses process errors during the fabrication of integrated circuits. It uses a data base of defect images stored on video disk for explanation during interaction with a process technician. It can also play back movies that demonstrate how to fix a wide range of problems. The system was written in HP-Prolog for the HP 9000 series. For more information call Terry Cline, Hewlett-Packard, at (415) 857-7559.

Hoist Diagnoser. Developed for internal use by Oxko.

Hoist Diagnoser isolates faults in the hoisting equipment used in plating processes, and recommends repair action. With the new system, problem isolation takes no more than one hour compared to four hours to four days previously. Hoist Diagnoser was developed with Insight to run on a PC. For more information, contact (301) 266-1671.

Welder Qualification Test Selection System. For sale by Stone & Webster Engineering.

There are many kinds of qualification tests for welders, depending on the type of job. The Welder Qualification Test Selection System saves time and money by helping managers pick the appropriate qualification tests for welders hired on major construction projects. The system was created with Exsys and runs on a PC. For more information, contact Gavin Finn at (617) 589-1567.

Rotating Equipment Vibration Advisor. For sale by Stone & Webster Engineering.

Rotating Equipment Vibration Advisor diagnoses unusual vibrations in rotating machinery. It provides help in interpreting vibration patterns and measurements. It was created with Exsys for use on a PC. For more information, contact Gavin Finn at (617) 589-1567.

Unit Commitment Advisor. For sale by Stone & Webster Engineering.

Unit Commitment Advisor helps dispatchers schedule power generating units. Developed with MAIDS, an internal tool, the system runs on a PC. For more information, contact Gavin Finn at (617) 589-1567.

IMP (Intelligent Machine Prognosticator). Developed for internal use by Texas Instruments.

IMP is a diagnostic system that troubleshoots problems with epitaxial reactors used in semiconductor fabrication. IMP was developed with Personal Consultant for use on a PC. For more information, contact Texas Instruments at (214) 575-2000.

Reis Service Expert. Developed for internal use by Reis Machines, Inc.

Reis Service Expert helps identify and solve problems with Robostar Series Factory Robots. Reis Service Expert was developed with KDS to run on an IBM PC. For more information, contact Greg Schuler (312) 741-9500.

Oleophilic Advisor. Developed for internal use by Rockwell International.

The Oleophilic Advisor is an expert system to be used by lithography R&D groups for selecting new materials based on whether they attract or repel oil. Oleophilic Advisor was developed with M.1 and runs on an IBM PC. For more information, contact Teknowledge at (415) 424-0500.

Dustpro. Distributed by the U.S. Bureau of Mines.

Dustpro advises coal mine operators on dust control and ventilation techniques. Dustpro was developed using Insight 2 + for use on a PC. For more information, contact Dr. Fred Kissel at (412) 892-6679.

Methpro. Distributed by the U.S. Bureau of Mines.

Methpro gives advice on controlling methane gas in coal mines. Methpro was developed using Insight 2 + for use on a PC. For more information, contact Dr. Fred Kissel at (412) 892-6679.

Expert Probe. Developed for internal use by Unisys.

Expert Probe allows workers on PC card production lines to perform quality control tasks formerly done by skilled technicians. Expert Probe was developed with KEE and runs on a Lisp machine. For more information, contact Unisys at (612) 851-3000.

RBT (Recovery Boiler Tutor). For sale by J. H. Jansen Co.

RBT simulates the operations of Kraft Recovery Boilers used in paper plants. It is used for training operators of recovery boilers. RBT was written in Fortran and C to run on an IBM PC AT. For more information, contact Beverly Woolf at (413) 545-0111.

Page-1. Developed for internal use by Honeywell-Bull.

Page-1 is a diagnostic system that troubleshoots Honeywell-Bull's high-speed page-printing system. In one case, Page-1 solved in just two minutes a problem that normally would have taken a customer service engineer six hours. Page-1 was created with Interlisp and Loops and runs on a Xerox Lisp machine. For more information, contact Chuck Strandberg at (612) 541-6578.

Mentor. Developed for internal use by Honeywell.

Mentor helps field technicians diagnose problems in air-conditioning systems. Mentor was written in Lisp to run on a PC. For more information, contact George D. Hadden at (612) 782-7769.

Turbomac. Developed by Radian Corp. for Hartford Steam-boiler Inspection and Insurance Co.

Turbomac diagnoses vibration problems in large turbomachinery. It can eliminate at least seven of eleven possible problems using frequency data alone. Turbomac was created with RuleMaster and runs on a Vax. For more information, contact Don Smith at (203) 722-5472.

BAISYS (Blast Furnace Operation Aid). Developed for internal use by Nippon-Kokan's Fukuyama Iron Works with Fujitsu, Ltd.

This is an on-line, real-time expert system developed to provide operational support in the blast furnace process. The blast furnace process is the first in the overall steel-manufacturing process and is used to create molten pig iron. Baisys performs a high-precision blast furnace diagnosis and standardizes blast furnace operation techniques. Since its use, Baisys has predicted the occurrence of abnormal furnace conditions, such as channeling and slippage, with more than 80 percent accuracy. The use of the system has increased the life cycle of the blast furnace considerably and has also eliminated human errors. Baisys was developed in a version of EShell that was modified for real-time processing. For more information, contact Fujitsu, Ltd. (in Japan) at (03) 735-1111.

MESA-1 (Marine Expert System 1). Developed for internal use by Ishikawajima-Harima Heavy Industries, Ltd.

MESA-1 helps in the selection of engines for merchant ships. The selection of engines is based primarily on a customer's requirements for specific tonnage and performance. In addition, customers' concerns about fuel costs, payment schedules, costs of dampening the engine vibration, engine costs, power plant requirements, and any special requirements are considered. It used to take four to five days to process two to three engines and two power plants. Now, with MESA-1, it takes between ten and fifteen minutes to process ten engines. MESA-1 was developed in EShell. For more information, contact Fujitsu, Ltd. (in Japan) at (03) 735-1111.

OPTEX (Lens Design Aid). Developed for internal use by Canon.

Optex is a design program that aids lens designers. Given a relatively high-level design specification, it produces a set of possible designs that meet the specifications. It also serves as an intelligent front-end to a CAD simulation program that evaluates the performance of lens designs, producing code that can be run on the simulator once the lens design is created. Optex currently knows about telephoto lenses. Although there is a cost savings from reduced design time (a factor of about ten), the main gain is in producing optimal designs for a given specification. For more information, contact Toshiaki Asano at Canon, Inc. (in Japan), at (0462) 47-2111.

ACEKIT. Developed by Mitsubishi Electric Company.

ACEKIT estimates the cost of manufacturing electric motors. Given a customer order for large industrial electric motors, ACEKIT produces a cost estimate by considering the parts required, whether a similar motor has been built before, and the material and manufacturing costs. ACEKIT was developed in Prolog. For more information, contact Mitsubishi Electric Company (in Japan) at (03) 218-2111.

Manufacturing Process Planner. Developed for internal use by Northrop Corp.

This system aids in the planning process for the manufacture of the approximately twenty thousand parts that go into a fighter plane. The system develops a plan that identifies the operations that need to be performed on a piece of raw material to transform it into a finished item, as described in the engineering drawing or model. The plan includes specification of the equipment to be used on the shop floor, any additional tooling needed, and the sequential routing of the part and its associated material through the factory. The system currently plans the manufacture of sheet metal extrusions. Manufacturing Process Planner was developed in KEE. For more information, contact Ken Lindsay (213) 332-1000.

LMS (Logistics Management System). Developed for internal use by IBM Burlington.

LMS is a system that aids in the process control of a chip fabrication line. The fabrication process involves between two hundred and three hundred steps. LMS maintains a snapshot, available to every manager of every operation in the line. It automatically slows, speeds up, or holds the line as conditions dictate. LMS was developed in XEN (eXpert ENvironment). For more information, contact Gary Sullivan (802) 769-3562.

Transformer Design Aid. Developed for internal use by Schlumberger.

Schlumberger's business involves building tools that take a variety of measurements in holes many thousands of feet below the surface of the earth. To operate the sensing tools, transformers are required. The transformers must be small and rugged. Transformer Design Aid helps Schlumberger engineers design these special transformers. The system was developed in STROBE. For more information, contact Schlumberger at (713) 456-0597.

PBA (Pocatello Burden Advisor). Developed for internal use by FMC.

PBA acquires and monitors data to control the process of manufacturing phosphorus. The goal of PBA is to reduce the cost of phosphorus production by optimizing the mix of raw materials and by controlling the production process. It is currently functioning as an advisory system, notifying operators of abnormal conditions and recommending corrective actions. For more information, contract Dr. Perry Thorndyke at (408) 289-3112.

Ash Mixer. Developed for internal use by Du Pont.

Ash Mixer analyzes the process for mixing radioactive ash with concrete prior to disposal. It was created with Exsys and runs on a PC. For more information, contact Paul D. Soper at (803) 450-6211.

Slurry Flow Diagnostics. Developed for internal use by Du Pont.

This system finds inadvertent water in a slurry process at a large manufacturing plant on the Gulf Coast. Water hoses are used to flush out clogged slurry from one or more of three hundred drain valves in the system. The problem is that the operators don't always know where the hoses have been left. Slurry Flow Diagnostics helps determine whether inadvertent water is in the system, and if so where. For more information, contact Du Pont Artificial Intelligence Program at (302) 774-1000.

Sales Tax Advisor. Developed for internal use by Du Pont.

Du Pont pays sales taxes on materials that are used in its plant or office, but not on materials that will be made into a product for further sale. Often there are gray areas, and often taxes are overpaid. Different states have different sales tax laws. Sales Tax Advisor not only saves Du Pont unnecessary sales tax payments, but it brings consistency to the whole process. For more information, contact Du Pont Artificial Intelligence Program at (302) 774-1000.

Mining and Geology Applications

Source Rock Advisor. Developed for internal use by Phillips Petroleum.

Source Rock Advisor provides field geologists with quick evaluations of the oil potential of rock formations. Source Rock Advisor was created with M.1 to run on a PC. For more information, contact Teknowledge at (415) 424-0500.

Mudman. For sale by N. L. Baroid.

Mudman diagnoses problems with drilling fluids (mud) and recommends new compositions. Mudman was created with OPS5 and runs on a Vax. For more information, contact Kenneth Bergen at (713) 642-6900.

Dipmeter Advisor. Developed for internal use by Schlumberger-Doll.

Dipmeter Advisor analyzes geological formations encountered in oil well drilling. This information is used in defining hydrocarbon reservoir structures and in designing draining methods. Dipmeter Advisor gives consistently better readings of dipmeter logs. Dipmeter Advisor was created with Lisp. For more information, contact Schlumberger at (512) 331-3000.

Medical and Scientific Applications

HP4765A Electrocardiograph. For sale by Hewlett-Packard.

HP4765A Electrocardiograph incorporates a knowledge base to aid physicians in diagnosing heart disease by interpreting ECG readings. The program was written on an ECL shell and runs on the processor in the ECG machine and on the HP1000 system. For more information, contact Ray Wardell at (503) 572-5101.

Microgenie. For sale by Beckman Instruments.

Microgenie analyzes long sequences of nucleic acids in RNA, DNA, and proteins. It comes with more than 3,000 sequences and can search the whole data bank for a sequence homologous to the user's sequence. Microgenie was written in Pascal and Assembly and runs on PC. For more information, contact Beckman Instruments at (415) 857-1150.

Spin Pro. For sale by Beckman Instruments.

Spin Pro advises scientists in the design of experiments using ultracentrifuge procedures. Spin Pro was written with Golden Common Lisp and runs on a PC. For more information, contact Ed Fong of Beckman Instruments, at (415) 857-1150.

Senex. For sale by Foundation Bergonie.

Senex is an expert system whose knowledge base incorporates the latest research in the management of breast cancer cases. Senex was created with Personal Consultant Plus to run on PCs. For more information, contact Cindy Smith at (512) 250-7984.

Pulmonary Consultant. For sale by Medical Graphics Corp.

Pulmonary Consultant interprets the output of pulmonary-function measuring instruments to help in diagnosing lung diseases. In tests of 144 cases Pulmonary Consultant diagnoses agreed with those of two physicians 93 percent of the time. Pulmonary Consultant was written in Pascal and runs on an IBM/AT or equivalent or Convergent 186 processor. For more information, contact Michael Snow at (800) 328-4138.

Oncocin. Developed at Stanford University.

Oncocin provides a graphic environment for managing clinical data of patients receiving chemotherapy on experimental treatment protocols. Using detailed knowledge of the rules for cancer treatment, Oncocin also advises on proper drug dosing and methods to avoid excessive treatment toxicity; it also provides reminders about laboratory tests and radiologic studies that should be ordered. Oncocin was written in Lisp for use on a Lisp machine. For more information, contact the Medical Computer Science Group in Stanford's Department of Medicine at (415) 723-6979.

Help. Developed for use at the University of Utah School of Medicine.

Help combines expert medical advice with a conventional patient-tracking system. Help has links between testing facilities, the pharmacy, and patients' rooms. Help makes 80,000 decisions a day. The system is accessed through terminals connected to a mainframe. For more information, contact Homer Warner at (801) 581-4080.

Interactive Poison Expert for Classification and Control (IPE-CAC). Developed by the Johns Hopkins University/Applied Physics Laboratory in collaboration with the Maryland Poison Center.

IPECAC helps diagnose human poison cases. The system is capable of handling 75 percent of telephone inquiries relating to antihistamines and decongestant ingestion. IPECAC was written with TI Personal Consultant with some algorithms written in IQ Lisp and runs on PCs. For more information, contact Dr. Andrew Goldfinger at (301) 953-5000, ext. 9292.

StrateGene. For sale by Intelligenetics.

StrateGene is a computer system that manages plasmid information and acts as an expert assistant in the design of cloning experiments. StrateGene keeps a central, readily accessible, and systematized record of the molecules used and created by a laboratory. It uses its information about molecules and cloning procedures to guide the researcher through complex cloning experiments. It was implemented on KEE and runs on Xerox workstations. For more information, contact Nancy Bigham, Intelligenetics, at (415) 962-7300.

TQMSTUNE. Developed for internal use at Lawrence Livermore Labs.

TQMSTUNE assists in tuning triple quadrupole mass spectrometers. The program was developed with KEE and runs on a Lisp machine. For more information, contact C. Kalina Wong at (415) 423-0193.

Metals Analyst. Developed for internal use by General Electric.

Metals Analyst allows users with no prior knowledge of metallurgy to make positive identification of commercially used metals and alloys with input from simple density, color, hardness, and chemical tests. Metals Analyst was created with Exsys and runs on a PC. For more information, contact Tom Anthony at (518) 387-6160.

Transportation Applications

Vibration Diagnosis Expert System. Developed for internal use by General Motors.

Vibration Diagnosis Expert System helps technicians diagnose auto problems associated with vibration and noise complaints. It was developed with S.1 and runs on a Unix workstation. For more information, contact Teknowledge at (415) 424-0500.

Hazardous Chemical Advisor. Developed for internal use by Air Products & Chemicals.

Hazardous Chemical Advisor gives expert advice on how to handle, label, and ship hazardous chemicals. It was developed with 1st-CLASS to run on a PC. For more information, contact Sam Shepard at (215) 481-8226.

Chart and Map Expert System. For sale by Human Technology, Inc.

Chart and Map Expert System provides guidelines to cartographers for compiling features on nautical maps and charts. The major benefits offered by the system are accelerated training of entry-level personnel, elimination of subjectivity in the compilation of map features, and improvement in productivity in compiling chart and map features. Chart and Map Expert System was developed with Exsys and runs on an IBM PC/XT. For more information, contact David Meyers at (703) 893-5305.

AALPS. Developed for the U.S. Army.

AALPS configures air cargo ship loads. AALPS can generate complex loading plans in a matter of minutes. AALPS was written in Quintus Prolog. For more information, contact Jim Treyens, of Quintus Computer Systems, at (415) 965-7700.

ATREX II (Automobile TRoubleshooting EXpert System). Developed for internal use by Toyota Central Research and Development Laboratory.

Atrex II helps diagnose the engine troubles of Cresta and Cressida models of Toyota passenger cars. The system is located in a central service department where dealers call in for help. Most calls concern electronic components and information not yet available in mechanics' handbooks. As of December 1986, Atrex II could handle eighty kinds of engine troubles. For more information, contact Toyota Central Research and Development Labs (in Japan) at (05616) 2-6111.

Truck Configuration Expert System. Developed for internal use by Navistar.

Navistar manufactures specialized trucks for particular uses. Truck Configuration Expert allows a Navistar customer to design a truck from different parts to meet particular needs. The system ensures that the designed truck can be manufactured and it plans the manufacturing process, including the identification of what parts will be needed at what point in the assembly process. Truck Configuration Expert System was developed in KEE. For more information, contact Gale Shirk, Navistar, at (312) 691-5700.

Tool and Language Vendors
Referenced in This Appendix

1st-CLASS 1st-CLASS, 286 Boston Post Road, Wayland, MA 01778
(617) 358-7722

ADS-MVS and **ADS-PC** Aion Corporation, 101 University Avenue, Palo Alto, CA 94301
(415) 328-9595 (Tom Halfaker)

ART Inference Corporation, 5300 West Century Blvd., 5th Floor, Los Angeles, CA 90045
(213) 417-7997 (Anne Hamlin)

BRAINS Toyo Information Systems Co., Ltd., Nihonbashi-Toyo Bldg., 7-24, Nihonbashi 2-chome Chuo-ku, Tokyo 103, Japan
(03) 535-6751

EShell Systems Engineering Group, Fujitsu, Ltd., 1-6-1, Marunouchi, 1-chome, Chiyoda-Ku, Tokyo 100, Japan
(03) 216-3211

Envisage Systems Designers International, Newcastle Corporation Commons, 55 Read's Way, Newcastle, DE 19720
(800) 888-9988

ES Environment VM and MVS IBM, P.O. Box 5577, 2321 Whitney Ave., Hamden, CT 06518
(203) 287-7127

Expert Edge Helix Expert System Limited, 190 Strand, London WC2R 1DT, U.K.
(01) 836-7788 (David Imberg)

Exsys Exsys Inc., P.O. Box 112477, Albuquerque, NM 87192
(505) 256-8356 (Susan Huntington or Dustin Huntington)

GoldWorks and **Golden Common Lisp** Gold Hill Computers, 26 Landsdowne St. Cambridge, MA 02139
(800) 242-LISP, (617) 621-3300 (Linda Bessette)

Guru Micro Data Base Systems Inc., P.O. Box 248, Lafayette, IN 47902
(317) 447-1122 (Gary Christie)

HP-RL Hewlett-Packard, 4 Choke Cherry Road, Rockville, MD 20850
(301) 258-2000.

Insight 2 + and **PRL3** Information Builders, Inc., 1250 Broadway, New York, NY 10001
(212) 736-4433 (Cornelius Willis)

IQ Lisp Integral Quality Inc., P.O. Box 31970, Seattle, WA 98103
(206) 527-2918 (Robert Rorschach)

KDS 2 & 3 KDS Corporation, 934 Hunter Road, Wilmette, IL 60091
(312) 251-2621 (William J. Wallace)

KEE IntelliCorp, 1975 El Camino Real West, Mountain View, CA 94040-2216
(415) 965-5683 (Lisa Sheeran)

KES II Software Architecture & Engineering, 1600 Wilson Blvd., Suite 500, Arlington, VA 22209
(703) 276-7910 (Ricki Kleist)

LES Lockheed Research and Development Division, O/92-10 B/257, 3251 Hanover Street, Palo Alto, CA 94304
(415) 354-5239

Loops and **Interlisp-D** Xerox Corporation, 250 N. Halstead Street, P.O. Box 7018, Pasadena, CA 91109
(818) 351-2351 (Ron Clarke)

M.1 and **S.1** Teknowledge Inc., 1850 Embarcadero Rd., P.O. Box 10119, Palo Alto, CA 94303
(415) 327-6600 (Judy Harris)

OPS4 and **OPS5** Carnegie-Mellon University, Department of Computer Science, Pittsburgh, PA 15213
(412) 268-2565

OPS83 Production Systems Technologies Inc., 5001 Baum Blvd., Pittsburgh, PA 15213
(412) 362-3117 (Diana Connan)

Personal Consultant Easy and **Personal Consultant Plus** Texas Instruments, 12501 Research Blvd., MS 2244, P.O. Box 2909, Austin, TX 78769
(800) 527-3500 or (512) 250-6785

Quintas Prolog Quintus Computer Systems Inc., 1310 Villa Street, Mountain View, CA 94041
(415) 965-7700 (Debra Staff)

RuleMaster Radian Corporation, P.O. Box 201088, Austin, TX 78720
(512) 454-4797 (Lori Baldwin)

STROBE (Developed by Schlumbeger) Sun Microsystems Inc., 2550 Garcia Ave., Mountain View, CA 94043
(800) 821-4643 or (415) 960-1300

TIMM General Research, 7655 Old Springhouse Rd., McLean, VA 22102
(703) 893-5915 (Wanda Rappaport)

Twaice Logicware Inc., 5915 Airport Road, Suite 200, Mississauga, Ontario L4V 1T1, Canada
(416) 672-0300 (Gordon Graham)

VAX OPS5 Digital Equipment Corp., 290 Donald Lynch Blvd., Marlboro, Ma 01752
(617) 490-8047 (Tom Madden)

XI User and **XI Plus** American Expertech, P.O. Box AF, Incline Village, NV 89450
(702) 831-0136 (Keith Clarke)

Glossary

artificial intelligence: Artificial intelligence (AI) is a subfield of computer science concerned with the concepts and methods of inference by a computer and the symbolic representation of the knowledge used in making inferences. A major goal of AI is to understand intelligence by building computer programs that behave intelligently. The term *intelligence* covers many cognitive skills, including the ability to solve problems, to learn, to understand language, and in general, to behave in a way that would be considered intelligent if observed in a human.

certainty factor: A certainty factor is a numeric or symbolic weight given to a piece of data, a relationship, or a piece of knowledge (a rule, for example) to indicate the confidence one has in the data, the relationship, or the piece of knowledge. As used in AI, the degree of confidence thus expressed contrasts with probability, which is the likelihood that an event (data, for example) will occur.

backward chaining: Backward chaining is an inference method in which a system starts with what it wants to conclude and tries to establish the facts that support the conclusion. Backward chaining is typically used in rule-based systems. Suppose, for example, Z is to be concluded. The system searches for a rule that concludes Z; for example, "If X and Y then Z." If X and Y are not available facts, then the system will try to conclude X and Y, and it will look for rules that make these conclusions. This process of "reasoning backward" continues until either the system finds all the facts to support the conclusion or it fails and the conclusion cannot be made.

domain: *Domain* refers to a topical area of knowledge, usually identifiable from the existence of specialists in that area. Medicine and engineering are broad domains; internal medicine is a narrower domain. Current expert systems operate in narrowly defined domains.

domain expert: A domain expert is a person who, through years of experience, has become proficient at solving problems in a particular domain.

domain knowledge: a Knowledge about the problem domain.

expert system: An expert system is an AI program that achieves competence in performing a specialized task by reasoning with a body of knowledge about the task and the task domain.

forward chaining: Forward chaining is an inference method in which a system starts with facts and moves toward some possibly remote conclusion. Suppose, for example, the system has facts A and B. It searches for rules that use these facts to draw conclusions—"If A and B then X." Given the conclusion X, the system then looks for rules that use X to draw further conclusions. This process continues until some desired conclusion is reached. To use a more formal explanation, forward chaining is the repeated application of the modus ponens rule of inference to rules and data.

frame (sometimes called **object, schema,** or **unit**): A frame is a knowledge representation scheme for describing entities (objects and concepts) in terms of their attributes and values. An attribute may be a property specific to the object with specific values, or it may be a relationship to other objects. For example, a person may be described with sex and age attributes, each having a specific value for a specific person. Another attribute may be a relationship with another person, such as, "mother of" the person.

heuristic: The term *heuristic* derives from the same Greek root as *eureka* (to discover), and it refers to judgmental, experiential knowledge—for example, a rule of thumb or a rule of good guessing. Heuristics do not guarantee results as algorithms often do, but heuristics offer results efficiently that are specific enough to be useful most of the time.

inference: *Inference* refers to various processes of logic or probability by which a program draws a conclusion from facts and suppositions. The most common inference method used in expert systems is to apply a modus ponens rule of inference to rules ("If A then B") and facts (A) to obtain a conclusion (B).

inference engine: The inference engine is that part of an expert system that contains problem-solving methods; for example, backward chaining in a rule-based system. Inference engines often include methods for dealing with uncertain knowledge and data, generating explanations, and interfacing with the user.

interface: An interface is a link between the computer and the user. An expert system usually has two interfaces, one for the developer or knowledge engineer (knowledge acquisition interface), and one for the end user (user interface).

knowledge: Knowledge consists of facts (statements whose validity is accepted), assumptions, and heuristics.

knowledge acquisition: Knowledge acquisition is a process whereby an expert system acquires knowledge about the task domain. The most common method currently in use is for the knowledge engineer to acquire knowledge from experts and books, and then encode it in some knowledge representation scheme for the program.

knowledge base: The knowledge base is a repository of facts, assumptions, and heuristics in the computer.

knowledge-based system, knowledge system: Often used synonymously with *expert system, knowledge-based system* and *knowledge system* refer to programs whose competence at a task derives from knowledge about the task domain. Often, the term *knowledge system* is defined more broadly than *expert system* and refers to systems that use textbooklike knowledge as well as heuristic knowledge obtained from domain experts.

knowledge engineer: A knowledge engineer is the person who designs and builds expert systems. This person is usually a computer scientist knowledgeable in artificial intelligence methods who can apply the methods appropriately to real-world tasks.

knowledge engineering: Knowledge engineering is a discipline that addresses the processes of designing and building expert systems.

knowledge representation: The knowledge representation is the collection of symbols and symbol structures used to represent knowledge. Knowledge representation is also a process of structuring, encoding, and storing knowledge.

LISP: LISP (LISt Processing) is a programming language designed for symbol manipulation. The name reflects the fact that symbols are stored in lists. LISP is the principal programming language of AI, especially in the United States.

Lisp machines: Lisp machines are computers especially designed to efficiently execute programs written in Lisp. Most Lisp machines are single-user, stand-alone minicomputers called workstations.

meta-knowledge: The prefix "meta-" indicates self-reference. Thus, *meta-knowledge* refers to knowledge about knowledge; *meta-rules* refers to rules about rules. In practice, meta-knowledge includes knowledge about problem-solving strategies, knowledge about how to solve problems efficiently, how to plan steps in solving complex problems, how to improve performance, and so on.

MIS (Management Information Systems): MIS refers to a department or a group responsible for computing and conventional data-processing within organizations. Its tasks involve designing, building, and maintaining various types of programs ranging from payroll programs, network programs, and special applications. MIS usually runs a centralized computer facility and the organization's computerized data bases. Over the years, various programming practices and methods, called software engineering methods, have evolved. Knowledge engineering methods are radically different from these conventional software engineering methods.

MYCIN: Mycin is an expert system developed at Stanford University in the mid-1970s. Mycin was a research system designed to aid physicians in the diagnosis and treatment of meningitis and bacteremia infections. It was one of the first systems to separate the knowledge base from the inference engine, reason with uncertainty, and provide explanations of its line of reasoning. The design lent itself to the creation of the first expert system shell, called Emycin. Designs of many of the current expert system shells can be traced to Emycin.

problem-solving model or **paradigm:** A problem-solving model is a scheme for organizing reasoning steps and domain knowledge to construct a solution to a problem. For example, in a backward-reasoning model, problem solving begins by reasoning backward, from a goal to be achieved toward known data.

Prolog: Prolog is an AI programming language based on logic (first-order predicate calculus), originally developed in France.

prolog: Standing for "programming in logic," the term *prolog* refers to any logic-based programming language. (The difference between Prolog with a capital P and prolog with a lowercase p is like the difference between *God* and *god*.)

rule-based system: A rule-based system is an expert system whose knowledge is encoded as rules.

shell, AI tool, skeletal system: A shell is a computer software package to aid in the construction of expert systems. A typical shell contains an inference engine, a support for one or more knowledge representation schemes (such as frames or rules), an explanation facility, user interface support, and a development and debugging environment.

symbolic processing: The "conventional" uses of computers to date have been in the area of data base management, data processing (for example, accounting or airline seat reservations), word processing, and engineering calculations. Symbolic processing refers to the manipulation of symbols (encoding primarily nonnumeric data and knowledge) to enable intelligent behavior in computer programs.

task: A task is a goal-oriented, problem-solving activity.

task domain: Task domain is an area of specialty or expertise within which a problem is to be solved.

tool: Refer to shell.